Praise for

CONTROL FREAK

"[A] witty memoir."

—*The New York Times Book Review*

"*Control Freak* will win over not just hardcore gamers but those appreciative of a self-deprecating, fun autobiography. Bleszinski's narrative is as animated as the games he played and created, his life story serving as advice for those looking to leave their footprint in any career."

—*Booklist*

"[An] entertaining and candid debut . . . Fascinating."

—*Publishers Weekly*

"Raw and real, [Bleszinski] does not shy away from any topic or censor himself as he shares his troubles with relationships and growth. From his small apartment to his Lamborghini, he shares the ups and downs of working with gaming industry leader Epic. He also provides insight into how major decisions were made in both the games he developed and his own life. Gamers will appreciate the bevy of name-dropping and insider revelations into the evolution of video games and how some popular games, including *Unreal* and *Gears of War*, were developed."

—*Library Journal*

"A behind-the-scenes memoir of the video games industry leavened with insight and self-deprecating humor."

—*Kirkus Reviews*

"This book is a fascinating dive into the grind of the games biz. Cliffy started as a fan of mine. And after he put me in his games, I became a fan of his. A solid guy I totally respect."

—Ice-T

"Modern game design is a high-stakes game. Cliff Bleszinski had a prime seat at the table, and won. In *Control Freak,* he gives us a gripping inside history of the games that have swallowed the world—and more than that, a deeply personal look into the mind and heart of a man behind one of gaming's all-time greatest hits. It's fun and heartbreaking and uplifting and real. So read this touching memoir of an eighties childhood and the birth of an artist, from the first person to score 9,990,950 on *Super Mario Bros.* It's the highest score you can get. You can't get any higher."

—D. B. Weiss, cocreator of *Game of Thrones*

"Cliff Bleszinski's career happened to exactly coincide with the rise of the modern video game industry, which transformed garage-band designers just out of their teens into multimillionaires. This fascinating and often moving book describes what that bizarre trajectory felt like from inside the rocket ship. But it's also about childhood, obsession, fear, and failure. I've known Cliff for fifteen years. Reading this, I realize I barely knew him at all, and I mean that in the best way possible."

—Tom Bissell, author of *Extra Lives* and coauthor of *The Disaster Artist*

"An honest, entertaining look at the life and career of one of the video game industry's biggest and brashest personalities. Bleszinski offers a surprisingly candid glimpse into the mind of an iconic designer: the ingenuity, the self-doubt, and the tense creative alchemy that makes video games come to life."

—Jason Schreier, *New York Times* bestselling author of *Blood, Sweat, and Pixels* and *Press Reset*

"From NES high scores to scrappy nineties shareware to the top of the triple-A heap, Cliff has been plugged in to video game history his whole life, and now we get to see what makes him tick. I loved this book!"

—Bryan Lee O'Malley, *New York Times* bestselling author of the Scott Pilgrim series and *Seconds*

SIMON & SCHUSTER PAPERBACKS

New York London Toronto Sydney New Delhi

CONTROL FREAK

MY EPIC
ADVENTURE
MAKING
JAZZ JACKRABBIT,
GEARS OF WAR,
UNREAL, AND
FORTNITE

CLIFF BLESZINSKI

Simon & Schuster Paperbacks
An Imprint of Simon & Schuster, Inc.
1230 Avenue of the Americas
New York, NY 10020

First Simon & Schuster trade paperback edition November 2023

SIMON & SCHUSTER PAPERBACKS and colophon are registered
trademarks of Simon & Schuster, Inc.

For information about special discounts for bulk purchases,
please contact Simon & Schuster Special Sales at 1-866-506-1949
or business@simonandschuster.com.

The Simon & Schuster Speakers Bureau can bring authors to your
live event. For more information or to book an event, contact the
Simon & Schuster Speakers Bureau at 1-866-248-3049 or visit
our website at www.simonspeakers.com.

Interior design by Lewelin Polanco

Manufactured in the United States of America

10 9 8 7 6 5 4 3 2 1

Library of Congress Cataloging-in-Publication Data has been applied for.

ISBN 978-1-9821-4914-7
ISBN 978-1-9821-4915-4 (pbk)
ISBN 978-1-9821-4916-1 (ebook)

To my amazing wife and soul mate, Lauren.

CONTENTS

LEVEL 5

LEVEL 6

LEVEL 7

LEVEL 8

GLOSSARY

AAA (triple A)—Shorthand for games that cost entirely too much money and time to create and market. By the time you read this, there will probably be six franchises in this space dominating the industry.

Baddie—A silly way of saying "bad guy."

Boss fight—After battling hordes of minions in any video game space, one is often faced with the challenge of dueling with one of these. Often a protracted fight that, when designed properly, is a proving ground for mastery of said title.

Bullet hell—A shooting game, often played from a side view or top-down, in which the player, often piloting a spaceship, must endure a bazillion shots from a never-ending menagerie of aliens.

Butt stomp—A tried-and-tested move in video games, often in character action jumping games. The player leaps into the air, usually over a foe, and careens down, squashing the poor enemy like a pancake.

Co-op mode (or cooperative play)—The ability to enjoy a video game with a friend, sometimes on the same screen at the same time, other times over an online connection. Everything's better with a buddy!

Cover system—The ability to hide behind a wall in a game in order to avoid getting shot. Makes sense, right?

Cut scene—Noninteractive movies contained within a game that are used to progress the story. Many gamers skip them in order to get back to the action.

Deathmatch—Tag, with guns, in a game, played online.

Demo—Short for "demonstration," a downloadable sample of a game. Players download them and try before they buy.

Demo package—The compressed final product one uploads to the internet for the trial version of a game.

Demo scene—A community of insanely brilliant programmers, usually centralized in the Nordic regions, in which the goal is to make the most visually stunning graphical display with as little code as possible. Many rock-star coders have come out of this scene.

Editor—A tool that allows a developer (or an aspiring one) to modify the game's rules and environment.

Emergent gameplay—Little happy accidents that come out of numerous systems interacting in a game. For example, in the classic shooter *DOOM* the player could lure the monsters into shooting one another.

Engine—Just like in a vehicle, the core of what makes everything work.

First-person shooter—Popularized by classic games *Wolfenstein 3D* and *DOOM*, the genre in which you see down the barrel of your weapons. Yes, usually guns. There aren't any first-person hugging games. Yet.

Frame rate—Simply put, how smooth one's gameplay experience is. The faster the frame rate, the slicker the game and the better the feedback time for interactivity.

Game jam—Kind of like a drum circle for development. A team splits off into smaller sets of people and has a set time limit to craft whatever prototype they think is interesting and/or compelling.

Gibbing—Overkilling a baddie in a way that sends flesh and body parts and buckets of blood flying across the screen. It's not just enough to vanquish your foe, you must turn them into mulch!

IP—Intellectual property. Characters, world, story, all of them add up to make an IP. Lawyers made me write this.

Mech suit—A suit that turns a human into a giant walking tank. Think Tony Stark's enormous Hulkbuster suit in *Iron Man*.

Modders—People who modify an existing video game. Could be as simple as tuning in-game values, editing environments, or creating altogether new ways to play.

Moore's Law—Moore's Law states that the number of transistors on a microchip double about every two years, though the cost of computers is halved. Although not an actual law, it has largely held true for the history of computers.

Multiplayer—A feature that allows you to play a game with other people.

One-off—One and done regarding a title. Of course, the last sequel is the one that fails to make money, so usually a bomb.

Pickups—Items in a game that you, well, pick up. Could be health, or ammunition, or goodies that expand the fiction of the world.

Platform—The venue on which a game comes out. The Xbox is a platform, as is the PlayStation, PC, and even the cell phone.

Point-and-click—A type of game that is driven by mouse input, usually 2D adventure games.

Polygon—The primary shape and building block of 3D graphics. Connect a few dots, or "vertices," to make a flat shape. Put a lot of them together to make, well, anything.

Power-ups—Goodies players acquire in games to run faster, jump higher, become more lethal, etc. . . .

QA—Short for Quality Assurance. The people that play a broken game and report what they find until it is no longer broken. However, few games ever ship without any bugs.

Resolution texture—The level of detail of a surface in a video game. Walk up that brick wall and examine every nook and cranny already!

Rocket jumping—Using the blast of an exploding rocket to reach extreme heights on a jump. Yes, you shoot a rocket at your feet and jump.

RPG—Role-Playing Game. Rules often derived from D&D-style games. The player usually goes on a legendary quest that features all sorts of progression, usually in the form of magic and/or combat systems.

Shareware—Popular in the early '90's, it was a guerilla way of marketing games. Release episode one for free, and then users could buy the other two episodes for a fee by mailing a check to the creators!

Shell—Shorthand for the prototype of an environment that has yet to have lovely art slathered all over it.

Ship—The term for when a game is done and headed out the door to store shelves. "Ship it!" is a common refrain in development circles.

Side-scroller—A 2D game in which the player usually goes from left to right in order to proceed.

Spherical harmonics—A fancy way of making a character or object look far more detailed than they are, using advanced lighting techniques.

Stealth game—A title in which the best way to succeed is to sneak rather than go in guns blazing.

Terrain-based game—Outdoorsy games in which the land sprawls as far as the eye can see.

UI—The user interface for a game or device. The DIRECTV channel browser, your phone's home screen, your car's dashboard—those are all UIs.

Vaporware—Slang for a game that is perceived to never, ever ship and release.

Versus mode—A fun way of competing against your friends, usually online.

GAME ON

They didn't kill me.

Bill Gates's security detail, if less disciplined, could've deleted me from the face of the earth. I am sure they knew how and I am equally sure they possessed the means, whether a Sig Sauer P229, a taser delivering twelve hundred volts of paralyzing electricity, a Krav Maga–inspired knee strike, a Mark 2 Lancer Assault Rifle (minus the chainsaw bayonet, obviously), or an old-fashioned kick in the balls.

It was May 2005, and it was the most important week of my life, a lifetime crystalized into one single event. I had flown to Los Angeles from Raleigh, North Carolina, for E3, the annual three-day video game conference where the industry's biggest producers, designers, retailers, wholesalers, journalists, and gaming fanatics gathered to see the latest in upcoming new games, platforms, and related technology. That afternoon, I was scheduled to walk onstage in front of nearly one thousand people and provide a live demonstration of Epic Games's much-anticipated third-person shooter *Gears of War*.

No one was more ready to step into the spotlight as a rock-star game designer. I had diamond studs in both ears and a gold chain dangling around my neck. I had let my hair grow and dyed it blond. I was outfitted in brand-new Affliction gear—it was the nanosecond that brand was cool—and had perfected a confident, reporter-friendly rap that made me sound like *of course* I should be the one leading a team of top-level designers toward the creation of a billion-dollar franchise. A publicist kept me on schedule, and an MTV camera crew trailed me for a documentary on *Gears*. I even had my own nickname: CliffyB.

But my ambitious public persona hid a personal life in tatters. I was not that far removed from being the kid on Accutane in high school who wasn't cool enough for the cool kids and not nerdy enough for the nerds. I was recently departed from a starter marriage, and most of the money I had made up to that point was lost down the black hole of divorce. I lived in a cheap, one-bedroom apartment across the street from the Epic offices with only my faithful dog for companionship. I was drinking way too much. I popped Claritin-D and guzzled Red Bull to defy fatigue and the need for sleep. I worked every day, all day, and through the night if necessary.

I had no plan B. Everything hinged on *Gears*, which had been officially three years in development but really was a lot longer if you counted the scribbles in my notebook, the ideas that were used in Epic's hit franchise *Unreal*, and the childhood traumas that led me to seek solace in designing video games in the first place, back in my early teens. It didn't take me long to realize this obsessive, maniacal work was either going to destroy me or make me rich. With the unveiling of *Gears*, I would finally find out which.

It wasn't just my fate that hinged on the game's success. It was the fate of everyone at Epic, especially co-founders Tim Sweeney, the genius programmer who had started the company in his parents' garage, and Mark Rein, the hard-driving businessman and master dealmaker. The pair had invested years of work and millions of the studio's dollars on *Gears*, essentially pushing all their chips onto this one number, hoping to establish the company as a major player in the triple-A video game space as opposed to making largely PC multiplayer shooters.

Perhaps more important than the game itself was the system on which it was built, the third iteration of the Unreal Engine, or the

Unreal Engine 3. It was the most advanced 3D creation platform in existence—and it was simple to use, enabling almost anyone with a bit of tech savvy to create a photoreal, immersive experience. This was Tim's baby, his version of Google, Facebook, or Windows, take your pick. The plan was to license the engine to anyone and everyone wanting to make a game, a movie, a TV show, a music video—anything involving real-time, AI, visual rendering of the highest quality. It would provide Epic with unlimited new revenue streams. If *Gears* succeeded, so too would the Unreal Engine. *Ka-ching!*

In addition to Epic, Microsoft was also betting big on *Gears*. The Xbox 360, their next generation of Xbox, was set to be released in the fall, in time for the Christmas season, when it would go head-to-head with Sony's PlayStation 3 and Nintendo's Wii. There was just one glitch: they had planned on a new version of the game *Halo* to sell it, but Bungie studios, the game's developer, had missed their deadlines, and Microsoft needed another game, a big game with which they could have an exclusive. They turned to *Gears*. And that's when all heads turned toward me. The new Xbox 360 was going to be revealed at E3 simultaneously during my demo of *Gears*.

That afternoon, I decided to walk from my hotel to the legendary Grauman's Chinese Theatre, where the event was being held. I wanted to get there in plenty of time and not have to fight nightmarish LA traffic. It was a warm, invigorating spring day. I was taking in the buffet of humanity on Hollywood Boulevard. The sidewalk and the street were jammed. The air vibrated with the *thump-thump-thump* of hip-hop pulsing from car stereos, boom boxes, and souvenir stores hawking Tinseltown T-shirts and tchotchkes. Tourists took pictures of pink stars on the sidewalk with gold-stenciled names of movie stars and celebrities. I stepped over Clint Eastwood, Jennifer Aniston, and Pat Sajak. Then I looked up and found myself on a collision course with the man whose fame, wealth, and influence transcended all of them combined.

It was Bill Gates. Not a celebrity lookalike. Not one of Madame Tussaud's wax figures gone AWOL. It was the genuine article, the co-founder of Microsoft, the inventor of Windows, the maker of the Xbox, college dropout, visionary, world's richest man, Warren Buffett's bridge partner, philanthropist, businessman, genius, and nerd icon. Dressed in a suit and tie, he was surrounded by a phalanx of Microsoft executives and security, but I wasn't intimidated. After all, we had produced *Gears* in partnership with Microsoft, which I thought, in some corner of this universe, made the two of us co-workers.

"Bill, it's me, Clifford!" I said with an outstretched hand.

That decision brought an immediate response from the largest and quickest dude in his security unit. He put his arm up, ready to end me, until one of the Microsoft executives whispered something along the lines of, "He's not a murderous douche nozzle," and everyone protecting Bill relaxed.

"Hi, I'm Cliff Bleszinski, and I'm designing the game for your console," I said.

"Nice to meet you, Cliff," he said in his high-pitched, scratchy voice.

We shook hands. For the record, he had the softest hands I have ever felt. God bless software development. I assured him that we were going to nail our release.

"Good." He smiled.

Then, like a busy head of state, he was moving again.

I stood there for a moment processing this remarkable intersection of my past, present, and future. When I was a little kid making a pretend computer with markers and a cardboard box, one of my older brothers dropped a book in my lap. I looked down and saw a picture of a skinny guy with glasses. "That's Bill Gates," my brother said. "You should know about him." Now our fates were inextricably linked.

I checked my watch. Just a few more hours until I would go on-stage and play *Gears of War*, in front of Bill Gates and the packed E3 audience, with gamers from Hollywood to Hong Kong to Hara-juku following along online. And as if that weren't enough pressure, I would actually be *playing* the game.

Most of the demos at E3 are canned, meaning they are pre-recorded, and in some cases are made specifically for the expo and thrown away afterward, a bit of digital smoke and mirrors that hides the work still being done. We'd decided to go another route, the high-wire route. We wanted to show the game's first level, which opened with our hero, Marcus Fenix, escaping from prison, his chainsaw gun flying amid Michael Bay–style blood and explosions. And I was going to play it live.

Which is just not done. Not when your microphone can shut down. Or your controller can fail. Or the monitor you're playing on can go on the blink. There are just a thousand different technical things that can go wrong.

I took a deep breath and headed into the theater to begin rehearsing. This was big. This was make or break. This was a boss fight that was either going to leave me decimated or power me up to a whole new level.

I hoped to fuck it worked.

ORIGIN STORY

Every game needs a hero, a larger-than-life figure adept at slaying every challenge thrown their way. Think Solid Snake from the *Metal Gear* series. Ex–Green Beret, special-ops good guy who demolishes nuke-carrying baddies.

You also have Master Chief from the *Halo* games, who shows up just in time to save the universe. And Mario, who rescues the princess.

Every childhood needs a similar kind of real-life hero who makes the world safe from monsters and their mayhem.

Mine was no exception. With four older brothers and sports legends like Yaz, Esposito, and Havlicek, who cast their shadows across Boston and its neighboring suburbs, including North Andover where I grew up, I had plenty of choices. But none measured up to the man who assumed that role for me—my father.

Take this one example: I was almost a teenager, hormones stirring shit up inside me, and I wanted to be a ninja warrior. No mutant jokes, please. This was serious stuff. I didn't *want* to be a ninja warrior. I *became* one. So did my friends Rick, Chris, and Mike. We found a catalog that offered authentic ninja outfits—black tunics, baggy pants, a cowl with cutouts for our eyes, and the split-toed shoes that ninjas would wear—pooled our paper route money, and bought the requisite outfits.

We also got a few *shuriken*, or ninja stars. Rick already had nunchucks. We were going to be truly badass.

Two weeks later, the stuff arrived. Since it was summer, we didn't have school, so the days belonged to us, and we blazed a trail on our Sting-Ray bikes to our secret fort out in the woods. There we excitedly transformed ourselves into the baddest clan of mercenary fighters ever to declare themselves ready to raise hell in suburban North Andover, Massachusetts. We were the way I imagined the band KISS was the first time they saw each other in full makeup and rock regalia—freaking ecstatic. *Look at us. Holy shit.*

We high-fived each other, posed, snarled, snorted, karate chopped, kicked, and were, as was popular to declare at the time, *ready to rummmmmble.* Oh, fuck yeah.

We acted as authentic, cool, and fierce as we looked—sort of. I was sneaking out of the house one night around three in the morning to rage with my friends when my brother Jeff came home from a night of heavy partying. I could see he was drunk, and I didn't want to get into anything with him. Quietly, stealthily, I crouched in the far corner of the dark front porch, hoping he wouldn't see me. He didn't seem to. He reached for the door handle and, without turning around, he said, "Hey, Cliff, what are you doing?"

"Uh, I'm doing my paper route early," I said.

"It's too early," he said. "Go back to bed."

"Okay," I said, before heading out to join my fellow *shinobi.*

A group of rival ninjas existed about a mile from us, over on a street like ours called Bridle Path. Like us, they also had a fort in the woods. We taunted each other, arguing about whatever was going on: Ray Leonard versus Tommy Hearns, Reagan versus Mondale. One day the tension reached a breaking point and war broke out. Our dojo versus theirs. The fighting took place over several days.

We ambushed each other without warning. We threw rocks and screamed threats and lodged complaints. *Dude, not in the eyes. You almost hit my eye.*

It was a miracle no one got hurt. Then late one night, being the true ninjas we were, my friends and I snuck out and trashed our rival ninjas' fort.

That ended the war.

My friends and I regrouped in our fort. While guzzling large bottles of Gatorade, we recounted the battles and compared welts and bruises from where rocks had hit us, or we had slid taking cover. Once our exploits had been thoroughly rehashed, our version of Hesiod's classic telling of the Titan wars, we moved on to the real raison d'être for our fort in the woods—this was where we kept and maintained our stash of porn magazines, *Penthouse, Oui, Playboy,* even the stray issue of *Swank.* Every religion has its holy book. These were the sacred scroll of puberty. And we were studying them with great intensity when all of a sudden my father paid an unannounced visit to our fort.

"Boys!"

The lot of us looked at one another, frozen with a mix of shock, fear, confusion, and panic. Our magazines were everywhere.

"Dad?"

I poked my head out, and he motioned for us to step outside.

"Safety check," he explained. "I want to take a look around."

After we had filed out and my father had gone inside, my friend Rick leaned close to me and whispered, "Dude, what the fuck?"

I shrugged. I didn't know.

"This really sucks," he said.

My father probably wasn't inside the fort for more than a minute, maybe two at the most, but the wait was interminable. When he stepped back outside, his expression was unreadable. He stared at each one of us. We were shaking in our sneakers. I'd spent my entire life decoding his looks and I had no idea what he was thinking about the glossy display of breasts and vaginas he had found in the fort. Finally, just before one of us developed a nervous tic, my father winked and said, "It's all good, boys. Everything looks fine. Carry on."

I watched him walk away. A total hero.

I loved my father. He wasn't cool. He was a dad. Serious, responsible, funny, stern, and occasionally crude, Walt Bleszinski was an engineer at Polaroid who married my stay-at-home mom, Karyn, and created a picture-perfect middle-class life in a quiet neighborhood that was pretty much straight out of *Stranger Things*, minus the parallel dimension and monsters. My parents were Catholic. They hoped to have a girl at some point, but every time my mom farted out a kid at Mass General, the doctor saw another baby boy weenie. Greg and Jeff were the first two, followed by Chris, and then Tyler and me.

Forgetting about the fact that after they saw me, they either said "Ugh, that's enough" or "Finally, perfection," the fraternal dynamic was important and inescapable. Greg was the original prodigal son, the home run, who attended West Point. He was buddies with Jeff. Growing up, I had zero in common with either of them. They were eleven and eight years older than me, respectively; in fact, Greg and I have the same birthday, which meant I ruined his party by popping out, and took away some of the spotlight every year thereafter. Chris, the middle child, was the black sheep of the family. Do the math. The two eldest sons paired up, as did Tyler and me, the two youngest, leaving Chris on his own and adrift.

He got sent home from eighth grade for showing up to class drunk and setting off a fire extinguisher. He fought constantly with my father, which caused serious discord in the house. In high school, he came home one night so hammered that my parents called an ambulance for him. Another time I woke up on a moonlit evening and saw a shape shambling out in the backyard, moving between the bedsheets on the outside clothesline that my mother had put up, and it scared the shit out of twelve-year-old me. I woke my parents and told them there was a ghost in the yard. It was Chris, unable to even find the door. Another time he crashed in Tyler's and my bedroom, and I awoke to the sound of him pissing on a director's chair we had in the corner, thinking it was a toilet. Then there was the time he totaled Jeff's brand-new Nissan on his way to get a fresh can of dip. The cops asked my father if he wanted to "let this one slide." My father shook his head no, his face a picture of frustration, his voice the hollow sound of resignation, and told them to take his middle son to jail for the night. Happily, Chris eventually got his shit together.

As the youngest, I had a unique vantage. Early on, I saw that raising five boys was rough, even on an engineer's salary. When our septic system at the house needed a repair, my father decided to fix it himself. To help him dig up the leaching field, he enlisted us, his sons, who were collectively referred to as "the boys." "The boys are helping me," he told my mother. We watched in disbelief as he put on a hazmat suit and climbed down into the tank, where he scooped up buckets of raw sewage and handed them up to us. We dumped them down the hill, into our neighbor's yard.

With one exception. Tyler accidentally sloshed one of the buckets over as it was being pulled up—they were heavy, and we were kids—and an ample amount of shit poured straight onto my father's face and into his somewhat open, astonished mouth. No words can capture the look of curdled disgust on his face as he was forced to taste the waste of the entire family of seven that had been sitting in that tank.

Growing up in the eighties, I enjoyed a freedom that today's kids may only know through movies and old farts like me. On Saturdays, I left the house after breakfast and hooked up with friends on Sting-Rays the same as mine. We went to the playground. Not some protected, prefab plastic; the slide was metal, and on hot days we burned our ass going down it. We spun the merry-go-round so fast it flung us off. If we found a hornet's nest, we threw rocks at it. Leftover fireworks in the woods were golden. I hunted for frogs and snakes in the woods.

It was fucking awesome. We rode our bikes all day, recovered the random porn magazine sticking out of someone's trash, played street hockey, lit fires with magnifying glasses, and only returned home when my mother summoned me with a voice that seemed to echo throughout the neighborhood.

"Clifford! Dinner!"

At age ten, I got a paper route. As a first gig, it was pretty good. My route consisted of about twenty homes, and it wasn't a morning edition, so I didn't have to wake up any earlier than I normally did to get my ass to school. Winter was the only time the paper route was rough. New England is famous for its brutal winters, four to six months of snow, wind, and ice—and those are the pleasant days in the dead of winter. Riding a bike through that garbage was a war to survive. Papers were dropped off at the end of my driveway. They came with the regularity of clockwork. Even in the worst blizzard, the stack of papers waited for me.

If I wasn't quick enough, the snowplows came and buried them and then, after futilely poking around in the snow like a member of the ski patrol looking for bodies buried in an avalanche, I said the bad word I had learned from my older brothers that is perhaps the most versatile word in the English language—*fuck!*

I trudged back inside the house and called the *Lawrence Eagle-Tribune.* "Yeah, this is Clifford Bleszinski and I need another stack of papers so I can do my route."

Eventually spring came, the enormous snowbanks blackened with soot, mud, and grime melted, and all across the front yard there would be stacks of newspapers, slowly emerging from the deep cold, a benign facsimile of those stereotypical scenes in horror movies where the jogger finds a body after stumbling over a foot sticking up out of the leaves. Ironically, and in another of what I would term heroic episodes in his role as head of our household, my father went through a phase where he wasn't making ends meet. Five boys were expensive. So he got himself his own paper route.

Unlike my two-dollar after-school job, he signed up to put the venerable *Boston Globe* on several hundred people's doorsteps before sunrise. At four a.m. every day, he woke one of us boys, guided us half-asleep into the shotgun seat of his Ford Fiesta, and drove to some pickup spot in Andover, where we loaded the papers and then barreled through the surrounding neighborhoods, quietly delivering the morning news. Sundays were a killer. Those papers, weighing at least five pounds each, were the big boys.

Like most kids, I loathed every minute of that exercise, which left me physically drained before the day had even begun, though in later years I admired the way my father had worked himself to the bone in order to provide for us and was enormously grateful for the work ethic he instilled in me. He did it all with humor and few complaints. He came home from work interested to know how the day had unfolded for each of us. He sat at the dinner table still in his shirt and tie. Only afterward did he loosen his tie and settle on the couch to watch TV while cradling a bowl of popcorn drenched in a full stick of melted butter and half a shaker of salt. The bowl never left his lap.

The amount of butter he consumed night after night bothered us. Heart disease ran in the family. His father had keeled over at age fifty-three, and he'd had his own bypass surgery following a mild heart attack of his own as a young man of forty. After that, he quit smoking cigarettes—though we were pretty sure he snuck one or two or three a day—and ran five miles three or four times a week, always "to the blinking-light intersection and back," as he proudly reported back to us.

If we mentioned the butter or the scent of tobacco on him, he got pissed off, so we left him to his vices. As the youngest and perhaps the most concerned of our brood, I sat close to him on the couch until he said it was time for me to go to bed, which was usually after Johnny Carson's *Tonight Show* monologue and opening guest.

Before I went upstairs to the bedroom I shared with Tyler, who was already asleep, I kissed my father good night.

"Sleep well, Clifford," he said. "I love you."

He did, too. He listened patiently when I, at a mere six years old, came home from my friend Mike Melvin's house gushing about the new high-tech gadget he had in his basement, an Atari 2600. "We played *Space Invaders*," I said. "On the TV!" I fired at alien soldiers, I explained. I nailed the pink UFO. I defended the Earth.

My father smiled at the way I was unable to contain my enthusiasm. For him, it was an *atta boy* moment straight out of *Happy Days* or *Family Ties*.

But for me, it was a pivotal event, the instance when the switch flipped in my brain. I went from a kid who had sat passively in front of the TV, watching shows like *H.R. Pufnstuf, ThunderCats, The Muppets*, and *Charlie Brown* specials, to being able to move the images on the TV screen. *I could move the images on the TV!* Suddenly, I was in control. And I liked it. I was a budding little control freak.

I wanted more. I wanted to make everything do what I wanted it to do. It was mastery of the idiot box. It was phase one of that glorious addiction of controlling the screen that would eventually lead me to making video games.

A few years later, my friend P. T. Luther, who had all the cool toys before anyone else, like the seven-foot G.I. Joe aircraft carrier, got a Nintendo Entertainment System with *Super Mario Bros.* I was incredibly envious. Nintendo's TV commercials had successfully, irrevocably permeated my brain. "Now you're playing with *power.*" Those ads were genius. Nintendo positioned itself as an entertainment system, not a video game, and it worked.

They reignited my interest in video games after I had lost interest in them, as had the rest of the world, due to Atari flooding the market with too many crappy games. My dog, Jazz, had chewed up my Atari power cord, so I couldn't even use it anymore. Not that I wanted to. Then Nintendo entered the fray and suddenly the entire world fell back in love with video games. But it was more than love.

It really was the *power.* I experienced a head rush the first time I made Mario jump onscreen. After finding a hidden block with an extra-life mushroom in it and hearing the subsequent 1-up sound, I was beside myself with excitement. "What kind of sorcery is this?" I exclaimed.

With my mind blown, I raced home for dinner and announced at the table, "It's in their living room!"

I told my family all about this pudgy little Italian plumber, running left to right, under crystal-blue skies, battling walking mushrooms, turtles, spiky desert-looking crawly things, heck, even a pair of upright turtles that, for some odd reason, could toss an infinite number of hammers at you. My parents smiled, amused but clueless as to what I was talking about when I told them about the extra-life mushroom I had discovered. "I mean, do they want us to find these secrets? Are they accidents? Or am I good?"

I continued to ramble about the game.

"The graphics are incredible," I said.

"Shut up, Cliff," one of my brothers snapped.

"It's as good as an arcade," I continued.

"Shut up, Cliff."

"You don't get it," I said.

"No, I do. You're annoying. Shut up."

Sorry, but they really didn't get it. I was obsessed. I went to bed with the game's music—that reggae island chiptunes song—still playing in my head. I can still hear it.

For Christmas, I saw a box under the tree and knew it was an NES without needing to unwrap it. It was for me and Tyler but mostly for me, because he was more into sports and chasing the neighborhood girls than video games. I wanted to hook it up to the color TV in the living room, the best set in the house, but with a family whose lives were deeply aligned with the ups and downs of the Patriots, Red Sox, Celtics, Bruins, and anything else related to New England sports, I knew better than to suggest something that would prevent them from watching *the game*. Even talking during the sports report on the local news was met with an onslaught of "Be quiet" and "Shut the fuck up."

My mom found a tiny black-and-white TV for the NES and let me take it up to the bedroom I shared with Tyler. We had bunk beds, and I drove him crazy by playing it with the sound up just enough so that he'd barely get his REM sleep. It was an early version of brotherly torture. I kept track of the games I vanquished. I taped a poster board on the back of the bedroom door where I wrote GAMES THAT I'VE BEAT (*Deadly Towers, Ghosts 'n Goblins, Contra, Solomon's Key, Mighty Bomb Jack*) and I put hash marks on my NES the way a World War II fighter pilot kept track of his kills.

For the record, I didn't cheat in any of the games. I saw it as validation. While my friends fantasized about becoming the best baseball or basketball or ice hockey player in the world, I wanted to be the best video game player in the world. I wasn't going to get there by using the cheat code.

I took it seriously. As Nintendo's reign continued, the graphics got better, the games grew more complex, and my ability became sharper and more sophisticated. I went from simple *Mario Bros.* jumping on a block to *Contra*, a side-scroller that had these two buff dudes with crazy sci-fi guns fighting aliens, to *3-D Battles of WorldRunner*, where you just run and jump over chasms and goofy enemies in what was Nintendo's take on Sega's arcade hit *Space Harrier*. Then Nintendo hits its stride with *Zelda*.

I topped it off with weekly visits to the public library and never left without a stack of books, including every title I could find about computers. I wanted to know everything about PCs. I was obsessed with RAM and ROM and cathode-ray tubes and how it all worked. One day I used a black Magic Marker to draw knobs and lights on my brother's aging 8-track tape machine to make it seem more computer-like. I pretended to code.

Then came the day I no longer had to pretend. My father brought home an Apple IIc and placed it in the living room. As an engineer, he saw the way PCs were becoming essential to the way people worked and younger people learned. He also heard me yammer about all the time I spent on the Apple at the public library and on my friend Rick's Commodore 64, on which we played *The Hitchhiker's Guide to the Galaxy*, that is until his parents upgraded him to an Amiga and we burned through *Chuck Yeager's Air Combat*, *Shadow of the Beast*, and everything we found from Psygnosis, the rock-star development team in the U.K.

But the Apple IIc was like parking a Maserati in the living room. I am pretty sure my father intended this fancy home computer for Tyler, since he wanted my brother to be thinking about college already and perhaps this new machine would help him get into a good school. But Tyler was too busy making out with girls in the woods, so I claimed it as my own and took to it the way the two Steves, Jobs and Wozniak, intended: no instructions, no problem.

I saw myself as a natural. One Friday night, my parents stopped for dinner at a local pub before dropping me at the mall. As my father enjoyed plates of potato skins and fried mozzarella sticks, I buried my face in the latest edition of *GamePro* magazine, which had the

Gradius side-scroller on the cover. My mother, bored of watching my father stuff his arteries with unhealthy apps, pointed at the magazine cover. "Clifford, how come the games don't look like that?" she asked. Not sure what to tell her, I shrugged and said, "Wait thirty years."

Lucky guess? Maybe not. Each month, I devoured the latest issue of Scholastic's *Family Computing* magazine, a publication containing computer-related articles, software reviews, and my favorite, pages of code for simple games and screensavers. I retyped each page of code, thinking I could train myself to be a coder, and over time I learned how to parse text to a small degree. Though I wasn't smart enough for that fancy poke and h=plot ( ) graphics stuff, I was able to produce simple ASCII art on my own.

My masterpiece was a crude dagger. During the summer, I spent one entire day writing the code. Getting all the backward slashes, parentheses, underlines, and semicolons in the exact right place made me dizzy, almost nauseous. But I stuck with it until the fancy handle and the blade with all its variations in shading was perfect. It was my first real solo project. I printed it out on our loud dot matrix printer and eagerly held it out for my dad to inspect after he got home from work, looking up expectantly for his reaction.

Like any kid, I wasn't just looking up because my father was so much taller than me. I was looking up from the vantage of being the youngest of five boys. I was looking up over the heads of my four older brothers. I was looking up for a glimpse into my future. He wanted me to go to Northeastern and get an engineering degree like him, and I wanted to hear him say I was on the right track. Ultimately, I was looking up for his approval. He was the smartest man I knew and the person I respected more than anyone else, and a nod from him or a pat on the back meant everything to me.

He had taken off his suit jacket but was still wearing a shirt and tie and dark slacks. *Come on, Dad,* I thought. Finally, after examining the image from all angles, which took at least a minute but felt like ten, he handed me back the printout, smiled, and ruffled my hair with his hand.

"That's great, Clifford," he said. "You're getting into graphics."

Yes! I held on to that moment for as long as possible. I had made him proud, and for the first time, I sensed this computer stuff might go somewhere.

THE LEGEND OF THE HIGH SCORE

"Clifford, come on over," said Rick Adams. "I want to show you something."

Rick, who was four years old than me, lived across the street. He was one of the accomplices in the ninja escapades. He and his sister were big stoners. For some reason, he felt it was his obligation to introduce me to knowledge and activities close to his heart. He taught me about groupies, showed me my first porn movie (a late-eighties video called *Pumping Flesh*), and let me play *The Hitchhiker's Guide to the Galaxy* on his Commodore 64.

He knew all this was true what-the-fuckery to me, and so when he told me to come over to his house, I made a beeline to his front door. He told me to follow him upstairs. We took the stairs in giant leaps and darted into his bedroom. He grabbed a booklet and thrust it toward me.

"Look at this," he said.

It was the instruction manual to *The Legend of Zelda*.

"My friend has the game," he said. "He told me that you can burn down a tree or bomb a rock and find a secret underground location."

"It's the hidden block in Mario taken to the next level!" I said, leafing through the instructions.

"And the cartridge is gold," he said. "Real, actual gold."

In reality, it was painted plastic, but like so many other kids, I bought into the fable. I put the instruction book down on Rick's desk and slowly raised my eyes until he could see my thoughts. *Holy shit. Zelda* was special. I had to have that game. That summer, after saving every dime I made from my paper route and a part-time job at a local golf course, I persuaded my mother to drive me to Toys "R" Us and I bought it. Back home, I unpacked the game, slipped in the cartridge, and played for the next twenty-four hours. Until I was able to put a notch on the back of my NES. Then I informed Rick.

"I beat it," I said.

"Dude, you just got it," he said.

"I know."

"Fuck."

"Yeah, and guess what?"

"What?"

"There's a second quest that opens up."

"No way."

"Seriously, you just keep playing it."

It was a prelude to more and bigger conquests. Starting mid-1987, I subscribed to the *Nintendo Fun Club News*, the quarterly promotional magazine started by former warehouse manager–turned–NES guru Howard Phillips. This was pre-internet, so news about games came from friends, coming-soon info on game boxes, TV commercials, and now this incredible new magazine, whose every word and picture I devoured.

Each issue in the *Nintendo Fun Club News* contained a message from Howard, articles about new games, tips and tricks, game reviews, jokes, and, later, a comic strip called *Howard & Nester*. It portrayed Howard in his signature bow tie as the gaming wise man and Nester as the snotty Nintendo know-it-all who was like all of us reading the magazine. In the second issue, delivered to my house in 1988, I noticed a feature that had escaped my attention previously—the high score section—and something clicked in my brain. I wanted to see my name on that list. Not just on the list. On top of the list.

At thirteen years old, that became my life's mission: to get the highest score possible in *Super Mario Bros.*—9,990,950.

The game only went up to that number before resetting to zero. Only a few others had achieved that score. Their names were in the magazine. I wanted to see mine there too. I read the rules: all I had to do was take a Polaroid picture of my high score and mail it to Nintendo. If approved, they would put my name in the magazine and . . . I would be famous.

Determined and disciplined, I played every day for hours. I developed my own strategy. I ignored the Warp Zones and took my time. Shortcuts were no good if the objective was getting a high score. In *Super Mario*, you had to milk every single level, take out every enemy, and get every coin. As I got close to the end, I jumped on the lumbering turtles and pushed their shells away, causing them to ricochet off the odd, medieval world's blocks. If I caught one on a staircase, I could keep a tight cycle of shells ricocheting as my score zoomed up.

As I navigated my way through the challenges in each level, the outside world disappeared, and I literally entered the game. I saw pathways, shortcuts, and opportunities. I thought like the people who had made the game, and I just knew how to win. It was that way with every game. But *Mario* was special.

Then came the day when I hit the high number: 9,990,950. I stared at the screen, nodded at the score, and thought, *Mission accomplished.* I grabbed my father's Polaroid camera and, sixty seconds later, I had the evidence in hand. I showed the photo to my family and several friends before mailing it to Nintendo. Then I waited. I thought I'd receive a handwritten note from Howard Phillips within a couple weeks saying, "Nice job, Clifford." But I didn't get a response. Nothing. Crickets.

A month later, the next *Fun Club News* magazine showed up in our mailbox. Though I still hadn't heard anything from the publication, I remained hopeful. I ran inside, slid into a chair at the kitchen table, and flipped through the pages until I came to the section. And there it was—my name, Clifford Bleszinski—at the top of the High Score list. "Yes!" I exclaimed, before showing my mother ("Look, Mom, I did it") and my brother ("Check it out") and later, my father ("Isn't it cool? What do you think?").

My name also appeared in the next two *Fun Club News* issues and the legendary next iteration of that magazine, *Nintendo Power*. I guessed the list didn't change that often. Evidence of just how difficult it was to make it in the first place. But there I was in black and white: Clifford Bleszinski. *Clifford Bleszinski*. Millions of people were seeing my name, including the Nintendo master himself, Howard Phillips. I was famous.

"Fuck yeah!"

At school, I was nicknamed "Nintendo Boy." I didn't especially like it, but the nickname was one of those things where if the shoe fits . . . I was a fixture in the computer lab, where I played *Oregon Trail* to death. Literally. I kept dying of dysentery. I spent so much time there, they should have called it the Cliff Bleszinski Computer Lab. One day it seemed they did. I got there and saw, taped to the door, the now famously ironic *Far Side* comic of parents watching their son playing video games as they imagined a future newspaper's Help Wanted section with six-figure job openings for a Nintendo expert and *Super Mario Bros.* player. My name was written in large block letters at the bottom.

I tore it off the door and threw it away. That wouldn't be my reaction now. Today we know the world has not only embraced but come to be defined and ruled by technology and the nerds who understand it. Video game creators, streamers, YouTubers, and cosplayers are the new celebrities. But back then, and especially in middle school, it wasn't easy being a gaming nerd. I couldn't change my skinny physique. I have no idea why I thought my fanny pack was essential (and cool), but I did (it wasn't). And being a gamer was me, who I was. I couldn't change that. Why would I even want to?

One reason might have been it made me easy prey to those who needed to prove they were better, stronger, and cooler—perhaps because ultimately, they were even more insecure and uncertain about who they were than me. The proving ground was the bus ride home in the afternoon. The twenty-minute trip was often a *Lord of the Flies*–like voyage of bullying and survival. I was routinely pushed, shoved, and teased. Once I had gum put in my hair. Another time a kid shook up a Coke behind my back and dumped it on my head while a chorus of his lame friends laughed.

That was the worst. Humiliated, I stormed up to the front of the bus and insisted the driver stop even though we were still a half mile from my house. He tried to ignore me, but I shrieked "Stop!" and he knew he had to pull over and let me out or something terrible was going to happen that he wasn't equipped to handle. As I bolted off the bus, someone behind me whined, "He's going home to play Nintendo."

I ran through the woods, hurrying past the pond where I played hockey and the junk pile where I hunted for snakes, until I was by myself in the middle of nowhere. There I finally stopped, caught my breath, and turned back toward where the bus had let me off. "Fuck you," I screamed at all of them. "Just fuck you!"

No one was home when I got back to my house on Russet Lane. That was fine with me. I relished the freedom and the lack of having to explain what had happened on the bus, why my eyes were red and I was out of breath. I took off my Coke-drenched clothes, put them in the washing machine, and showered, scrubbing furiously, as if trying to shed a layer of skin from my awful day at school.

Still, I think kids growing up in today's hyper-connected world have it tougher than I did. At least the bullying didn't follow me onto Facebook, Twitter, Instagram, and TikTok. And in some way, those assholes on the bus motivated me. As Frank Sinatra once said, "There's no better revenge than massive success."

I had an antique key that I thought was lucky. I got it at a yard sale one weekend when I was tagging along with my parents. In every video game, you're looking for keys to open doors. This one spoke to me. *I'll unlock doors for you. I'll unlock secrets. I'll help you find your way when you seem lost.* It was the last thing I stuck in my pocket before I walked out of my bedroom in the morning to face the day.

I was fumbling with it the day I went over to my friend Ralph Barbagallo's house to make a confession: I'd cheated on my NES.

The guilt was weighing on me. I had to tell someone. And Ralph was the guy.

"I was at Lechmere's," I said, referring to the local electronics store. "They had a Sega Master System, and I couldn't resist. I played *Alex Kidd in Miracle World* for two hours."

"Cool," he said.

"No, not really." I shook my head, troubled. "I cheated on Nintendo."

"Dude, it's okay," he said. "It's just a game."

He didn't understand. To me, it was much more than a game. My bedroom walls were covered with pictures and posters of Nintendo games and characters. Everything I could find. I even fueled up on the short-lived, fruit-flavored, and aptly named Nintendo Cereal

System. This was at the very outset of the console wars, but people still wanted to feel like they were part of a team. I didn't belong to a team or a group at school. Nintendo was my team; now I would refer to it as my community. Nintendo had helped create and define my identity. It was cool, much more so than Sega, and despite this, I'd strayed.

"I couldn't resist," I said.

"On behalf of Nintendo, I forgive you."

Ugh, if only it were that easy. As with all sins, I had to forgive myself. Sega's Master System had none of the magic and mystery of Nintendo's games. *Alex Kidd* was a case in point. You were a little kid who punched things. It was anemic. But Ralph got me through the crisis. He was my gaming Sherpa, teaching me about basic game theory and, more important, which games were good, and which were a waste of time and money, and why that was.

I would play anything, as my fling with Sega made apparent, but my friend helped me become more discriminating by pointing out the details of gameplay, the quality of the graphics, the same with the sound, and the overall feel. He was the first person I heard use descriptors like "bullet hell" and "side-scrolling beat 'em up." And when I was blown away by *Mystic Defender*, he matter-of-factly said, "Dude, it's the graphics."

I don't know how he knew all this, but he did. He understood the pacing of games. He knew they should have a sense of mystery. And he realized the best games had a cool world you wanted to live in. After he got the Shoot-'Em-Up Construction Kit for his Commodore 64, we set about creating our own games. Sleepovers turned into all-nighters, and we produced two games. His was *Adventures in Stupidity*. Mine was called *Thunder Burner*.

Despite all the hours Ralph and I spent talking about pixel art and textures, I couldn't program that well. Still, it was a preview of things to come. My little *Thunder Burner* game had a helicopter that scrolled upward and took out enemy aircraft carriers and supporting ships. It was crude, but it gave me that same excitement of manipulating things on the screen, except now I was making them.

Those efforts were put on hold when Ralph informed me of the upcoming Nintendo World Championships, a touring competition the gaming manufacturer was sponsoring across the U.S. This was Ralph's forte—knowing stuff before anyone else. I was immediately interested. He showed me a flyer for a three-day event in Boston happening in about a month. It was one of twenty-nine cities across the U.S. hosting similar events in a lead-up to the first-ever Nintendo World Championships at Universal Studios in Los Angeles. The grand prize was a $10,000 bond, a new Geo Metro convertible, a 40" TV, *and* a Mario trophy.

"We have to enter," said Ralph.

"Duh," I said. "And I have to win."

We learned the competition was going to consist of three timed rounds, each one a different game, starting with the first level of *Super Mario Bros.* Next was the really bad Nintendo racing game *Rad Racer*. And the last round was *Tetris*, a flat-out one-on-one against your opponent for the high score. Ralph and I trained every day. Since we could play *Mario* in our sleep and we hated *Rad Racer*, we just played the hell out of *Tetris*.

The April date of the competition arrived quickly. My parents drove me, Tyler, and Ralph to the Boston Garden arena in downtown Boston. I saw my first concert there, a double bill of hair metal from Poison and Warrant. Inside, the immense floor where Bret Michaels had belted out "Nothin' but a Good Time" was filled with people and games, consoles and handhelds, blinking lights, the sound of electronic jumps, coins, and mushrooms. All the games on display could be played for free. "Amazing," I said repeatedly.

It was my first time at a gaming convention, and the excitement of breathing in the cool scent of freshly unpacked computer gear and being among other video game enthusiasts and obsessives made me feel like I had finally found my people—guys with mullets and acid-washed jeans, girls with crimped hair, everyone trying to hide their acne and insecurity.

I cruised through the first two days of prelims, which put me into the Sunday finals for the Boston city championship. I woke up that morning excited and confident. I put on a fresh white polo shirt and baggy gray cargo pants, buckled on my fanny pack, and shoved my lucky key deep in my pocket. "Ready," I announced to my family.

My championship round was at the end of the day. The wait fueled my desire to win and gave me time to enjoy the free games on the floor. I played a kid named Jason, who had a mullet like mine, and, as it turned out, a steadier hand. I cruised assuredly through *Mario*, which I had done a million times before, but then, sadly, I buckled under the pressure of playing a really good kid in front of a crowd of people hooting and screaming and watching the giant screen behind us. I wiped out while playing *Rad Racer*—I still blame the controls—and I choked on *Tetris*. One misplaced piece and I was toast.

During the awards ceremony, I was numb from the shock of losing to Jason. I wore a blank expression through the whole thing. Jason's prize was a new pair of Reebok high-tops. I got a T-shirt and the soon-to-be-released *Super Mario Bros. 3*. Even though I thought I made out with the better prizes, I walked slowly out of the arena with my head down. I felt like such a loser. My dad put his arm around my shoulder and pulled me toward him. "Forget about tonight," he said. "You did good. I'm proud of you."

I rallied the next weekend for another try when the championships moved to Hartford, Connecticut. The same group of people drove me there.

"You can still win and go to Cali," Ralph said.

"Yeah, if you get your shit together," my brother added.

I didn't manage to. I went down in flames in the first round. I played even worse than before. I was furious with myself. On my way out of the convention hall I flung my so-called lucky antique key into the bushes. *Fuck good luck charms*, I thought. *A lot of good that did me.* I slid into the back seat of my dad's Honda Civic and let the shoulder belt snap into place across my cheek. I wanted to feel that sting. I deserved it. My dad pulled onto the highway and Tyler turned up the radio. I leaned my head back. My eyes were shut. Aerosmith's classic "Dream On" came on and I felt as if the lead singer of this band with Boston roots was singing directly to me. *You've got to lose to know how to win . . .*

I had no idea of this at the time, but my childhood came to a stop then and there, and so did I, frozen seemingly forever, at age fifteen, trying to hang on to that last moment when life, even in the dismal wake of defeat, felt normal and right, with Mom and Dad in the front seat and all of us heading back home, as we always did.

THE PALACE
OF DECEIT

I burned through the NES classic *Ninja Gaiden*, digging the badass hero Ryu who swung his sword, tossed ninja stars, jumped walls, and performed a variety of other awesome moves to get out of trouble. Like everyone who played the game, I wanted to be Ryu in real life. I still had the gear in my closet. Not that it mattered. Being a ninja is the ultimate nerd fantasy—you're the outcast who turns out to be the biggest badass and saves the day.

Ninja Gaiden was famous for its cinematic "cut scenes," mini movies that advanced the plot along. In the game's opener, two ninjas raced across a field under a full moon that was way too large, anime-style, and leapt high into the air where they clashed swords. One of the ninjas was Ryu's father, Ken, who seemed to die in the scene. However, at the end of the game, Ken returned very much alive, only to save Ryu by leaping in front of a fireball shot by an angry demon. He then died for real, but Ryu survived with the girl he loved.

The twist delighted young ninjas like me and planted in my subconscious a comforting dream that my father would always be around to protect me.

———

I have a photograph of my father running in front of the cemetery where he was later buried. I frequently look at that photo as a reminder to eat healthy and work out because genetics are an unsentimental motherfucker.

That fact was slammed home on August 13, 1990, a Monday that seemed like any other summer day except that my father had taken the week off from work. He was in a good mood all day as he puttered around the house. At lunchtime, he fixed himself something to eat, gave our dog, Jazz, a playful rub, and changed into his golf clothes. He was going to play eighteen holes with my brother Chris at the Far Corner golf course in nearby Boxford.

I was upstairs in my bedroom, playing *Blaster Master*, when he was ready to leave. I heard him pause by the front door. He yelled up to me.

"Clifford, pick up after the dog in the backyard."

I shut my eyes, annoyed that he was asking me rather than Tyler and interrupting my game.

"Fine, Dad," I yelled back, but in a tone that let him know I was irked.

That turned out to be our last conversation.

Those words.

That moment.

You never know.

I didn't.

Hours later I was still firing the *Blaster Master* tank and hypnotized by that dark musical riff when Tyler burst into the bedroom we shared and barked, "Get your shit. We need to go to the hospital. Dad's had another heart attack."

I stopped playing and turned toward him. "What?"

"It's bad," he said. "Get up. Get your shit."

How does that happen?

It just does.

How is there no warning?

There just isn't.

Our family friend, Lori, took us to the hospital. First, she picked up me and Tyler at home. Then she raced to get my mother at work. My mother, who had gotten a job now that her boys were older, was too upset to drive herself. I'll never forget the sight of her waiting for us in the parking lot. Lori didn't even come to a complete stop before my mom got in the front seat and we were back on the road.

My mom's face seemed to be in shock, or maybe it was her valiant effort as a strong mother to hold it together in front of us boys. I saw Lori squeeze her arm as if to say, "Be strong. It's going to be all right." Lori turned abruptly into the police station to see if we could get an escort to the hospital. They said no and she peeled out of the station, the tires screeching at the cop cars parked behind us. She never slowed. I can't recall her stopping once.

It was and still is the most terrifying car ride of my life—and I once tried to impress a friend by driving my Lamborghini 150 miles an hour to the local shopping mall.

A hospital usually has two places for families to wait for the prognosis of a loved one who has been admitted: Either the main waiting room with the horribly uncomfortable chairs, bad coffee, and weirdly buzzing snack machine that never works. That is the place where people thank doctors, smile, and hug each other. The other option is a smaller room off to the side. This is where bad news is delivered in private so people can cry and wail without embarrassment. Being directed there is not a good sign.

When we told the nurse we were there to see Walter Bleszinski, she pointed us to that tiny room and said in a hushed voice, "You'll be comfortable there." We were in there less than fifteen seconds before the doctor stepped in and shut the door. He looked at each of us before discerning that my mother, with her red face, puffy eyes, and trembling limbs, was his patient's wife, and said, "I'm sorry, your husband died today at four twenty-four p.m."

Died.

Today.

That's all I heard.

Walter Bleszinski was dead.

My dad was dead.

We didn't see him one last time, and whatever we said or didn't say there in that sterile little room has been erased from my memory. My mother didn't want to sleep in her bedroom that night, so Tyler and I camped out in the living room with her. She fell asleep on the sofa with the TV droning in the background. Tyler and I cocooned in our sleeping bags, staring up at the dark ceiling, trying to come to terms that we would never see our father again and wondering what life would be like without him. It was inconceivable to me.

I was fifteen years old.

I heard his voice from a few months earlier. *I'm proud of you.*

I heard my voice from a few hours earlier. *Fine, Dad.*

Now he was dead.

It's profoundly disturbing to think about that night and those that followed because not a single thing in the house had changed or even been moved except for my dad. His clothes were in his closet. His papers were on his dresser. The dishes from his lunch were in the dishwasher. His car was in the garage. He was everywhere, and yet he was never coming back. Everything was different. For me, home was no longer a safe place. My father would never go to work in the morning and come home at night, sit down for a family dinner, tell a corny joke, ask me to pick up after the dog, talk to me about computers, put his arm around me as we watched *The Tonight Show* and laughed at Johnny Carson, or give me a good-night kiss and tell me he would see me in the morning.

There were no more tomorrows with Dad.

Life couldn't be trusted. Only death was for sure.

The idea that he would always be with us was a lie.

Home was a palace of deceit.

I was never a good sleeper. When I was a baby, my mother used to take me to bed kicking and screaming. My sleeping got worse after my dad died. I had nightmares, including a recurring one where I woke up in the middle of the night having to pee and saw the floor covered in tarantulas trying to climb up onto the bed. I had no idea how I was going to get to the bathroom without being eaten alive by the spiders. They wanted to kill me.

The urge to pee and my fear of dying intensified until I jolted awake. The relief of realizing I had been trapped in a bad dream was quickly replaced by another nightmare from which there was no escape. Awake and unnerved, I lay in the dark, listening for my father's thunderous snores through our thin walls. I didn't hear them. I didn't hear anything. Until in the quiet I heard my own voice. *Fine, Dad.*

Except it wasn't fine.

I was a mess. At night I sat in my brother's black Nissan Sentra parked in our driveway, listening to Roxette's "It Must Have Been Love" on repeat. I spent hours there, crying until my entire body ached. In typing class at school, I sat at my desk, stinking of Drakkar Noir by Guy Laroche, trying not to sob out loud as I filled page after page with

DAD IS DEAD DAD IS DEAD DAD IS DEAD DAD IS DEAD. At one point, the teacher walked over to see what I was typing so feverishly. She glanced at my paper from behind me and walked away.

I spent hours playing *Willow*, a decent *Zelda*-style game based on the Val Kilmer movie. I played until I disappeared from reality. I probably would have disappeared for good if my mother hadn't dogged me about participating in the funeral arrangements. She wanted all the boys involved, including me.

We chose an oak coffin since my father always made such a big deal out of not scratching our kitchen table because it was oak and had cost him an arm and a leg. At school, I heard kids whisper, "His dad just died." I didn't mind the attention. I even tried to use it to my advantage by asking a cute girl to be my date to the funeral. I thought it might lead to my first kiss, maybe more if we hit it off. She declined.

I hated my dad's funeral. He was there in an open casket, looking like he was taking a nap in front of everyone. I reluctantly followed my mother and brothers. I didn't want to see him dead. Then I couldn't not look. I was creeped out by the stupid, fake smile the embalmers had given him. I started to panic, or maybe I felt sick. Whatever it was, I wanted to run the fuck away as fast as possible.

My mother misread the look on my face and leaned into me instead. "It's okay," she said. "You can touch him."

I bent down and kissed my father good night and goodbye. He felt cold and waxy. I wish I hadn't listened to my mother. Later, at the cemetery my dad had jogged past only a week earlier, we tossed white roses onto his casket as it was being lowered into the ground. I looked down only once, quickly, and then trained my gaze past the headstones toward the street, hoping to see Walt Bleszinski in his running clothes, thinking, hoping, and praying I would see him still alive, like Ryu's father in *Ninja Gaiden*.

SHAREWARE

My mother had experienced family upheaval before. When she was in her teens, her mother peaced out to Cali, leaving her to take care of her father and brother. Her parents eventually divorced, and her mother remarried and had a daughter, my aunt Lisa. They had grown close, and in the wake of my father's death, Lisa and her husband, Bob, came out from their home in Glendora, California, to support my mother and help with me and Tyler.

I liked Bob. He was a British transplant who spoke with a pleasant accent and shared crazy, exciting stories of driving rally cars in his younger days. He owned a small PC sales and repair store. He didn't try to take my father's place. But I did like it when they visited and I could come home from school and talk with him about computers, about which he was quite knowledgeable.

One day I came home from school and he asked if I played *Space Quest*. I was on my way upstairs, eager to throw my books on the floor and fire up my computer, but I stopped and turned back with a curious look on my face.

"You know *Space Quest*?" I asked.

"Surprise." He laughed. "Old fuckers like me play games too."

We bonded over our mutual love of Sierra On-Line games. Before they left, Bob and Lisa suggested to my mother that she move near them in California, where she could be close to Lisa, enjoy better weather, and restart her life. *The boys are going to be out of high school soon*, they said, and she was still a relatively young, attractive woman. Thanks to Bob, my mom also came home one day with a new IBM 386SX PC. I had talked about wanting an Amiga, but Bob insisted this was good for all my gaming and online needs.

"It's fast," he said, knowing that was all he needed to say.

Few adults understood the internet at the time. It was invisible to them. To me, it was a portal to a world that had been waiting for me to arrive, the party I had been missing out on until the day my friend and fellow nerd Ralph had showed me his dial-up modem and introduced me to BBSs—bulletin board servers or worlds consisting of message boards, games, videos, and so many other things hosted on computer servers.

I loved going over to his place. His family had moved to a brand-new house, with carpet that had a fresh-from-the-factory smell. Everything was clean and perfect. His older sister was hot, and his mom dug UB40's hit "Red Red Wine." Before going up to his room, he told his mom that we were going on the internet and to stay off the phone so as not to interrupt and disconnect us.

"I love that sound," he said, referring to the high-pitched whine of his 300-baud modem digitally shaking hands with the local internet server.

"I know," I said. "It sounds like two robots getting it on."

To me, the internet was a different version of my old fort in the woods. Here was this other space where people hung out, communicated, played games, and left messages for each other. We downloaded files, compressed games into zip files, and transferred files. It was our invisible superhighway, with activities and language that separated insiders from everyone else. We connected to it and with each other. It may not have been obvious at the time, but the internet was a new tool beginning to change the world, not just a new toy for nerds and so-called video game addicts, and you were either on it or left behind.

Very soon I couldn't imagine life without the internet. It wasn't just the games and the message boards. It was also the pictures and videos. Specifically, those of naked women. And more specifically, the scene of actress Phoebe Cates getting out of the swimming pool and unhooking her red bikini top in the movie *Fast Times at Ridgemont High*. The movie was fantastic. The ripped video on the internet was even better.

We spent hours hunting for naked celebrities. We weren't mature enough to consider the morality or lawfulness of such images, nor did we stop to ask how they even got there. When you're a horny teenage boy, you don't pause to think about those issues. You just want to see boobs and butts—and famous boobs and butts are best of all. Jerry Seinfeld explained this in a riff on men and sex in the first season of his classic TV series:

"What do we want? We want women! It's the only thing we know for sure: we want women! How do we get women? Oh, we don't know that."

At sixteen years old, we sure didn't know that. But we knew we wanted women, especially naked women, and famous naked women. And now we knew where to find them. Those pictures and animated porn, very early versions of GIFs, which took an excruciatingly long time to download and about two minutes to enjoy, replaced the skin magazines we used to hide in our fort in the woods.

But there was more than celebrity skin. When I got my own dial-up modem at home, I was able to spend more time exploring this universe of geeks and gamers obsessed with the same things that interested me. I played simple ASCII online games like *Trade Wars* and an early version of *Tetris*, whose leader board obsessed me. I connected with people in forums, traded information, left messages, and hung out. I joined a BBS group called Modem Warriors, whose posts had witty taglines like "Pope goes to Mount Olive. Popeye almost kills him," and I learned to communicate online with coolness and humor.

I was part of a community where I could be myself in a way that wasn't possible at school. I was accepted.

But, as would become ever more apparent over time, there was a dark side to this world. Early on, my primary BBS hangouts were *Trade Wars* and *Tetris*. Then I drifted over to Software Creations, a popular BBS for game developers and shareware distribution— selling, trading, playing, and talking about games. To maximize my modem speed, I searched for local BBS phone numbers instead of dialing into Los Angeles or London. The upside was obvious. The connection was faster. The downside? The trolls were nearby, and they got more personal.

After posting a simple screensaver I made, someone wrote, "Did your dead dad write that?" Enraged, I fired back: "Fuck you. I will find you and fucking kill you."

That earned me a warning from the BBS's moderator and advice from my brother Chris, who told me to "be careful."

Wise words. Soon I had a new friend on that local BBS, a guy named Phil. Phil and I became good friends. He was an older dude who was friendly, open, gently inquisitive, eager to answer questions and offer advice.

Through our back-and-forth exchanges, he got to know me. He took his time, starting with seemingly innocuous, general questions about my interests in games, computers, and school. He got me to reveal that I was a misfit, a nerd; that I struggled to make friends, hated that I had acne, and missed my father. He said he understood these wounds, he offered sympathy, and though I was too naïve to realize it, he had found his opening.

"You can ask me anything, anytime," he wrote. "School. Girls. Sex."

"Okay."

"Growing up is hard, isn't it?"

"Yes."

Our conversations took place in early versions of private chat rooms, but I knew Phil presented himself the same way to others on the BBS, in the role of confidant and advice expert on growing up, dating, relationships, and sex—especially sex. Within the relative anonymity of the BBS, sex was discussed with a willing openness. Lulled into a sense of privacy, safety, and intimacy, I admitted my ignorance and confusion and insecurities, and of course, Phil was there to listen and respond.

"How hot are the girls at your school?" he asked.

"Some are pretty fucking hot," I said.

"Have you had sex with any of them?"

"LOL."

"Still a virgin?"

"Yup."

"Sorry about that, pal. Bummer. Your day will cum."

";)"

"Do you know how to put on a condom?"

"Pretty sure it's obvious."

"They come in different sizes."

"Definitely a large."

"I have videos if you're ever interested."

I didn't know what to say. I had already opened up to Phil about losing my dad, the fears I had of going forward without him, and other things I hadn't told anyone else. When Phil said he cared about me, I believed him. It got to where some days I came home from school and I couldn't wait to fire up the BBS and talk with Phil. Nothing was off-limits: zits, loneliness, girls, sex. It was like an addiction, and Phil was the gatekeeper of all that was illicit and intoxicating, like he had the fastest internet connection and had hooked up with a bazillion girls. But watching videos with him?

"Think about it," he said. "I think you'll learn a lot about sex and what women really like."

He sounded doctor-like. Periodically he would remind me that he was local, like me. Then one day he asked if I wanted to come over to his place and hang out. He didn't mention the videos this time. It was more like a friend saying he was as bored as I was and we should get together and be bored together. Everything else was inferred.

I said yes.

We picked a date and time. After school, I hurried downstairs and told my mom I was going to a friend's house. She was vacuuming the living room. "Okay, have fun," she said. Phil's gray Honda was in front of our house. I got in and he drove us to his town house. In his mid-to-late thirties, Phil was nondescript physically, ordinary-looking. Nothing about him stood out then or now. He gave me a casual nod and made some forgettable small talk.

I was nervous about being in the car with this older dude but tried to play it cool and no doubt failed miserably. I mean, we were going to his house to look at porn. But he was practiced enough to go with it and get us to his house.

"Favorite radio station?"

"Nah."

"Cool. We're almost there."

Inside his place, he showed me his PC and collection of games, stuff that he knew would interest me and help me relax. I did get a sense of familiarity from seeing this spot where he sat when he was online, talking to me and everyone else. He remembered my computer was in our living room, and he commented about the luxury of having privacy. "It helps," he said, laughing as if we were sharing a secret.

Which was exactly what we were doing. He went online and jumped around to a few sites. It was like riding shotgun in a friend's car as we cruised around town. When he sensed me relax, he clicked on links that brought up pictures of naked chicks and steered the conversation toward sex. Soon he offered to show me one of his porn videos.

"Want to?" he asked. "It's the stuff that really teaches you how to fuck."

I was still jacking off to animated GIFs. Phil's promise of real hard-core porn was too much to resist.

"Fuck yeah," I said, trying to echo my online bravado.

I thought this was going to be like watching porn or paging through a *Penthouse* with one of my friends. It wasn't. Phil led me into his bedroom, where he had a VCR connected to a TV. He looked through a shelf of tapes before selecting one, holding it up for me to see, and said, "This one is unbelievable." Phil made room for us to sit on the edge of his bed. As we watched, he commented on the action onscreen and nudged my shoulder as if to confirm the quality. *See, what did I tell you? Good shit, right?*

I nodded. "I'm going to bust out of my clothes," he said, using that as an excuse to take off his shirt and pants. Clad only in his underwear, he looked at me. "I can see you're enjoying this too." I nodded, embarrassed. Then I learned his real intention. He asked me to touch him, and in exchange, he offered to show me "what it was like to fuck a girl." He busted out a tube of K-Y Jelly, told me to pull down my pants, and said, "You use this stuff, you'll go off like a rocket. Let me show you."

Although I knew this was wrong, Phil had won my trust long ago. I would later realize that BBS was full of characters like him—the stereotypical pervert who disguised himself as a nice guy, a knowledgeable friend, a sympathetic older pal, a father figure. Whatever worked in terms of gaining your attention and access to your imagination.

I was perfect prey for him. I was emotionally vulnerable, curious, bright, and hungry for connection and validation. All these years later I still struggle with what happened: Was I that naïve? Or did I know? I mean, I was going to this guy's house to watch porn. Of course the dude was going to do something to me, you know?

Afterward, as I cleaned up and he got dressed, Phil maintained an easygoing, friendly chitchat, as if what we had done was normal and no big deal, just the fun he had promised we would have at his place.

"Finished?" he asked.

I nodded.

"Good. I'll drive you home."

The ride home was quiet, excruciatingly so, and horribly uncomfortable. I stared out the window. I knew what we had done was wrong, but I didn't know exactly where to put it on a scale of bad, very bad, illegal, or scarred for life. "So this is probably one of those things we don't tell anyone about," I said.

Phil turned toward me and nodded. "Yeah, let's just keep this between us."

As soon as he stopped the car in front of my house, I bolted out the door. I think I managed to say "See ya." I walked through the front door and headed straight toward the stairs, intending to go directly to my room and lose myself in my Nintendo. The more you don't want to deal with the real world, the more you jump into the virtual one. It's the reason thirty-plus years later, people are signing up to live and work in the metaverse.

But my mother intercepted me.

"Are you okay?" she asked.

"Yeah, sure."

I turned around to look at her but stared down toward her feet.

I didn't want to look up and make eye contact. I knew she would see through me and know something was wrong. I think she knew anyway.

"I was worried that guy was going to molest you or something," she said.

I was well into adulthood when I thought back on this moment and felt a surge of resentment and heard myself ask, "Then why didn't you do something before I got in that pervert's car?" At the time, though, I said, "Nah, I'm good," and raced upstairs back to my Nintendo, my retreat from the real world into the virtual world.

I never spoke to Phil again. Though he tried multiple times to connect with me online, probably to arrange a second playdate, and then, after I went incommunicado, to make sure I didn't call the police, he dropped off my radar. I was left feeling more confused than anything else. Had I been raped? Was I gay? Was I still a virgin? It was all stuff I thought I needed to figure out but eventually buried under layers of other shit and got on with my life.

Like many people who've been molested, especially boys, I never told anyone I had been molested. If someone had asked if I had ever been sexually abused, I would have said no. Then one night in 2019 I was having drinks with a bunch of game-developer friends and the topic came up, as happens when alcohol gets people talking. It wasn't the shocker I might have thought. "Shit, man, *everyone's* been molested," one of my friends said. His statement was confirmed as hands went up around the table, including mine. I thought, *How many bastards like Phil were out there fucking up people's lives?*

Soon after Aunt Lisa and Uncle Bob visited, my mother announced that we were moving to California. It was just like her own mother had done. She was pushing reset after her life had gone tilt. We were going to pack up and head west in the summer. The move wasn't going to affect my two older brothers, Greg and Jeff, who were in the army and navy respectively, or Chris, who was out of the house, but Tyler and I would finish the school year and then say goodbye to our friends.

Seeing a FOR SALE sign go up in front of our family home was more traumatic than my rendezvous with Phil. The wound from being molested could be managed. Losing the sense and security of home would be something that never went away. As word spread that Tyler and I were moving to Los Angeles, something unexpected and different happened at school. For the rest of tenth grade, I was considered cool. Instead of referring to me sarcastically as Nintendo Boy, I was envied for being that Cali Boy.

Ever the opportunist, I tried to take advantage of this change in status with the ladies. I hit on Laura DeLuca, the Julia Roberts of our grade, but without success. She stuck with her sports-stud boyfriend. (Hey, you can't blame me.) I also tried to convince my other crush, Tammi Kent, that my last summer could be her best summer if she ditched her loser boyfriend. "Life is too short," I told her. "We don't want to miss out on something special." Amused, she gave me a tiny kiss and said, "You're sweet."

That was progress. But I didn't want to be sweet. I wanted to be hot, special, unique, and famous. I decided to show Tammi what she was missing by designing a video game that would make me all that and more.

I created *The Palace of Deceit: The Secret of Castle Lockemoer*. The game, a single-player text adventure, was about a good wizard trying to rid a faraway land of an evil wizard who is terrorizing its inhabitants. The fighting took place in a castle full of traps and treachery. I plugged away every day after school and late into the night. My mother was obsessed with the soundtrack to *The Phantom of the*

Opera and played it nonstop; but Sir Andrew Lloyd Webber's masterpiece couldn't have been a more appropriate backdrop. I was the Phantom, a genius hiding in the dark beneath the Paris Opera House, aching for love.

The instruction book to *The Palace of Deceit: The Secret of Castle Lockemoer* read like the opening voice-over to a coming-of-age movie starring sixteen-year-old me:

"This adventure was produced through many hours of toil and labor on the author's part. He blew off his homework many a night to fix bugs, and his grades suffered. He was severely beaten by his mother with a spatula repeatedly. His spelling is now pitiful, and he can only groan once for yes and twice for no. On top of it, the only girl he ever loved outside of his spatula-wielding mother, the lovely Tammi Lynn Kent, decided to stay with her ugly boyfriend instead of going for this talented, handsome, moderately built dude.

"He is emotionally crippled from this experience. He needs your donations to get back on his blistered feet and write games, fight off his mother, do homework, and somehow defy the odds and prevent his relocation to California and marry this pretty thing. Hasta la vista, baybeeee."

The game was beta-tested by a couple of friends and uploaded onto CompuServe, the best platform for sharing and selling software. I slapped a price tag of five dollars on it and then got to the real work of telling everyone I knew to buy it. My English teacher purchased the very first copy. Several friends and acquaintances from my BBSs also bought copies, and somehow word spread. I got orders from around the country.

It was only one here, two there, but the game was selling. I affixed a large order number on each game—5006, 5007, etc.—to give the impression that I was selling thousands of them when the actual number was in the high dozens. Then I bubble-wrapped each game, stuck it in a manila envelope, and asked Tyler to drive me to the post office, where I dropped them into the mailbox and once again bid them *hasta la vista, baby*.

As my bank account grew into the hundreds of dollars, the time came to say goodbye to North Andover, the woods where I had so many adventures, my friends, and Tammi, who missed her chance at hooking up with a hard-working, self-proclaimed boy genius. I was already plotting my follow-up game. What did she have going for her besides hotness?

Long live shareware.

DARE TO DREAM

I dug myself into the seat and stared out the window of the plane, watching the clouds and the checkerboard landscape thirty-five thousand feet below us. Gradually, the view gave way to mountains and desert, and then urban sprawl. I took a final sip from the tiny bottle of booze I had snuck off the flight attendant's drink cart and nursed for much of the flight. I figured it might help calm my fears about the move.

My mom had gone out to LA, done her homework, and used the money from my father's life insurance to buy a house on a golf course. It sounded fancy. But I was scared. I didn't know what to expect on the West Coast. I didn't know how to skateboard, and I was frightened of the gangs. I had listened to NWA and Ice-T, and through their lyrics, I learned that people were shot in some LA neighborhoods just for wearing the wrong color T-shirt.

Although I was sixteen, I had only recently stopped sleeping with my teddy bear, Pudgy. How was I going to deal with being in the crossfire of the Bloods and Crips?

Uncle Bob picked us up at the airport and drove us to our new home in La Verne. As we pulled into the driveway, I was listening to Madonna's "Like a Prayer" on my Discman. She sang, "And it feels like . . . home." I hoped it would.

La Verne was a tapestry of middle-class housing developments about forty-five minutes east of downtown LA but devoid of the city's culture and diversity. The opening of a Chili's and a new Edwards cinema was a big deal here. It was near Raging Waters, the popular water park that Tyler and I renamed Raging Hard-Ons as soon as we saw the bikinied girls there. My new school, Bonita High, was an expanse of small buildings and bungalows surrounded by a large chain-link fence. It reminded me of a minimum-security prison.

My first day was terrifying. When I got to school, I realized I had worn a red T-shirt. I spent the first half of the day thinking I was going to get shot. Fear finally got the best of me, and I asked a kid if I was in danger. He looked at me like I had just arrived from Planet Dork. "Dude, we're in La Verne, not Compton," he scoffed. "Jesus Christ, get a grip."

I tried. I made a couple friends, but otherwise I was invisible to my new classmates. Or else I was lame. Like the day I wore a hockey jersey to school, and people were like, "Hockey? What the fuck?" It could have been worse. Considering the dislocation of the move, my father's death, the molestation, starting a new school, and the severe acne that erupted after I got there, I could've gotten into drugs, suffered depression, or succumbed to the isolation and alienation of being the new kid. It's a miracle none or all of the above happened.

Not that it wasn't hard. Every morning I stared at myself in the bathroom mirror and saw nothing but the most hideous outbreak of acne. How could anyone be friends with me when I didn't like looking at myself? How was I ever going to get a girlfriend? Even my brother's poster of Heather Thomas seemed to turn the other way when I looked at her. It was in that frame of mind that I then left the house and went to school.

Luckily, I had a safety net: video games. One day I was doing errands with my mother, and we pulled into this fancy place I had never heard of called Target. Compared to the Bradlees department store back in North Andover, this was next-level shopping. Inside, I split from my mom and wandered the aisles while she shopped. I was a tiny vessel drifting in an ocean of so-what and who-cares until I turned a corner and came face-to-face with a stack of Super Nintendo game consoles. I stopped and stared as if the display was a sign from God—or maybe my father. *Clifford, don't give up.*

Whether it was out of pity, love, or some leftover largesse from my father's life insurance, my mother bought me one. I didn't even have to beg.

At home, I sat on my green comforter and fired up *Super Mario World.* I had pulled back from playing games while I tried to make new friends, but suddenly I felt like my best friend in the world had come back to rescue me and I knew that somehow, some way, we were not going to be apart ever again.

In the spring, my mother fell in love with a decent man whom she eventually married, and on her way down the aisle, she basically abdicated her responsibilities as a parent. Although she didn't leave the same way her mother had, she did peace out emotionally. Tyler and I were basically on our own. I got a job at McDonald's. I also bought a copy of *Introduction to Programming Using Visual Basic* and worked on updating my game, *The Palace of Deceit.* My life was narrowly and purposefully focused. I went to school, worked a four-hour shift at Mickey D's, and then toiled on the game.

Updating the game took priority. I worked late into the night. My midnight trips to the kitchen for Mountain Dew refills made me privy to the sounds of my mother and her new man from her bedroom, which I didn't need to hear, and so I hurried back to my room, shut the door, and continued mapping out the details of my game. In *The Palace of Deceit: The Dragon's Plight,* as this next version was titled, a baby-blue dragon named Nightshade is held captive by the evil wizard Garth (*Wayne's World* was popular at the time) in the kingdom of Salac (inspired by the salicylic acid I took for my acne). The object is to escape the castle's dungeon, obtain the magical sword, slay Garth, and save the kingdom.

The graphics were crude and cobbled together in MS Paint, and the game lacked animation and music, but the point-and-click adventure was still a significant leap for me in terms of programming and storytelling. I finished it over the summer and typed out a five-page instruction manual. "It's not a good idea to go pushing strange buttons or pulling levers you don't know about," I wrote. I added encouragement in the Help section. "Don't give up. Explore every room in the castle! Good luck!"

Lastly, I included a small pitch for my uncle Bob's store ("Bob gets the finest computer parts wholesale and sells them to you for incredible prices") and a troubleshooting section with my home phone number. "Leave a message. Or ask for Cliff."

Palace 2.0 posted on CompuServe in August 1992, and sales were better than its predecessor. At one point, I was getting close to ten registrations per week and the pace stayed relatively steady for about a year. I never counted the exact number of registrations, but I might've totaled a couple thousand sales.

Encouraged and now even more ambitious, I jumped straight into building my next game, this one fittingly titled *Dare to Dream*.

Unlike the two previous games, this point-and-click adventure was distinctly and perhaps disturbingly more personal. Its protagonist, Tyler Norris, was a ten-year-old boy being driven crazy by nightmares that plagued his sleep after his father's death. I borrowed my brother's name, obviously, but the nightmares unfortunately belonged to me. Snakes in the closet, tarantulas on the floor, monsters chasing me. I suffered all the classics and, as a result, was and still am a terrible sleeper.

Sitting on my bedroom floor, I sketched out the game scene by scene. Some nights I was surrounded by dozens of drawings. Once I had enough, I tacked them next to my computer in storyboard fashion, opened Microsoft Paint, and chipped away. I wasn't aware of it at the time, but I was working under the influence of Accutane, the powerful drug my dermatologist prescribed to nuke my acne. Depression was one of its many side effects, and indeed, it put me in a dark, hazy fog where I was able to access the anxieties and grief that had been eating at me since my father died.

I hadn't talked about these feelings with anyone, but they flowed straight into the game without any difficulty. It opened with a photograph of Tyler poking out of the top of a large manila envelope. Next to it was a page from a psychiatric case study detailing the anxiety, depression, and manic episodes he suffered due to his fear that a demon named Christian (my middle brother's name) was coming for him. "How much stress can a young boy be put under?" the file read.

"First the grades, then the paper route, and of course the loss of a father that has been eating away at you for the past eight months. You're now the MAN OF THE HOUSE . . . Awfully big responsibility for a kid who turns eleven in two weeks. Life sure couldn't get any worse . . . Stormy, uneasy clouds greet you as you fall deeper and deeper into the depths of your soul."

The game was basically a fever dream. The objective was to guide Tyler through his troubled subconscious to a place where he was at peace with the loss of his father. The game's final screen showed Tyler's father's grave (his name was Walter, of course) with the year of my father's birth and death on his headstone, and the words "Forever and Then," which was the phrase engraved on the inside of his and my mother's wedding bands.

I don't think any of the puzzles in *Dare to Dream* ever made sense, and the characters were weird amalgams from my life and Clive

Barker's *Hellraiser*. I cringe whenever I see video of the game on You-Tube, but making it was probably more effective than talking to a therapist.

I n the second semester of eleventh grade, I signed up for a drama class and finally made a few friends. The drama kids were nerds too—just a different type. I shared their same passion for the theater, and I thrived from being involved in the school's productions. During senior year, I was Mercutio in *Romeo and Juliet*, the lead in *Ten Little Indians*, and Lenny in Neil Simon's *Rumors*. I loved being onstage. The applause substituted for the praise and encouragement I missed from my father. The hugs backstage were the reason most of us lived for drama class. We were accepted for being our quirky selves.

I thought those small claims to fame might make me popular with the school's cool kids no matter how uncool I was. One day the hottest surfer dude in the school and his girlfriend, Miss Teen La Verne, shouted "Hey, you" as I wandered past them at the start of lunch and motioned for me to come over to where they sat on the quad with their little clique of genetically blessed wunderkind.

"You go here, right?" Miss Teen La Verne said.

I nodded. "Yeah."

"How come I haven't seen you at any parties?" she asked.

I couldn't tell her the truth without destroying the dignity I was holding on to as if it were driftwood in the ocean.

"Not into 'em," I said.

"What do you do instead?" someone else asked.

"I make money," I said.

I thought that sounded cool. So did they.

"How?" Surfer Dude asked.

"I make video games and sell 'em," I said.

"You have a store?"

"No. Shareware."

I saw they had no idea what I was talking about. I explained that shareware was software that was uploaded onto servers where people could log in and *share* the software, meaning they could download and use it for free. Their eyes glazed over. Though we attended the same school, we belonged to different worlds, and as much as I enjoyed meeting Mr. Hot Surfer Dude and Miss Teen La Verne and her friends, we ran out of conversation.

Besides, I had work to do.

A company called Apogee was killing the shareware market with side-scrolling platformer games on the PC. In 1990, they released *Commander Keen: Invasion of the Vorticons*, featuring a young boy in a football helmet who battled aliens with a little laser. I was used to games like this on my Nintendo, but I played *Commander Keen* on my PC and recognized that being able to do so was new, crazy cool shit.

Eager to find out more about how this came to be, I learned that Apogee published *Commander Keen*, but the game itself was developed by id Software, a company founded by John Carmack, John Romero, Tom Hall, and Adrian Carmack. In the spring of my junior year, they released *Wolfenstein 3D*, a first-person shooter with a simple and irresistible premise. You blasted Nazis. You shot guard dogs. You blasted more Nazis as guards shouted "Mein leben!" And blood splattered—in 3D! The blood looked like it was coming straight at you. The game was an instant classic.

Wolfenstein 3D established John Carmack and John Romero as the Paul McCartney and John Lennon of video games. They had created a game that was as catchy and cool as any pop song, and they understood how to market it. *Wolfenstein 3D* consisted of three episodes—the first was free, and then once hooked, you had to pay to get the next two. They were well worth it. In the third and final episode, you went after none other than Hitler, whom the bad boys at id had outfitted in a teal mech suit. It was truly a bloody good time.

One of the other rising stars in the shareware space was a company called Epic MegaGames. I played their hit game *Jill of the Jungle* on my IBM 386, which my mother bought at a deep discount from Uncle Bob. Jill was a blond vixen in a unitard careening through a variety of environments—not just jungles—collecting power-ups, tossing knives at nefarious jungle creatures, and collecting all sorts of loot. "Find the magical icons, and Jill will transform into a flaming bird, a leaping frog, or even better, a fish who can shoot bullets!" read the description. It was standard character platform stuff on a console, but *not* on the PC.

There was something about *Jill of the Jungle* that made it unique. After I played the game for the first time, I noticed the end credits contained a message from Epic MegaGames inviting talented game makers to contact them about a job. "Come work with us," it said. I had never seen a message like that in a game. I felt as if that was intended for me. My first two games were still selling, and I was hammering away on my third. Partnering with Epic could help me sell more games and add legitimacy to my budding aspirations as a game maker. If they wanted to hire me, I was more than ready to quit my shift at McDonald's.

I saw that Epic was headquartered in Maryland. I had no idea that its founder, twenty-two-year-old programming genius and future billionaire Tim Sweeney, had launched it from his parents' basement in 1991 and had only recently added a second employee, businessman Mark Rein. The company's name, Epic MegaGames, was supposed to give the impression it was a massive operation. It convinced me. I wondered what it would be like to work there, making games full-time.

What if they wanted to hire me right away? Would I wait till graduation? Drop out of high school? Would I have to get my mother's permission?

I wrote a letter to Tim Sweeney and Epic MegaGames, responding to their call for talent with a brief description of myself as an ambitious young game builder and a copy of *Palace of Deceit* on a 3.5-inch floppy disc. I dropped the envelope in the mail, hoping for a response but not counting on it. Even if I got one, I didn't think it would actually change my life.

Weeks passed. High school continued. I had nearly forgotten about the letter. Then one day my phone rang and a fast-talking man on the other end said, "Cliff?"

"Yeah," I said.

"Mark Rein," he replied. "You sent your game in to Tim Sweeney. I'm Tim's partner at Epic MegaGames. Got time to talk?"

"Yeah, sure," I said.

Caught off guard, my head spun.

"We got your game and . . ."

He spoke faster than any human I had ever encountered. But I picked up the gist: he liked *Palace of Deceit*, but it could be better.

"It needs work," he said. "Better graphics, add music and audio . . ."

It sounded like he was suggesting that I start over on this game. What the fuck? I was still receiving orders and making money off it. I kept my cool, but I was pissed.

Who the fuck was this guy?

Where was this mysterious Tim guy?

No, I'm not redoing my entire game. Why should I?

Do I even want to work with these people?

Is this what working in video games was like?

"But you're pretty good," he said.

That calmed me down. All of a sudden I liked this guy. He thought I was *pretty good*. Damn.

"What else do you have?" he asked.

I told him about *Dare to Dream*. "It's going to have higher-rez graphics, music, things like that," I said.

The call ended with us promising to speak again. I continued to work on *Dare to Dream*. I mapped out the first three episodes and when I completed the first one, I sent it to Epic. Within days, I got a response. The phone rang and this time it was Tim Sweeney, sounding upbeat, enthusiastic, and open. In other words, he was the opposite of Mark.

"Hey, what's up?" I said casually, like I would to a friend, which was the way Tim sounded, and no doubt why it made Tim laugh.

"Oh, I'm just looking at a beautiful moonlit dock in your game. It's great. Keep going!"

"Thanks, man," I said.

"Let me know when you're finished."

Tim sent me a publishing agreement, which offered a small royalty, and which I signed without having any idea what it said, even though my man Ice-T, in his song "Rap Game's Hijacked," warned: "Read everything before you sign." I didn't even know if the contract was legally binding since I wasn't yet eighteen. But who cared?

Epic released *Dare to Dream* on March 1, 1993. They uploaded the first episode to CompuServe and every BBS they could find. As was standard practice, the first one was free and the next two had to be ordered. They arrived by snail mail. I got excited when I heard Epic had created an inventory of several thousand games. I imagined *Dare to Dream* was going to make me enough money to dodge the inevitable college train.

But my first royalty check was only six hundred dollars. The next one arrived a month later for half that amount. And so on. *Dare to Dream* was a flop. I was crushed. I didn't understand why it had failed. The game had all the elements that I loved: it was personal, whimsical, and the puzzles, though odd, weren't, in my opinion, too hard. Tim disagreed.

By this time, Tim and I were speaking several times a week, and we had developed a good rapport. He was only five years older than me, but that gap was immeasurable in terms of maturity, experience, and brainpower. I felt similarly about Mark, whose single-minded focus on making money impressed me as much as it intimidated me. I knew he liked me, but it was Tim with whom I really clicked.

We traded opinions about Epic's releases, like *Ken's Labyrinth*, *Xargon*, and *Castle of the Winds*, and those put out by the competition, like Apogee and id Software. He loved the notes I gave him, all the tiny details about why I thought a game was or wasn't good, and similarly, what made one game better and more fun than another. I was often blown away. He was equally obsessed, but his obsession was with making games, not playing them, which I realized early on when I asked him a question about *Wolfenstein 3D*.

"Have you ever noticed when you kill Nazis and their bodies are laying there, if you rotate around the zombies, the Nazis' feet are always facing you?"

"Oh yeah," he said. "That's because they're not actually 3D. They're just pixelated sprites that are ray-casted in front of you."

I was like, *What?*

Even then it was clear Tim knew things about games other people didn't and would never know. So when he said *Dare to Dream* was pretty good but the puzzles were too difficult and way too weird, I listened.

"Look, Cliffy, at one point, the player has to find a jar of Vaseline so they can slip into the sewers to meet a talking country gator." He laughed. "That's weird."

"I guess."

He heard the dejection in my voice. "Don't give up. The next one will be better."

Would there be a next one? I had spent a year working on *Dare to Dream* only to see it bomb. Tim's encouragement helped, but I didn't have any ideas and I didn't feel like I had the drive or desire to make another game. Thank God I got a free meal with every shift I worked at McDonald's.

ALL THAT JAZZ

One night Tyler drove me to Subway and a blond girl around my age was taking orders behind the counter. As we stepped up to the counter, she greeted us with a hello and a smile. I volleyed with a few quips of my own, made her laugh, and before we moved on down the counter, she wrote her name and number on a napkin and thrust it into my hand. "Call me," she said with a playful wink.

At home, I sat down at the kitchen table and stared at the napkin as if it were a word problem on the SATs. My brother stood next to me, impatient and kind of incredulous that I didn't get what was so obvious to him.

"Call her," he said. "What's the worst that can happen?"

Divorce?

Having to give her all my money?

Ah, but that was far down the line and unforeseeable.

So I called. Her name was Marcy, and she reminded me of a slightly plumper and less permed Bridget Fonda in *Drop Dead Fred*. Although we went to the same school, our paths had never crossed. She was involved with choir, and I was in drama. They were as different as California and Florida. But we started to date and liked each other. Her travel agent mom and police officer father were divorced, which gave her an independence similar to mine. Basically, we called our own shots. Neither of us had been in a serious relationship before, and we got close quickly. We spent all our free time together.

Since I didn't have a car or a driver's license, we cruised around town in her '67 Mustang. We saw all the films at the new Edwards cinema, including *The Crow*, *Pulp Fiction*, *Speed*, and even *Milk Money*. We ate at Chili's and McDonald's, drove into Claremont for Mexican food, and listened to Nine Inch Nails, Enigma, and *The Crow* soundtrack.

About a month into our relationship, Marcy and I had sex in our spare bedroom downstairs, which doubled as my room because my mother never ran the air-conditioning and my upstairs bedroom got too hot. I'd be like, "Mom, I got two computers running in here. I'm trying to work on my career. I'm going to school. It's ninety-eight degrees outside, about ten degrees hotter in here, can't we run the fucking air-conditioning?" But no, it was too expensive, she'd say.

That first time doing the deed was clunky and awkward and also the greatest thing that had ever happened to me in my entire life. I was convinced that I was the only person my age who hadn't done it, and now that I had, I felt a sense of relief and confidence that wasn't there before. I also wanted to do it again and again and again . . . and we did. Usually with the Nine Inch Nails song "Closer" on repeat in the background. I was in love.

In fall 1993, I enrolled at Cal Poly Pomona, where Tyler was already studying journalism. I signed up for computer science classes and discovered how woefully unprepared and behind I was compared to my classmates. They had lived and breathed math and programming in high school. I had done drama. Our big assignment was to create our own operating system. I had taught myself to code in simple Visual Basic, but creating an operating system required extensive knowledge of C++ or an even more hard-core programming language, Assembly, and that was way out of my league. It depressed the hell out of me.

I could have gone to the library and tried to catch up, but I believe you go where you need to be, not where you should be, and for me that was the campus arcade.

There I found not just fellow gamers but hard-core gamers, students who were total badasses at *Mortal Kombat 2* or *Street Fighter 2*. I spent at least fifty dollars in quarters before I was able to take several down and prove my own badassness. It probably sounds crazy when I say that playing *MK2* or *SF2* with such obsessiveness could be mentally healthy, but it was my way of working through the sense of failure I had after *Dare to Dream* bombed and my lack of programming know-how compared to my fellow comp-sci classmates.

Tim and Mark did nothing to discourage me from school, but our conversations and emails continued as if it were incidental. That was substantiated when an envelope from Tim arrived in the mail. Inside was a check for one thousand dollars and a note that said the money was an advance on "whatever Cliff's next game is." I had barely finished my shopping spree at the mall when a $20,000 SGI Indigo computer showed up at my house with a note that said, "Play around with it. Tim."

Such largesse seemed like a setup. Soon another surprise arrived: a silky-smooth 2D-platform game demo made by a talented Dutch programmer named Arjan Brussee. Arjan was a standout in Europe's demo scene, a subculture of leading-edge programmers who staged semi-competitive events where they showed off their work. It was like a graphical Bake-Off for video game programming. After sharing this background, Tim asked me to play with the demo and let him know my thoughts. "It's pretty cool," he said.

He was right. Arjan's demo lit up my screen. I thought I recognized the snippet of game as a micro clone of an Amiga game called *Turrican*, which featured a gun-wielding mutant warrior fighting a random assortment of foes. The frame rate was buttery smooth, and the graphics were crisp. Nice job. But Arjan's demo was really all about its user-friendly editor, the tool nontechnical programmers like me used for building levels, animating characters, making pickups, and crafting weapons. It gave me skills I didn't have and the ability to build a more sophisticated game. Never mind learning C++. Screw my computer programming major.

"This guy is a mind reader," I emailed Tim. "I love it. The editor will let me go from creating 2D point-and-click games to a character-action platform game."

"Great," he replied. "I can't wait to see your new game."

Ah, so there it was: Tim's plan revealed. He had sent the advance to keep me on the hook. The computer was to keep me excited. And now the editor would let me create at a new and more sophisticated level. It worked. Inspired, I sat down on the carpet in the spare bedroom I had since converted into an office, busted out my sketch pad, and started to doodle. I didn't have an idea for a game. But I sketched and wrote out thoughts as they came to me. I let my mind wander and hoped I would bump into something good.

My sketch pad filled up with evil panda bears, sci-fi guns, goofy giant turtles, and *Sonic the Hedgehog*–inspired environments. Later, as I sorted through them, one stood out: a tough little rabbit wearing a headband and goggles and firing a big fucking gun. The heavily armed rabbit reminded me of John Rambo blasting bad guys with his M60. At the bottom of the drawing I scribbled the words *Jaz the Jakwabbit*. I liked it. "This just might work," I said to myself.

I don't know if I was learning how much of this type of work, like most artistic endeavors, was a highly individualistic, often lonely, and intensely personal journey inside my imagination or if I understood all that intuitively, but, despite my otherwise short attention span, I seemed temperamentally suited to long hours staring at a sketch pad or a computer screen. My drawing of that badass jackrabbit triggered ideas.

I knew that character platformers were a thing on consoles, but I also knew the side-scrolling character mascot genre was way underserved on the PC. *Commander Keen* came to mind, but I think what really happened is that I ripped off *Sonic*. I saw an opportunity to come out swinging with a Rambo-like rabbit.

But that was it. I sat in front of my $20,000 SGI Indigo computer and played. Maybe that was the reason I didn't mind the long, lonely hours: it seemed like play. The first iteration of this character stretched my artistic abilities to the limit. Then came the fun part: updating, tweaking, animating, and bringing the final image to life. I used Deluxe Paint's gradient auto-fill function to put him in a cool environment. Finally, I played with the name until it not only sounded right but also felt right on my tongue: Jazz Jackrabbit.

Next, Jazz needed foes. Mario had Goombas, Koopas, and Lakitu. Who were Jazz's enemies? I flashed back to the days I spent exploring the woods beyond our house in North Andover, fishing in ponds, catching critters, looking for snakes, and listening to toads; a thought hit me: What about turtles?

Other than some French chefs, I can't imagine many people have asked that question, but it resonated with me. Why not turtles? As soon as I thought about it, I knew I had found my story: the tortoise and the hare from Aesop's Fables were still fighting three thousand years later. In this case, it was a gun-toting jackrabbit and an evil genius tortoise. They were locked in a timeless battle. With those two elements in mind, the game began to unfold. I worked on it during my computer science class in school. At home, I sat in front of the computer turning my notes into animated scenes.

Life got very focused. I quit my job at McDonald's, popped NoDoz, pounded Mountain Dew, and within two weeks I had animations of

Jazz, several turtles, some wizards, a weapon or two, and whatever else my amateur ass could draw. I also mapped out the first level. The work was crude, but I saw potential, as did Tyler and Marcy, who gave their approval. That was all the encouragement I needed before sending it to Tim and Mark.

Tim responded with an email formally introducing me and Arjan Brussee, the Dutch programming whiz. Unbeknownst to me, while I was playing with Arjan's demo and sketching out my first iteration of *Jazz Jackrabbit*, Mark Rein had traveled to the Netherlands to recruit Arjan. He was on board. "Let's see what you guys can do with Cliffy's idea," Tim said.

Tim had a knack for putting people together in the hope that something good might result, and in this case, it did. Arjan and I talked on the phone several times before relying almost exclusively on email. The nine-hour time difference between California and the Netherlands was not an impediment. He spoke excellent English, with a slight accent, and very fast. I also spoke quickly. Together, an hour-long conversation for most people took us ten minutes.

He liked *Jazz*, and we fell into an easy partnership. I asked for features, and he obliged: Springy jump pads. Velocity tubes. Different movement patterns for enemies.

"I want force fields that you climb going up and down the level," I said.

"You got it," he said.

Nothing fazed Arjan. With his editor, I was able to construct characters, objects, and environments, and then hand them over for him to code. For example, he added the artificial intelligence to the enemies, coded the boss fights, and made sure the frame rate was good. It was the same playbook Tim Sweeney would perfect later with the Unreal Editor. Make life simpler for the creatives so they don't get hung up on technical aspects.

Arjan's coding genius made me feel insecure about my art and animations. I suppose that was to be expected, to some extent, especially as my grades dropped at school, though that was mostly from lack of attention. I didn't have the interest or the time for classwork. I cobbled away, drafting ideas for each level and of course the requisite boss fights that needed to be won before graduating to the next one. There was something about the boss fights that came at the end of every level that reminded me of real life.

I wasn't yet twenty years old and I'd had my share of them: losing my father, moving to a new city, struggling in school . . . and now trying to turn this idea into a game that would lead to a career that would make me a rich and famous game designer. I was like other young guys practicing guitar or the drums in their bedroom and dreaming of rock stardom. It happens to a few. Most fail. It's life without a safety net. If you have a plan B, you're probably going to fail at plan A. The odds are against you anyway.

But I saw myself following in the footsteps of John Romero, the successful, flashy rock-star game designer. I wanted that so fucking badly.

Tim and Mark decided Arjan and I should meet and collaborate in person for a few days. We decided to meet at Mark's house in Toronto. The flight there was my first time traveling on my own. Tim and Mark failed to mention that I would need a passport to enter Canada. I showed my Social Security card at customs and the snarky official held it up, looked me in the eye, and said, "This is not worth the paper it's written on."

Another official ushered me through a nearby door and into an empty side room. It looked like a place criminals and shady characters were interrogated, which I suppose was its purpose. Another agent joined us. They were not amused or sympathetic, which would have been the appropriate response. After asking a few rapid-fire questions, they could tell I was inexperienced, terrified, and not going to single-handedly destroy the Canadian economy. Come on, guys, where's your sense of humor? Our countries aren't at war!

They eventually let me go to try to find these guys named Tim and Mark who, as I explained, were meeting me in the baggage-claim area.

I had never seen either Tim or Mark—not in person or in photographs. All I knew was what Tim had told me: that he was about six feet tall, had brown hair, and wore glasses. I saw someone fitting that description to my right.

"Tim?"

"No." The guy shook his head.

"Sorry."

A moment later I heard someone say my name and I spun around. "Cliff?"

It was Tim. Tall, gangly, and glad to have recognized me. Next to him was Mark Rein, who was built like a beer-drinking frat boy and fanning himself with an ad flyer he had picked up somewhere in the terminal. The man was always hot. We drove to Mark's house in a suburb outside Toronto. Canadian flags hung in front of homes throughout the subdivision. It was Canada Day, Mark explained.

Mark's house was large and new and impressive. His soon-to-be wife was beautiful. Prior to Epic, he had been president of id Software and I could see he was punching upward in life. He was an openly ambitious capitalist, who talked about making money as often as he complained about being hot, which was all the time. Over the years, Mark has gotten plenty of well-deserved credit for being the hungry business bulldog behind Epic, but Tim is equally smart in that area, if not smarter, and I didn't have to hang around them too long before I sensed they were destined to build an empire.

When I finally met Arjan in person, I did a double take: he was a dead ringer for the actor Alfred Molina. Regardless, we already knew each other. Hours on the phone together and the dozens of emails we'd exchanged had given us a familiarity. We spoke to each other in a shorthand, and we wasted no time getting to work. For the next few days—we were there for less than a week—we spent twelve to fifteen hours a day in front of our computers. We ate lots of pizza. Mark and I debated which city had better pizza, his beloved local pizza chain, Pizza Pizza, or my favorite, Regina's, in Boston. We also talked about games, sales, and money.

"*Wolfenstein 3D* sold something like four thousand copies in its first month," Mark said. "The first royalty check was around a hundred grand. And the money kept coming."

I could only imagine. I pictured trucks full of cash. I also showed that I had a sense of humor.

"With royalties from my game *Palace of Deceit*, I treated some kids at school to a lunch at Taco Bell," I said. "Then I was practically broke again."

My jokes worked, and although I was the youngest in the group, I sensed I fit in. Mark was the most extroverted among us. His energy filled the room. He liked games, and he liked talking about how to sell them. Tim was more complex but similarly ambitious, and open to answering my questions about his background. His father had worked for the government making maps and he had an older brother in the computer business. At eleven, he wrote his first game on an Apple IIc. At nineteen, he switched to a PC, and a year later, while attending the University of Maryland, he built a text editor that turned into his first game, *ZZT*. He started Epic Mega-Games in his parents' garage in Rockville, Maryland, near where he still lived.

By our last dinner together in Toronto, the four of us had developed a friendship, and Tim and I had bonded. I saw what would become apparent over the years: Tim was more interested in making games than playing them. In me, he saw a kid who loved playing games. More than that, I think, he saw a kid who lived to play games with the same passion he had for programming them. He asked for a progress report on *Jazz.*

"Well, we've got this classic tortoise-and-the-hare thing except it's a rabbit and turtle in outer space," I said. "Devan Shell is the evil leader of the terrorist turtles. He's conquering planets, including Carrotus, home of the hares and the beautiful princess Eva Earlong, who he kidnaps. Enter Jazz Jackrabbit and his tiny bird sidekick Hip Hop. The fate of Carrotus is in the hands of this one awesome rabbit."

"Tell me about Jazz," Mark said.

"He's Rambo with long ears," I said.

Tim smiled approvingly and said, "When you're a little rabbit, you carry a big gun."

Bingo.

Not a lot of people were needed to make a 2D game like *Jazz*, but it did require a division of labor among a few folks. In our case, it was four. I designed the game and came up with a good chunk of the characters and environments; Arjan coded everything; after Toronto, Tim introduced me to classically trained animator Nick Stadler, who took charge of animation and did all the cinematics; and a guy named Robert Allen was waiting to produce the music.

First and foremost, Nick raised the quality of the art. He changed my version of Jazz from purple to green, which was an instant improvement, and when I suggested Jazz needed a sidekick, he drew a funky little bird that could be freed from its cage and shoot enemies. He wanted to call it Flip—as in flip someone the bird. I didn't feel it. But I loved the bird.

A little later I was listening to US3's song "Cantaloop (Flip Fantasia)," one of the outstanding hip-hop/jazz blends of the decade, and the little bird's name popped into my head: Hip Hop. I knew it was perfect. I shot an email to Nick. He liked it, too. So did Arjan. We had our characters: Jazz and Hip Hop.

Toward the end of production, Tim sent me to Northern California to work on the music with Robert Allen, a musician who had composed original music for many of Epic's games. He and his wife lived in an RV in an old logging town near Yosemite. There was nothing to do there but work and hike. We got right to business. We ran the game through Robert's computer and discussed the sounds and music needed in every scene. I suggested the catchy keyboard on Prince's "When Doves Cry" as an overall theme. I also cited the gothic "Overture" from *The Phantom of the Opera*.

He did manage to tear me away for a day of spelunking, something I'd never done or even heard of. By the time he explained we were going to explore caves, I was in a harness, descending hundreds of feet into darkness, until my feet touched the floor and I was in this world of hidden passageways, stalactites and stalagmites, mega crystals, soda straws, and flowstones. They sounded like environments in a video game. Indeed, it felt like we had slipped inside a video game.

One day, after we spoke to Arjan about building a tool set for some of *Jazz*'s cut scenes—the animated, movie-like scenes that told the story—I saw Robert fooling around with some new 3D software. He said it was a new editor Tim had sent him. Robert was a smart dude; on top of composing music, he also produced games. He described the editor as better brushes, paints, and canvases. "This is going to be big," he said.

He let me sit down and test-drive it, and I saw what he meant. It was easy to make a box, a spear, or a staircase in 3D.

"You can get buried in this pretty easily," he said.

I could see why. But I was so deep into *Jazz* and Arjan's tool set that I was unable to fully comprehend this new editor. I do remember the ease. And I do remember being impressed and thinking this was one more thing that confirmed my belief in Tim. It took a tremendous amount of faith to work with these guys with only the slimmest agreement between us, if it was even legally binding since I had signed it while still a minor. But this was what I wanted to do—make games—and I wanted to do it with Tim and his crew.

I made several trips to Rockville, where Tim lived and Epic MegaGames was headquartered. The company's output to that point included *Overkill*, *Jill of the Jungle*, *Electro Man*, *Solar Winds*, *Zone 66*, *Ken's Labyrinth*, and *Xargon*. Tim kept an extra apartment there for developers to live and work. He referred to it as the company's studio. Those of us who stayed there called it the "Epic Apartment" or simply "the apartment"—as in "I'll be at the apartment next week."

It was a three-bedroom/three-bath place with a living room furnished with card tables for computers and a TV where we watched *The X-Files* and drooled over Gillian Anderson. Hey, it was the nineties. The apartment was basic digs, a place where I plugged in, slept—uh, that was optional—and met cohorts such as Robert Elam, who was working on his side-scrolling fighter *One Must Fall: 2097*, and James Schmalz, who had made the company's biggest hit thus far, *Epic Pinball*, a shareware sensation that put Epic on the map and transformed James from a gamer with a degree from the University of Waterloo into a multimillionaire who founded his own company, Digital Extremes, while continuing to partner with Epic.

I didn't know about the name of James's company. I thought the word Extreme had been played out by the eighties' hair metal band. Otherwise, I was in awe of him—and intimidated. He was one of the rare individuals who could do it all—programming, art, concepting, everything. He also had the good looks of Gaston from *Beauty and the Beast.*

Before I entered the picture, James had begun work on a new level editor, the tool used to make video games. It was the first step in making his next new game. Then Tim took over developing the editor, leaving James to focus on the game itself. This was the same remarkable editor I had played with at Robert's house, only it kept improving. The quality of the graphics was moving in a very impressive direction, but Tim's real breakthrough was in making it easier for someone with limited programming skills like me to create indoor and outdoor environments and layer in various colors and textures. Tim was very focused on this project. It made me even more envious of James.

The two of us spent a lot of time together in the Epic Apartment, working on our separate projects but also engaged in another game, *DOOM.*

All of us were more or less obsessed with *Wolfenstein*, but then Mark and Tim saw a demo of something similar and said, "Wait until you see id's new game." As always, they were on target. *DOOM* took 3D programming to the next level. When the first episode was released free of charge in December 1993, so many people tried to download it that computer systems across the country crashed. The game's multiplayer *deathmatch* function crippled some university computer networks.

In the Epic Apartment, *DOOM* deathmatches often kept us up until dawn. One time I was enjoying solo time with Tim and Mark, playing deathmatch, while Arjan was out of town for several days of work on *Jazz.* Each of us stared intensely at our screens. Although we were in the same room, we could have easily been a thousand miles apart: Mark in Toronto, Tim here in Rockville, and me at home in California. The potential of multiplayer gaming hit me.

"Fucking Carmack and Romero," I said. "This is going to change everything."

Mark shrugged. "It already has."

G etting *Jazz Jackrabbit* ready to ship that summer required endless patience and a devotion to perfection. The only way to find all the bugs, errors, misspellings, and glitches was to play it. Endlessly. From start to finish. All six episodes, each one consisting of multiple worlds, with two levels, thousands of challenges and possibilities, various modes of play from hard to easy, and secret levels offering even more challenges.

I had no patience for QA. Testing was the equivalent of telling someone with a house to inspect every wall, window, and floor, as well as turn on every faucet and light switch, to see if anything is broken, warped, or out of alignment, and then do it again and again until someone declares it's finished. It's a miracle any game ever ships, and not surprising so many go out with bugs.

The hardest part for me was seeing my inferior art on the screen, the parts that hadn't been replaced with Nick's work, and I wasn't alone. Epic had an ace pixel artist, a Norwegian guy who went by the name Pixel, which fit him, and every time one of my drawings passed in front of him, he laughingly said in his thick accent, "Ah, stupid Cliff art."

I agreed.

I wanted perfection, and seeking it is the surest path to insanity.

I was at home in La Verne when I received the congratulatory email from Tim announcing that *Jazz* was finished and ready to ship. I thanked Tim profusely, feeling like Christopher Moltisanti pledging undying allegiance to Tony Soprano. I even said it to myself: *I will follow that man into hell.*

Jazz was released on August 1, 1994. Epic's press release said, "Fasten your seatbelts for the ride of your life! *Jazz Jackrabbit* is coming toward you at light speed, and this little bunny carries a REALLY big gun." By then, Mark had the team working on a CD-ROM version with three more episodes, new levels, animations, and music. He also scheduled a special Christmas edition, while Epic sold *Jazz* T-shirts for twelve dollars. This was the difference between a business with a sophisticated strategy and a kid working out of his bedroom.

It wasn't the only difference. That fall I received a royalty check for five thousand dollars. I realized this was likely the first of at least several such checks I would receive, and my life changed. I went on a shopping spree at the mall. I left with a new Miller's Outpost wardrobe and bags of games, music, and books, including Stephen King's short story collection *Nightmares & Dreamscapes*.

That was the start. I bought a GM Saturn, which had a sporty look and a fleeting coolness, and rented a one-bedroom apartment where I could have sex with Marcy without my mother barging in to yell at me for making too much noise. For the pièce de résistance, I dropped out of school. It was the inevitable leap of faith I had to take. It didn't matter that I had an older brother who went to West Point and another brother thriving in his studies at Cal Poly, no one challenged me when I announced I was leaving school to concentrate on making games. I was on a path, and I had to see where it was taking me.

Or taking us. I was tight with Marcy despite subtle signs that we weren't the best fit. For instance, during my splurge at the mall, I purchased the entire set of mini fighter jets and alien spacecraft toys from the movie *Independence Day* and hung them from my bedroom ceiling. It was proof of my nerd cred, and I thought it was cool. Unfortunately, Marcy hated looking up at them. She gave me an ultimatum: take down the air force or sleep by myself. I unfastened the toys one by one and made crash-landing sounds—*kaboom!*—as they dropped onto the bed.

A few years later, our relationship would make the same sound. Until then, I didn't want to give up the sex, even though in my head I was very clear on how my career and my relationship ranked. And after all those toys came down, I announced to Marcy, with a defiant edge in my voice, that I had work to do.

And I did.

LEVEL

3

UNREAL

Half an hour after hearing an ad for Home Depot on the radio, I was at my local home improvement store, walking up and down the aisles with my camera, snapping pictures of things that looked like they would make interesting environmental textures in video games. I took dozens of close-ups of plywood, siding, fencing, veneer tiles, slate, chains, screens, flooring, insulation, sandpaper, concrete, and dozens of other items.

I got funny looks from employees. I didn't care. I was working.

Most people wouldn't have understood that I was gathering material to make textures for a new video game, but most people didn't understand video games, period. It was the Rodney Dangerfield of the entertainment industry: it didn't get any respect. One person who did understand everything about it and didn't worry about respect was Tim Sweeney. In gaming, the revolution is always now, and Tim was a little bit ahead of that. That's what made for a visionary, someone whose thinking is in front of everyone else.

Driven by the innovations in *DOOM*, 3D gaming on PCs was the next wave in video games. Tim was on it—and moving forward. He had already envisioned shifting Epic strategically from a shareware company into a major game developer. The key was his new engine and editor, the one he had begun with James Schmalz but then taken over on his own. One day he sent me the latest version of his new editor with a simple request, one I had heard before: *Play with it. See what you can make.*

This was now a familiar refrain, a prod to get started on the next game, whatever that might turn out to be. The easy-to-use editor made creating games a much simpler task for game creators of all skill levels, including nonprogrammers like me. It rendered 3D color, light, action, and perspective with a speed, clarity, and sophistication that not only took advantage of state-of-the-art technology, it redefined what that meant. It was as if Einstein had created a tool kit for the average person to understand space and time, capture it, and mold it into cool shapes that would appear on their computer screen.

But that was only half of Tim's genius.

The other half involved monetizing this innovation. Epic would use the engine-editor, but non-Epic game developers, including Epic's competitors, could license it, too—for a fee.

This was the birth of what would be known as the Unreal Engine—and what Tim called and has continued to call the most difficult project he had ever undertaken. But that doesn't begin to capture the nonstop iterating and updating of what was to become his life's work. He was reimagining Epic's place in the landscape of video game developers and his own path to becoming a multibillionaire, but he was also doing nothing less than reimagining the entire video game industry and, as it would turn out, all of the visual arts.

I'm humbled to think I was there at the beginning.

Play with it, Cliffy. See what you can make.

James and others had already embarked on making a new game using Tim's new tool, and I was folded into the mix, but the thing about game making is that in most instances the story is secondary to the cool shit you create. The story emerges from environments that get sewn together. It's like a relationship. You have a picture in your head of someone. You go searching for that person. When you find that person, you go out a few times to see if the pieces work, if there's chemistry, if your individual interests complement each other, and if the sex is good.

Then, if everything feels like it will fit together, you move in together, arrange your stuff, and build a life. That becomes your story.

We had no idea what the hell the next game would be other than a great first-person shooter, and we were going to work on it together, as a team.

I taught myself how to use Tim's editor polygon by polygon. The tool let me build things as if I were assembling LEGO bricks. It was simple, solid geometry. James had already created various terrains and a flying dragon that set the creativity bar high. But as new creatures and toys were made, we abandoned the terrain and dragon. I scanned the dozens of photos I took at Home Depot and used them to create environments. I also bought a decent library of stock photography. It was as if I were chipping away at an invisible slab of marble that would eventually become something.

I plugged into conference calls and nonstop email chains with Tim and James, who was driving the creative while Tim focused on the engine.

Marcy thought I worked too much. Too much for whom? She didn't understand my ambition or the addictiveness of the work. I wanted to be a rock-star game designer more than anything and always knew if push came to shove, I was willing to sacrifice my relationship for my career. One of my favorite movies, *Swimming with Sharks*, came out around the same time *Jazz* did. It was about the levels of abuse and degradation a guy accepted while carving out a career in Hollywood and, while I didn't encounter any of the treachery and debasement he did, I related to his determination to succeed.

Sometimes I spent twenty hours straight working in this new 3D realm, manipulating images, creating the rugged terrain of a distant planet, an underground cave, a surreal light display. In my early twenties, sleep was an afterthought. Like everyone, I battled imposter syndrome. Is this really happening? When are they going to realize I'm not that good? I wanted and in fact needed to prove myself, especially to myself. Ice-T's songs "New Jack Hustler" and "Prepared to Die" gave me late-night motivation.

> *Watch me flip and rip*
> *On the freedom tip*

James Schmalz and his team at Digital Extremes were operating the same way in Waterloo, probably not with gangster rap blasting in their headphones, but they were churning out the work.

We communicated 24/7 via email. Our email program was called Eudora. Every email that popped up was a puzzle I had to solve. It was my own version of mental *Tetris*. I was easily hooked on the sound of a new email arriving, a new response needed, a new texture arriving that I could paint on the walls . . . It was that constant drip-drip-drip of dopamine and serotonin being injected into my brain, and it was intoxicating.

After receiving my next royalty check for *Jazz Jackrabbit*, I upgraded to a two-bedroom apartment in Alta Loma. I converted the second bedroom to a home office, and when I told Mark Rein that I could see the snow-capped peak of Mount Baldy out the window on a clear day, he said, "Sounds fancy." It wasn't—and I blocked the view by tacking a Mexican blanket over the window. I didn't want the distraction. I had a computer, two screens, and a scanner; that was all the view I needed. Well, that and a poster from the movie *The Craft* for, uh, inspiration.

I was a pop culture junkie. *Entertainment Weekly* was my bible, and the Ontario mall was my place of worship. I saw *Jerry Maguire* opening night at the Edwards cinema. I read Garth Ennis's *Preacher* in the back of Virgin Records, which stocked a robust collection of graphic novels. Marcy and I played the first-generation *Dactyl Nightmare* VR game in Steven Spielberg's arcade chain, GameWorks. After scarfing dinner at Salsa Fresh in the food court, the two of us wound up browsing the games in Electronics Boutique.

Many nights I stood in front of that store with my arm around Marcy and mused, "Someday one of my games will be displayed in the window."

It seemed possible. In 1995, *DOOM* was the most popular software downloaded on PCs. Microsoft Windows was second. Video games were blowing up without much notice by the mainstream entertainment media, which was focused on the O. J. Simpson trial, crazy-ass white people doing the Macarena, and Brad Pitt's long blond locks. I bought Spawn action figures and arranged them on my desk.

We needed more environments for the game we were building, more than I could produce on my own, and I was tasked with building and managing a team of level designers like James's in Waterloo. I recruited guys known as "modders." Modders were programmers who created their own *modifications* to existing video games and posted them online for others to incorporate into their game-playing. It was a great way to find a job. They were typically super-bright guys who ranged from genius-level show-offs to obsessed fanboys who were hoping to turn their passion into a job.

Their levels typically included contact info, and I hunted them down and hired the best, assigning them to produce environments— castles, dungeons, battlefields, distant lands, and futuristic rooms.

"We're making a new 3D game and we could use someone like you," I said.

"What's the game?" they asked.

"We don't know yet. Just make cool shit," I said, sounding like Tim.

This being the nineties, I wore a pager, and it went off at all hours.

I would be at the store buying Kraft mac and cheese and have to race home and call my team to see what they needed or fire up my computer to see their latest level. Marcy once said the designers I managed either kept the strangest hours or they didn't sleep.

"Correct," I responded, without explaining that it wasn't one or the other, it was both. And sometimes you needed to talk to someone about the brilliance of *Duke Nukem* at three thirty in the morning.

On February 24, 1996, id Software released a test of the new Carmack and Romero creation, *Quake*. It shook the ground under our feet.

Not an actual game, the *Qtest*, as it was called, consisted of three multiplayer deathmatch maps that could be played and explored and drooled over in anticipation of the real thing. The main purpose of the test was to let a bunch of gamers play it and see if it worked. It was buggy and clearly a work in progress, but that was the point. Carmack and Romero wanted a performance benchmark. They wanted to see how it would perform on people's PCs, what the frame rate was, and other technical insights.

But it was also a shot across the bow. It was unquestionably brilliant. It busted open the idea of 3D space. It also lit a competitive fire in me that I wanted to share. I dashed off an email to Tim, Mark, James, and a few others. "It's not that cool, guys. We can do better."

That was, of course, the larger game we were playing, and Carmack and Romero raised the bar to new heights. Released in June 1996, *Quake* was among the bestselling games of the year. It was a bombastic, chaotic shooter set to Trent Reznor music in a weird H. P. Lovecraft–style universe, where this dude in a football helmet and weird armor ran around annihilating demons with a rocket launcher. Carmack cared more about premise and gameplay than actual story, but there was more than enough to satisfy everyone.

Critics and gamers lauded the game's 3D graphics, sound effects, and over-the-top, blood-splattered violence. "No one kills like these guys," I shouted to Marcy one night as I leaned into the game, impressed at how Carmack and Romero had perfected gibbing. I mean, it was the first time a rocket strike would explode someone into chunks of flesh. To this day, that's one of the most satisfying ways to take someone out in a first-person shooter. It's also one of the most misunderstood elements of gaming.

Non-gamers recoil at such violence, but they don't understand that it's simply good, satisfying feedback. It's not enough to shoot someone and watch them fall over—not in movies and not in video games. It's like fireworks on the Fourth of July or New Year's. It's immensely gratifying to our lizard brains. And *Quake* delivered.

Shortly after *Quake*'s release, Carmack and Romero rattled the industry again, but in a different way. They split up. The Beatles had called it quits before I was born, but I understood the impact of that decision, and this one was similar. *Quake* was Carmack and Romero's *Abbey Road*, a masterpiece and a farewell.

I heard the same gossip as everyone else: apparently, they'd had a falling-out while making *Quake*. I figured it was the age-old conflict that everyone in the industry faced: science versus art. As the überprogrammer, Carmack was all about efficiency and technology. If you wanted to talk about ray casting, binary space partitioning, and surface caching—and few could—he was your man. Romero, though a deft programmer himself, was a game designer who turned the dark corners of his imagination into really fun, really bloody games, which was what he liked. One guy was an engineer. The other was a creative. They complemented each other until they didn't. Both had enough money to do their own thing—and they did.

I hadn't encountered this problem at Epic, thanks to Tim's openness to collaboration and respect for the array of talents needed to make a great game. We embarked on those efforts ourselves. But video games were and remain a balance of science and art, and I wondered if such a clash was inevitable.

Rocking high-top Chuck Taylors with Sonic the Hedgehog lace clips, I recruited more *DOOM* modders to make more environments. Our mantra was, simply, *more*. In Waterloo, James and his team conjured up a menagerie of bloodthirsty enemies, including tentacled monsters; flesh-eating, acid-spitting, lizard-like amphibians that we named Slith; and the reptile-like baddies who were the smartest, most ruthless, powerful fighters of all, the Skaarj. My spelling of these creatures (pronounced "Scar") irked some of my more logical, left-brained colleagues.

"Why do you need the *J*?" they asked.

"I want there to be snobs," I said. "You know, people who condescendingly say, 'The *J* is silent.'"

"But why?" they asked. "What's the point?"

"It's cool," I said, with a certainty that ended the discussion.

Tim, having assessed the *Quake* engine and editor and found the areas where he could improve upon it, was fully in his element. The features he was adding to the engine were going to give our game higher-resolution textures than *Quake*. For example, the texture of light on the water's surface looked astonishingly realistic. Tim found a Dutch programmer who coded a system that enabled us to draw gorgeous, animated particle effects, or what we called "painting with fire." Colored lighting was added to the engine, which was huge. A rocket could be launched, and it would illuminate the hallway and blend with the existing lights. No game had ever done this before, not even *Quake*.

Then our ace 3D animator created a sea ray–like creature that flew through the air. This dangerous-looking reptile, which we called

"Manta," was smooth and unlike anything I had seen in real-time 3D. It had red eyes and a long tail that killed. The detail looked phenomenal. The lighting was breathtaking. The breakthroughs fed off each other and added up to truly next-level shit. It was exciting to not only see it come together but to use these tools to create environments and creatures that popped onscreen like nothing before.

We had *Quake* in our crosshairs, but it wasn't all more, better, faster. We had to be cognizant of how much detail we were putting on the screen, because the more polygons that were on a screen—polygons were the building blocks of images—the more memory that was required. The more memory the game sucked out of a PC, the slower the game played, and, of course, that ruined the whole experience.

Add to that the fact this had to be balanced with the range of speeds of people's personal computers and the rate at which those speeds kept changing thanks to new and improved PC technology. For us mortals, it was a mind-bender.

But no worries. Tim was on it.

So was Mark Rein. Recognizing the work that needed to be done on the business side, Mark hired former id executive Jay Wilbur, the ace dealmaker who had helped Carmack and Romero get very rich, and then followed Romero out the door. At Epic, he was given the title of Imperial Advisor.

Tall, with sandy hair, a bulbous nose, and an infectious laugh, Jay had what I referred to as a teddy-grizzly personality. One moment he was an easygoing, joke-cracking teddy bear, and the next, he shifted, suddenly and without warning, into serious grizzly bear mode, making it clear that he wanted his directives followed or else.

I liked him. He referred to his laptop as "Never Cold." It described his work ethic. In his first major piece of business, he ordered us to name our new game. "If I'm going to sell it, I have to be able to call it something," he said. I suggested *Dark Earth*. I knew it sounded like a fake game in an Adam Sandler movie, but it was still better than most of the other suggestions. It didn't matter. Tim wanted to call the game *Unreal*.

I mentioned that *Unreal* was an old Amiga game and there might be an issue with the rights. Tim thought about it. He still insisted on *Unreal*. He wanted to call both the game and the engine *Unreal*.

And so it was.

Jay got the trademark.

Word about Epic's new game got out, and *Next Generation* magazine offered us their February 1997 cover. It was a holy crap moment. *Next Generation* was the *Vanity Fair* of gaming magazines. It was a high-quality glossy that was well-researched and well-written. It meant something to be in the magazine, and they were offering *Unreal* the cover. The buzz would be incredible. Not just among fans, but also among industry insiders. The problem was we barely had a game. What we did have was basically a tech demo. But that didn't matter. This was an opportunity we couldn't pass up.

Tim, Mark, James, and I were interviewed together in the Rockville office. We sat close together in a small room dominated by computer screens. We took the reporter through a deck I had put together from dozens of screenshots I'd captured. Then we showed him the demo and bluffed our way through the rest. As the lead designer, James provided background on the development, Tim gave an in-depth dive into the technical advances, and Mark spoke to the strategy of making a user-friendly level editor available to fans who could script and mod their own worlds. I provided game-playing color.

We worked well together. We talked frame rates, textures, lighting, the increased speed, and the enormity of the stakes, which was the writer's main question, the one he kept returning to throughout the session: What were we doing to beat *Quake*?

This time, I didn't look around and wait for one of the others to answer. I sensed the moment was mine and leaned toward the reporter.

"If you think of *Quake* as a car, it's like a really good base model that runs really fast," I said. "With *Unreal*, we're hoping to give you air-conditioning, power brakes, power steering, and a real sense of style that's lacking in some of those other games."

I n the days that followed, Tim realized that working remotely on a project of this size was too slow and unwieldy. He was working on the engine in Rockville, Mark was in Toronto, I was managing level designers from my Alta Loma second bedroom, James and his company were modeling creatures and weaponry in Waterloo, and we had team members and freelancers across the country and in Europe. All of a sudden it was apparent the org was too decentralized to pull a game together that would meet our ambitious goal.

Tim's solution was just as obvious. He wanted everyone to go up to James's office to establish a beachhead and "knock this one out."

I had mixed feelings. Marcy and I and our two cats had fallen into a comfortable routine. In the morning, she went to a sales job at a clothing store at the mall. I got up a few hours later, said hello to the cats, dealt with emails, gave feedback to my level designers, played the clunky builds they sent me for review, and worked on my own levels. At night, we ordered a pizza and watched *Friends*. Then she went to bed, and I returned to my computer. This was as normal as our life together got, and it was pretty good.

Then I started traveling to Waterloo. At first, I went there for a week and then returned home for three. Marcy was supportive. She buried herself in work, our cats, and spending time with her family. When I came home, I kissed her and my kitties, then we ate at the mall and came home and watched *American Idol* and caught up on Ross and Rachel as if they were real people. After Jay Wilbur secured a publishing deal for *Unreal* with GT Interactive, the same company that had put *Quake* out, the trips up north increased in length.

My commute was Ontario to Dallas to Toronto. I got to know the Dallas–Fort Worth airport like the back of my hand. I laughed at the picture I had of myself only a few years earlier, fumbling nervously through customs without a passport. Now, after landing in Toronto, I got a rental car, drove an hour to Waterloo, got Curry in a Hurry to go or sushi or East Side Mario's, and thought it was as normal as getting on the 57 freeway back home.

I got to the point where I stopped thinking about the inconvenience of the travel and the stress it put on my personal life as much as I did *Unreal*. The game was always top of mind. That's what it means to put career before anything else. It takes over and consumes everything in its path. It wasn't just me. One night I was at home playing *Ultima Online* and I ran into James in a dungeon. We updated each other about the status of our work.

Something began to happen. A game emerged. And as it did, so did an idea for a story: all of this existed in the Bermuda Triangle of the galaxy where the protagonist is a prisoner being transferred to some hellish fate and crashes on an alien planet. To survive, the prisoner must escape from the planet and its predatory aliens, a path that takes them through all the different environments and baddies.

That's what made the Bermuda Triangle idea perfect: We had so many different styles of environments and creatures, and we had to come up with a reason all of them were there; this explained it. Details would come. But the structure was there.

The hype was there, too. The February 1997 issue of *Next Generation* magazine finally arrived with *Unreal* on its cover. The image—which Tim and Mark had told the writer was straight out of the game—was of a giant Skaarj looking like it was ready to leap off the page and tear into the reader. It was everything we could have hoped for and more. The headline screamed, "*Unreal* could be the best looking PC game of 1997."

Now all we had to do was make the damn thing.

NA PALI TO WATERLOO: ALL ABOARD

It was spring 1997, and Jay Wilbur was wearing the grizzly half of his teddy-grizzly face as he walked into the conference room at the Digital Extremes offices in Waterloo. All the key players had gathered around the table, including Tim, Mark, James, and myself. We had recently missed the original delivery date on our contract with GT and were continuing to make up our production schedule as we went along. Jay wanted to put us on a stricter schedule, as did the publisher.

He explained that when he was at id, people would ask when this game or that game was coming out and the answer he gave was always "When it's done." But with Epic having invested millions in development and essentially betting the company's future on *Unreal's* success, we couldn't afford to go on forever.

"This could be big, really big," Jay said. "But we need to do things different. We all need to be here as much as possible."

He wanted everybody involved to relocate to Waterloo until the game was done. All of us working under one roof. In the same time zone. Singularly focused. Development had already run two-plus years and we still had considerable work to do to finish it, never mind getting it out the door and onto shelves.

James scrambled to find accommodations for everyone. I started out in a dingy dorm room on the University of Waterloo campus and moved to the basement of a nearby boarding house that was also used for student housing. I would stagger into my room after working all night and fall into bed, only to hear the college girls upstairs blare the Backstreet Boys as they woke up a few hours later. Eventually I upgraded to a three-bedroom, one-bath town house that I shared with Tim and one of the level artists.

The Digital Extremes offices could barely hold all of us. I doubled and tripled up in an office with artists and level designers that I had talked to for more than a year but was now meeting for the first time in person, including animator Dave Carter, designers Pancho Eekels and Cedric Fiorentino (who went by the name Inoxx), and a *DOOM* level designer named T. Elliot Cannon, who I knew only by his online handle Myscha the Sled Dog. Likewise, he knew me as Grand Master Ice Shaft. The two of us played the cult movie *Fear of a Black Hat* on our office TV, quoting it nonstop: "We anti-violent, and anyone says different, I'll bust a cap in his ass."

Not everyone adapted as easily. I once saw two coders seated back-to-back at their desks, arguing through email instead of turning around and chatting face-to-face. And during one unseasonably hot day, the air-conditioning broke, turning the office into a nerd sweat lodge. We continued working, shirtless and sweaty. Inoxx ate ice cream, but apparently the relief it provided wasn't enough. He slammed down his spoon and exclaimed in his thick French accent, "Dis sucks!"

Fortunately, inspiration was more common than perspiration. There's no better example than the arrival of brainy computer engineer Steve Polge. At this point in development, we didn't have any artificial intelligence for the baddies who roamed our dangerous planet. Without AI, they would just stand there like stationary targets. We needed the Skaarj and our other enemies to evade, threaten, and kill—and generally behave as menacingly as they looked.

Steve solved this problem. A computer engineer at IBM with a fascination for AI and gaming, he had created an extremely popular and innovative *Quake* mod called the Reaper Bot. The Reaper Bot injected countless computer-generated-and-controlled foes—or bots—in *Quake* that got smarter and deadlier the more they were engaged. In other words, they learned the game. Mark persuaded Steve to leave his job at IBM and add this bot AI to *Unreal*. It was like throwing nitro against the screen.

Amid this cacophony of inventiveness, I continued to add clarifying details to the story. The player was Prisoner 849, who emerges alive after crashing on this planet called Na Pali, where the murderous Skaarj have taken over from the indigenous Nali. It was classic colonization. To survive, the prisoner had to traverse maze-like mines, destroyed villages and temples, sky castles, caves, and wrecked ships—all the environments we had made—and ultimately breach the Skaarj mothership and kill their queen before escaping in their shuttle.

Our protagonist, Prisoner 849, was female. I didn't think of it as a terribly radical idea. *Tomb Raider*'s Lara Croft was a big success for the PlayStation console, though we frowned at the low resolution of detail on the PlayStation, and there were plenty of other female leads with nerd cool, including Xena, Warrior Princess, Gillian Anderson from *The X-Files*, Princess Leia from *Star Wars*, and my fantasy girl, Buffy the Vampire Slayer.

But there was some pushback. James made a model, and we showed Tim. He let the troops choose whether they wanted Prisoner 849 to be female or male, and though the gender of Prisoner 849 was never explicitly defined and has remained something of a mystery, it was and still is clear to me.

I knew many guys in tech who married their first and only girlfriend, and I was no different. I suppose the reasons were similar: I was more frightened of not being together and finding myself alone than I was of being in a relationship that wasn't perfect. I was insecure, inexperienced, and emotionally immature. How would I ever meet someone else if Marcy and I broke up? My world prized efficiency, and I told myself that it was most efficient to stick with Marcy regardless of the possibility that we might not be soul mates, that we might be growing apart as we grew up.

I decided we should get engaged. During a trip home, I purchased a diamond ring from the fancy jewelry store at the mall and, per the suggestion of the saleswoman, I planned a romantic proposal at the beach. After a seafood dinner at Gladstone's 4 Fish, a famous hot spot in Malibu, Marcy and I took a walk on the beach, and when she turned to look at the waves, I got down on one knee and surprised her with the ring. She opened the box, which lit up like the briefcase in *Pulp Fiction*, and said yes.

There wasn't time to set a date. In Waterloo, we had wanted to ship *Unreal* in time for Christmas, but that second deadline came and went as the game sprawled. Rumors that we couldn't pull together thousands of environments and all the new technology spread through the industry. *Wired* magazine referred to the game as "vaporware." As if I weren't busy enough, I was involved in producing a sequel to *Jazz* with Arjan, who had opened his own studio in the Netherlands, and animator Nick Stadler.

Arjan forwarded me builds of all the new toys he devised, including a multiplayer mode, and Nick created the environments and characters. The tiles were sent to me for assembly, which was like putting together a familiar jigsaw puzzle. It was all muscle memory and a welcome break from the pressure of *Unreal*. I could also be found ducking into online chat rooms and forums where fanatical gamers who knew about the demos of *Unreal* we had shown at conferences asked about our progress.

It was 1998, and as spring approached, we scaled back the levels to a sane and manageable number, a sign we were reaching the end. "Cutting features ships games," Apogee founder George Broussard once said. I added, "Only the cool stuff gets in." All of us pounded on the game, playing it endlessly as we looked for bugs. I felt like I was in the movie *Groundhog Day*. "What if there is no tomorrow? There wasn't one today." Finally, Tim said, "Have Cliff go through it one more time," which I did lightning fast, and then, amazingly, we were done and ready to ship *Unreal*.

On May 18, we went gold, meaning we produced a gold master of the game from which all copies would be made, and delivered it to our publisher. Four days later, *Unreal* was online and in stores. I was still in Waterloo, and the magnitude of the project suddenly hit me. So did the irony of all the effort that suddenly struck me as a perverse tease. We had spent three years creating and building and playing a game that was broken every day until it finally worked, and then once it worked, we had to give it to everybody else to enjoy.

I walked outside the Digital Extremes offices for a breath of fresh air. The temperature was almost fifty degrees, and the locals were running around outside in shorts, pretending it was already summer. I was eager to go home and fool around with Marcy and bask in the California sun before taking on whatever was next.

I spotted James enjoying the sunshine. We looked at each other and shrugged like two soldiers who had climbed out of their foxholes after surviving a firefight, as if to say, "Well, that just happened."

But it was what we didn't say that hung in the air between us.

Over the past few years we had labored on *Unreal*, we had traded thousands of emails and spent countless hours exchanging ideas, debating character and story ideas, and pushing the game forward. Our interactions were never less than amicable. Often, they were much better. But as we moved toward the finish line, I sensed something else enter the conversation: the question of who was going to be the main guy pitching and designing the next game.

James never said anything about it and neither did I. In fairness, he was a millionaire with his own company and may not have had such egocentric concerns the way I did. But I doubt it. In the month or two leading up to this moment, there were too many times when I went into his office with his giant wooden executive desk, as square as his Bruce Campbell jaw, and saw him tab away from whatever he was working on so I couldn't see what was on his monitor. It caused me to worry. I had new ideas too.

Our emails had a cache file on a main server. It wasn't password protected. Anyone could click into it and read. One day I burrowed in there and found out that I wasn't paranoid. James was rallying his Digital Extremes troops to make sure they got to co-create Epic's next big hit after *Unreal*. "This is a war," he wrote, "and we need to win it."

Any jockeying for position, though, would have to wait. *Unreal* debuted at number three on the list of the bestselling games the week of May 17, behind *StarCraft* and *Titanic: Adventure Out of Time*. The latter game drafted on the phenomenon of the James Cameron film, and *StarCraft* was an instant classic, though I preferred my real-time strategy games with soldiers and tanks as opposed to aliens. *Unreal* climbed to number one the next week, and it stayed at the top of the list or among the top three for most of the summer.

By year's end, *Unreal* would rack up a pile of accolades, including the Editor's Choice Award from *Next Generation* magazine and a listing among the Top 50 Games of All Time from *PC Gamer*. But the thing that meant the most to me had nothing to do with rankings or awards. It took place the day after I flew home from Waterloo. Marcy and I drove to the mall for a celebratory dinner at the Rainforest Cafe. Afterward, we walked to the electronics store to see the new games, as we had done for years, and there in the window, as I had always dreamed, was a large, beautiful, full-color standee for *Unreal*.

"There it is," I said. "My game."

"You always said you wanted to see one of your games in that window," she said.

"I know. I mean, holy shit."

The scene was both symbolic and real, a pivotal marker in my young life that was like my graduation from the college from which I had dropped out. Diploma in hand, it was time to march forward into the serious business of forging a career and becoming an adult. This next phase began with an important lesson when Epic's message board lit up with complaints: *Unreal*'s multiplayer mode was broken. It worked on a local area network—a LAN, where PCs were on a network in close proximity—but connecting to the internet in the wild with a low-bandwidth modem, as most people did, resulted in frustration. "Believe me, these shortcomings are very much on our minds, and improving internet play is the team's top priority," Tim said in a press statement.

The fuckup was considered an all-hands-on-deck emergency, though for some reason—perhaps because this was related to tech and not design—I was more philosophic than upset. I saw that video game development was and still is and always will be like real life— less about perfection and more about fixing your mistakes.

RALEIGH TIMES

After the intensity of nine straight months in Waterloo and all the travel that preceded it, I was ready for a few laughs, and I got them thanks to our two cats, Disco and Tango.

One day Tango climbed onto my scanner and instead of shooing him off, I scanned him and shared the picture on a new website I created for that purpose. I called the site Cat-Scan.com and launched a contest for the oddest, weirdest scans of their cats. I blasted out a call for photos. The winner would get a bunch of *Jazz* merchandise.

Entries poured in, and the site went viral before viral was a thing. Write-ups appeared in the *Guardian* and *San Francisco Weekly.* "It was like chocolate hitting peanut butter," I told one reporter.

Not to cat lovers, who thought it was abuse. Soon I was getting almost as much hate mail as entries. I posted the hate mail on the site, too. I also scanned my own eyes—wide open, of course. I wanted to make a point that it wasn't a big deal. I knew what I was doing. At twenty-three years old, I was just having fun. I enjoyed the attention.

Then we were back at it, addressing *Unreal*'s faulty multiplayer. Tim led an effort to improve the network coding. We became obsessed with *Quakeworld*, which id had launched while we were still heads-down on *Unreal*. It was Carmack's clever way of expanding *Quake*'s multiplayer. The browser allowed players to pick their preferred server and easily download modifications for the game. It was what *Unreal* should have had but didn't.

What we did have, though, was Steve Polge's ability to code AI foes that mimicked multiplayer gaming, and since all of us were too burnt to go through another long, grueling slog of development, we decided to make what we dubbed the "botpack." It was to be a multiplayer expansion for *Unreal* that could be played online or entirely offline. Though it wasn't the best fix, we began making new levels, until Mark Rein announced a change of plans.

After determining the botpack offered minimal return, he ordered a new stand-alone product. Not entirely new, but a game that kept the best of *Unreal*, while adding new levels and game types completely focused on multiplayer. We were still partnered with Digital Extremes, and he thought a streamlined product like this could be built remotely with the two studios working in sync rather than under one roof, which was a relief to everyone.

The past few years had taken a toll on everyone, and Tim wanted Epic to do as much as possible on its own. That led to talks about merging with Digital Extremes and finding a new home for Epic itself. Just as Epic MegaGames had outgrown the garage where Tim had started it, he wanted a new headquarters beyond Maryland. The question was where.

Everyone wanted to know. It wasn't like Tim solicited suggestions, but with so many of us affected, we offered them anyway. I pitched the Washington State peninsula. Marcy and I had recently visited *Jazz Jackrabbit* composer Robert Allen and his wife at their new home in Battle Ground, Washington, and I thought the area was beautiful and full of potential. But I was too late. Steve Polge had already sold Tim and Mark on Raleigh, North Carolina, where he resided and had worked at IBM before joining Epic.

Several of us went there to check it out. Steve drove me and an animator who lived in Chicago around Raleigh. I saw its quaint, quiet charm, but as someone who craved pop culture and already lived in a place where hitting up the Del Taco drive-through at night passed for an event, the quiet scared me. As we passed through the grittier southeast part of the city, I quipped, "My hood can beat up your hood." A few minutes later, we were parked on the main drag downtown and the animator muttered, "Nothing's going on around here."

But I think that's what appealed to Tim. The man was a visionary with vanilla taste. Raleigh was ideal for him.

That night I stayed in the hotel across from the Crabtree Valley Mall. I bought a six-pack of Red Oak beer and watched Bill Clinton on TV proclaim, "I did not have sexual relations with that woman." I called Marcy and gave her a recap of the tour. "At least they have a mall and all the same fast-food places," I said. Eventually I passed out, my head spinning not from the beer but from wondering what the future had in store for me.

I knew the move was a done deal. Open to leaving Southern California, I could picture myself in Raleigh. Marcy was amenable to the change, too. I might be bored on Saturday nights, but I saw opportunity for growth. The part that was cloudy had to do with Digital Extremes and James Schmalz. If the merger happened, I knew James was a shoo-in to land the title of lead designer. Where did that leave me? I was still just a contract freelancer.

I didn't want to relocate and find myself like Prisoner 849—crash-landed and fighting for survival in a strange place.

I thought about going to Mark Rein, but I instead expressed my concerns to Epic's Imperial Advisor, Jay Wilbur. I made it clear that I was a loyal soldier fully committed to the company and its future, but as a key player—a description with which I thought Tim would concur—I wanted more security to make such a big move worthwhile. I also wanted to pursue my own idea for a new video game, as I had done with *Jazz Jackrabbit*.

"Do you have something in mind?" he asked.

"Yes, it's called *Overfiend*," I said. "It's inspired by a Japanese horror manga."

Jay nodded. "Haven't heard of it," he said. "But I hear you. I get it."

He told me what I wanted to hear, and I felt a little better, a little more emboldened for the conversation I knew I needed to have and ultimately the only one that mattered, and that was with Tim. We met in person. I was sure he was having similar talks with other people, but none had the relationship we did, and for that reason, as we got into things, I chose not to mention my concerns about James and the merger with Digital Extremes and instead cut right to the part that mattered most to me: I wanted to be a full-time employee, and I wanted a six-figure salary—one hundred thousand dollars.

Tim ran his fingers through his hair as he considered the request. "Oh geez, Cliffy, that's a lot of money," he said. But a moment later he stuck out his hand and we shook on it. Both of us knew I was worth the money. Both of us knew Epic could afford it. And both of us knew our handshake was more about friendship and loyalty and me having a place to call home than it was about money.

I called Marcy and told her to start packing.

Marcy and I had trouble finding a comfortable house in Raleigh that I could afford. Later, after having lived there awhile, I learned that I wasn't seeing the whole picture. Most neighborhoods, especially those off the highways, were either built behind large brick walls or enormous trees, and the homes were completely hidden. That wasn't a bug, I realized. It was a feature. Eventually, we settled on an apartment in North Raleigh.

Epic took over space atop a relatively new office building in a beautiful business center with parklike grounds, including a small lake. As we got back to hammering away on this new game, the Digital Extremes folks came down regularly. We also expanded the crew in Raleigh. The energy was good. I bonded with a new level designer over a mutual love of *Transformers*. We almost got teary when Optimus Prime died in the original movie.

One day I invited skinny programmer Brandon Reinhart out for a beer after work. The kid from Kansas crossed his arms and said, "Straight edge! Death to alcohol!" I took a step back. I wanted to stick out my hand and welcome him to the Land of Misfit Toys.

Talk of a merger faded.

The new game was feeling great, and Mark insisted on the name *Unreal Tournament*, and it stuck.

Before leaving LA, I gave myself a crash course in multiplayer by attending several LAN parties in Orange County. Known as Bastard's Beatdowns, they were weekend-long events held in the offices of GameSpy, the company that provided a slick server browser for multiplayer games. Their offices were outfitted with strobe lights and disco balls; dozens of gamers plugged their computers into a high-speed T1 line, guzzled Jägermeister, and spent Friday through Sunday playing *Quake*, *Unreal*, *Tribes*, and other shooters.

I loved it, and I shared all the insight and crazy good fun people had shooting at each other with our team in Raleigh. We improved *Unreal Tournament*'s user interface, the UI in the original *Unreal* having been an afterthought, and introduced new game types, including Domination and Capture the Flag. Old maps and environments were repurposed, and new maps and environments were created. Stunning work was done; I thought the Capture the Flag map "Facing Worlds"—an asteroid in space with two opposing towers across from each other and Earth rotating in the distance—was a museum-quality piece of art.

I saw *The Matrix* the day it came out. The scene in which Neo had to jump off a building reminded me of the low-gravity Ziggurat Vertigo map in *Quake* that turned the otherwise hyper-fast action into a slow-motion drift through danger. As I left the theater, I called one of my level designers and suggested he make a deathmatch map with several towers that leveraged the low-gravity gimmick. The result was "Morpheus," a map I named after the wise Zion teacher played by Laurence Fishburne.

We debated whether *UT* should have more traditional deathmatch maps or more artistic and gimmicky maps. I thought we needed both. The maps "Peak" and "Hyper-Blast" might not have been the most challenging tournament maps, but they let players frag in exquisite environments and gave the game a visual wow factor. I thought that wow factor could itself be a distinguishing part of the game.

One of the things *Duke Nukem* did extremely well and arguably better than *DOOM* and *Quake* was present a sense of place. You were in a movie theater. In a strip club. You knew it was *Duke Nukem*. That resonated with me. In *Unreal Tournament*, you could be on a Spanish galleon, inside a castle in the clouds, or on an asteroid circling Earth. As a result, we wound up with over fifty exquisite maps.

It may have been overboard, but we wanted to appeal to the broadest audience. "You can't please all the people all the time," I said to my design team, quoting the old showbiz adage. Then I quickly added my own twist: "So why not make most of the people insanely fucking happy some of the time?"

You go into video games because you want to remake the world as you wished it were or because you have the ability to create whole new worlds. If I wanted to name a Capture the Flag map after my favorite Italian restaurant because I loved their chicken parmesan, I did it without asking for permission. There's a reason programmers are often accused of having a God complex, basically an insufferable sense of privilege and infallibility, especially after a couple beers or a couple quart bottles of Mountain Dew. In high school, you are too shy to talk to girls, too uncoordinated for sports, and too smart for everyone in class. But then you discover that you can create entire worlds, and populate them with monsters; invent the sickest, most lethal ways to kill; make energy ebb and flow; manipulate gravity; return the bleeding to battle and give the dead another chance at life; pit real-life human beings against each other in deathmatches; find yourself revered and reviled on message boards, and make money doing something your parents told you not to do and other kids teased you about . . . Come on, who isn't going to think of themselves as a gaming god?

Me, for one. I had to work up to that stature. I left Brandon in charge one week when Marcy and I visited her father in Florida. While I was away, he came up with the game's story—in the future, deep-space miners are pitted against each other in a battle to the death. It was the glue that made *UT* gel, and the fact that it did, and was excellent, and filled with all sorts of cool details that tied many of our disparate maps together made me terribly insecure.

I told Tim that I needed to take a walk around the lake behind the office building so I could talk about it with him.

"Maybe I'm not the right guy here," I said.

"During the course of a day or a week, you're in a lot of different meetings," he said. "You don't have to be the smartest guy in every meeting."

"Yeah," I said, weakly.

"You want to be smart enough to know who the smartest guy in the meeting really is."

He taught me one of the hardest and truest lessons of management: hire talented people and get the hell out of the way.

In December 1999, Epic announced a new two-game deal with GT Interactive for *Unreal Tournament* and *Unreal II*. Talks about a merger with Digital Extremes surfaced again. It triggered an alarm in me, and I arranged a meeting with Tim and Mark to discuss my status.

When we got together, I shared my concerns and asked them to give me the title of lead designer. It was not the most strategic move, as I had very little leverage, but there it was, all my cards on the table.

My frankness caught them off guard.

"I don't know," Tim said, trying to be diplomatic and not hurt my feelings.

Mark rubbed his face.

"We're a small company," he said. "Very small. Less than twenty people. We don't really have titles. Tim has his company. James has his company."

"Cliff, are you unhappy?" Tim asked.

"No," I said. "But I am—"

Mark cut me off.

"I have an idea," he said. "We're a collaborative company. Everything we do here is based on collaboration. We'll let the employees of both companies vote."

"An election?" I asked.

"Yes."

The next time the DE crew came to Raleigh, everyone gathered in a conference room in the musty North Raleigh Hilton for an all-hands meeting, and we voted. For weeks, I had quietly campaigned for the role, positioning myself as a champion of ideas, asking some directly to vote for me and dropping hints to others. There was nothing negative to say about James. It was mostly about me and what I wanted, like an election in fifth grade for class president. I think developers at both companies thought the whole thing was crazy, and in retrospect, it was totally bonkers.

When I walked into the conference room, I wore a politician's fake smile and hoped that no one saw I was shaking from nerves. A short time later the votes were tallied, and James was the clear winner. If the companies merged, he was going to take the lead. Devastated,

I went home and cried to Marcy. Later, we drove to Borders, and I bought books on architecture, design, and how to draw comic book characters. I wanted more and better skills.

Then, for complicated reasons of immigration and taxation, the merger was dropped. Work continued as before, and James and I fell back into a collaborative, productive, and supportive rhythm. To James's credit, he didn't hold anything against me. I felt like we were Rocky and Apollo Creed after they became friends at the end of *Rocky II*; then Apollo went on to train him in *Rocky III*.

One day I was at my desk, making notes about *UT*'s flaws and shortcomings, as was the curse of my job. Look for the mistakes and weaknesses, not the innovations and gee-whiz magic. I was forever walking into restaurants, hotels, theaters, and airports, and seeing the features and flaws in systems and ways to improve them. It's not a terribly pleasant or healthy way to live. It can annoy the hell out of the people around me, except when I was at work where this was normal and valued behavior.

The list I compiled was short but significant: The sounds were tinny and weak. The muzzle flashes on the weapons were polygonal and boring instead of hot and flashy. The baddies looked small in the environments. If we wanted to compete with the legacy of Carmack and Romero and forge our own reputation, we had to master the art of gratification across the board, from the basics of firing a weapon to the outrageous thrill of destroying enemies. We needed something like the feedback players got in *Quake* when a foe exploded into giblets, only it had to be uniquely and identifiably ours.

I walked into Brandon's office to see what my straight-edge colleague was up to, not concerned about interrupting him, because such considerations did not exist in our offices. When an idea hit or when searching for one, it was standard procedure to dive-bomb into someone else's space and tell them about it, which was what I did with Brandon, acting as if I were the Kramer of game design. Bursting in and blurting something out as if I were already in the middle of a conversation.

"We need to come up with better ways to incentivize players to kick ass in the game," I said.

He looked up from his monitor and took off his headphones.

"What's up?" he asked.

"Like id's gibbing," I continued. "I love that shit."

"Keep going," he said.

"Beautiful chunks of ham hocks flying into your monitor in glorious 3D after you nailed that perfect rocket shot . . . Something like that."

Brandon got it and began to think.

It wasn't like *UT* lacked firepower, I said. We had an impressive rocket launcher. We had the Shock Rifle, whose precision laser could knock enemies off a map. It also had an alternate firing mode that shot a slow-moving plasma ball that ended in a massive explosion— an idea that came to me after seeing Jean-Claude Van Damme in *Hard Target* kick a gas can into an enemy's face and then shoot it to trigger a devastating fireball.

"But we need more."

Then it came to us. Since first-person shooters are largely about aim, we came up with *UT*'s multi-kill system. If you shot a foe in the head, it did much more damage than a body shot, for instance. Some of our weapons could knock the enemy's head clean off. When that happened, text popped up onscreen that said "Headshot!" When a player destroyed numerous other players in sequence without dying themselves, we said they went on a "Killing Spree!" If they kept going, it was called a "Rampage!"

There might have been some subliminal reference to games that had something similar, like *Mortal Kombat* ("Fatality!" and "Finish him!") and *NBA Jams* ("He's heating up," "He's on fire"), but this idea struck me as different enough and unique to *UT*, and I loved it. But I wanted to take it further.

"How do we push the envelope?" I asked.

"We keep going," Brandon said.

"What about an announcer? The voice of . . . not God. The voice of SATAN!"

If you fragged someone and took another out seconds later, you heard a deep-voiced announcer say: "DOUBLE KILL." It sounded like Lucifer himself was coming through the screen to offer high fives. Three kills got you a "MULTI-KILL." At four, it was: "ULTRA KILL." After that, it was the ultimate: "MONSTER KILL." We kept going. If you notched twenty-five frags without dying, you were "GODLIKE."

We hired a radio announcer with a classic baritone voice to record those kill rewards, and as soon as I heard the playback, fireworks started going off in my brain. It was like my nucleus accumbens, the little pleasure chest in my prefrontal cortex that lit up when playing video games, had ordered a Big Gulp of dopamine. I'd felt this kind of thrill before: the first time I played *Jazz Jackrabbit* and was able to run around in a level I'd created. Also, the first time I coupled together a level in Tim's new editor, the future Unreal Editor. We'd done it. Our little fragathon feature was destined to be an instant classic. Brandon knew it. I knew it. And everyone who emulated it in countless other future games knew it, too.

In April 1999, six months before *Unreal Tournament* was released, Eric Harris and Dylan Klebold murdered twelve students and one teacher at Columbine High School in Columbine, Colorado. The shooting took place late morning in Colorado, which was lunchtime in Raleigh, and I didn't hear about it until I got home that night and turned on the television. Like everyone else, I was stunned and horrified by the initial reports, and then, as I learned more, I was profoundly, deeply saddened and shaken. Tears poured out of my eyes as I watched the news.

I talked about it with people at work—the guys with whom I shared my office, some of the others as we waited for meetings to start. All of us were struggling to process it and asking the same questions as everyone else: How could this happen? Who would do this? Why would they do it?

Over the next few days and weeks, as Harris and Klebold were discovered to be obsessed fans of *DOOM*, blame for the school shooting found its way to video games. Senator Joseph Lieberman renewed his call for regulating the industry, as he had done a few years before when he led congressional hearings about the impact of violence in video games. Lieberman and other politicians may have sounded good on the evening news, but as far as I was concerned, he didn't know what he was talking about, nor did so many of those who added to the chorus of criticism.

Had they played video games? Did their children or grandchildren play them? Were they turned into killers? Video games and pop culture were an easy target.

As I grew up, my parents were the archetypal American parents who deemed what was okay versus not okay. Sex and nudity were off-limits. My mother had tossed a coat over my head when we went and saw *National Lampoon's European Vacation* and the girl flashed her breasts to Rusty. But violence was acceptable. After my father took me and Tyler to see *Indiana Jones and the Temple of Doom*, I walked out shaken from chilled monkey brains served as a meal, Mola Ram pulling out a still-beating heart, and crocodiles that ate Ram's Thuggee guards.

One night my father rented *Poltergeist*, a masterpiece of horror. Another night it was *RoboCop*, which has the best blood squibs of all time, as well as a scene of a bad guy falling into a vat of toxic sludge and getting squished by a speeding car. And still another night we watched *Predator*, complete with skinned bodies and countless mercenaries falling prey to the dreadlocked alien. "What'd you think?" my father always asked. Wide-eyed and pinned to the back of the sofa, I said, "Cool."

Then one fateful Saturday my father brought home a VHS copy of *Rambo: First Blood Part 2*, and I cheered as Sylvester Stallone mowed down legions of fighters who had double-crossed him. He even took down an enemy chopper with an explosive arrow shot from his bow, a scene that was re-created in the Sega Genesis classic *Rambo III*, which I devoured when I had my affair with Sega.

American pop culture is composed of equal parts violence, blood, gore, and sex. It's part of who we are. We entertain ourselves with our strongest fears and desires.

To educate myself on both sides of the debate, I used a relatively new website on the internet called Amazon to order two books on the subject: *Stop Teaching Our Kids to Kill* by Dave Grossman, which argued that video games desensitized kids and made them more likely to commit Columbine-like atrocities; and *Killing Monsters* by Gerard Jones, who wrote that fantasy and make-believe violence helped kids defeat the proverbial "monster under their bed." I thought both missed the mark.

To me, the problem was abuse. Too many kids were abused emotionally, psychologically, or physically at home and school and it went ignored or excused. As someone who had been picked on at school, suffered the loss of a parent, been molested by an adult predator, ostracized for having bad skin, and moved across the country in the middle of high school where I had to make new friends at a most fragile time of adolescence, I knew what it was like to experience the pain of isolation, loneliness, alienation, and insecurity. I knew how easily that could turn into anger and desperation. And I knew how easily that could've been me.

I wondered how many other people deep down saw the same potential in themselves. I wished someone could have gotten to those kids sooner.

In a tape Harris and Klebold had made before carrying out their massacre, the killers both talked about being motivated by their rage and anger. Harris spoke about having moved five times, being "at the bottom of the food chain," and being made fun of—"my face, my hair, my shirts." Klebold also spoke of being the runt of the litter. I knew what that pain and rage felt like. I knew how overwhelming it could be. And I'd been even more obsessed with video games. So why hadn't I killed anyone? The answer was that there was no answer. That's why the politicians and media were so eager to place the blame on video games. There needed to be some simple explanation because the truth—that this happened for reasons too hard to comprehend or for no reason at all—was too scary.

However, there *is* a simple explanation for why there is so much violence in video games: it's quick and easy to design and build. Shooting is a rudimentary interaction, much easier than the complex animation needed for a fighting game where players grapple with each other. In a shooter, you trace a line or toss a projectile and hit your foe. As for the blood, games are based on the idea of a feedback loop. Actions and outcomes. Risk and reward. When you're finished playing, you're supposed to walk away feeling satisfied.

After Columbine, we never considered abandoning or scaling down the violence in *UT*. If anything, the attacks from politicians and pundits brought us closer together and made us more determined to deliver a great game.

LEVEL

4

LIVING PRODUCT

Summer 1999. I watched it through the windows of the Epic offices, where we were holed up while pounding *Unreal Tournament* in search of bugs. The routine was familiar to everyone who makes games. In the process, though, we discovered some emergent gameplay, the happy accidents that programmers didn't remember coding, and no one knew how they got into the game.

For instance, we had created the ability to dodge, which led to some emergent gameplay—similar to id's rocket jumping—double tap left or right on the arrow keys and you leapt to the side or even forward or backward. But it turned out that if the player did that on a sloped surface, they could ride it up and find shortcuts in the arenas. Who knew?

We also had lift jumping. If the player rode an elevator in a map to the top and jumped at the exact moment they reached that high point, they got a super jump, which we later leveraged by placing power-ups and other secret goodies way up high for players to find.

For game designers, emergent gameplay was the Holy Grail—and having it was a good sign. The basics were covered too. *Unreal Tournament* was all about multiplayer deathmatches, and Tim and the coders had built a slick auto-download feature that made sure we weren't going to wake up and find our message boards stuffed with complaints about the multiplayer. Even so, I pushed for messaging on the box that made it clear an internet connection wasn't necessary to enjoy *UT*.

"We have AI," I said in the forums. "You can have fun offline."

In September, we released a demo of *UT*, tinkering up to the last minute in a race against the impending release of *Quake III Arena* and the arrival of Hurricane Floyd in Raleigh, which we feared might cut power and also prevent Mark Rein from catching a flight to New York and hand-delivering a physical copy of the master to our publisher. Our offices did, in fact, lose electricity the day after Mark flew out of town.

Reaction to the demo surpassed our boast that the game featured "more bells and whistles than in all the Rhineland's cuckoo clock shops." GT wanted to double down on the tournament aspect and picture a trophy on the game's cover.

Unreal Tournament went gold on November 15 and was released a week later. Mark's decision to build a stand-alone product stood out as a brilliant read of the game board. A "technical and game-playing marvel," crowed one reviewer. Others praised the different modes, the levels, the weapons, the bots, and the engine's easily accessible and powerful editor. But above all else, *UT* was a hit where it mattered most—the stores. By the end of the year, sales topped one hundred thousand, and revenue was two million and counting.

But we weren't finished. Mark convinced Tim that we needed to port *UT* to Sony's PlayStation 2 as a way of showing off our tech on that platform and expanding our licensing fees. It was well known in the office that I wasn't a PlayStation fan, and I wasn't in favor of shipping our game with less fidelity and weaker controls. It was going to be a thankless job and a pain in the ass. However, one day I went into Tim's office and found him tinkering with an early PS2 kit. He looked up at me and grinned. "Hey, Cliff, I'm a console programmer!"

I realized something about the industry that has been true ever since: work on games never stops. Just as humans keep evolving throughout their life, so do games. Between those who make them and modders, they're living products. It would get to the point where instead of *Halo 6*, *7*, and *8*, you just get new seasons of *Halo Infinite*. We shipped the PlayStation 2 version in February 2000, and for the record, I hated the experience.

It's hard enough to get a decent game out the door, never mind one that's exceptional, but then to do an inferior version of it while working super-long hours and sleeping at the office? Not fun. I made up for it by posting about *UT* on the company's website and hanging out in fan forums. "I'd love to see more servers running these maps online," I wrote. "Shit, I'd love to see more servers!" In retrospect, I can say that I was carving out a position at Epic as the company's most engaging spokesperson and creating a public persona for myself, and while that would be true, I was having a fuckload of fun.

I was first and foremost a gamer just like the fans, who knew me by my junior high school nickname, CliffyB. In the forums, they treated me like one of their buddies. I enjoyed the cool factor and popularity I had craved since high school. I was quick, funny, snarky, occasionally outrageous, and always informative. I was also an insider who was accessible, perhaps an updated version of Nintendo know-it-all Howard Phillips.

I shared news and tips. I suggested specific maps for old-school shooters and other maps for players who dug the beautiful design. I pointed out which maps played well in low-gravity mode. I also jumped into deathmatches. "I fragged CliffyB," one guy boasted. I saw it and snapped back, "Sheesh, like anyone can frag me."

I knew of only one person who was not fond of my work ethic or impressed. I happened to live with her. Marcy was usually winding down or already in bed by the time I got home, and instead of curling up next to my fiancée, I usually grabbed a beer, went upstairs, and sat in the chat rooms. It's not the most flattering picture of me, but I was hooked on connecting with the masses. I was creating a club where I was the president.

I bleached my hair blond, and when I walked into Epic's offices and heads turned, I thought, *Mission accomplished.* For kicks, I installed a webcam in front of my desk and posted what I called the CliffyCam on the web for anyone who wanted to watch me at work. It was an early livestream, sending out still photos every few minutes. I never knew if the audience was two or two hundred. It didn't matter. I was just being me. I was my own living product. In perpetual, irrepressible development.

For many of us, the office was an extension of our personal lives. We didn't only work there. We grew up there. One of our more uninhibited artists seemed to begin every story, "One time when my boys and I were drunk . . ." Southern folk, gotta love them.

The lack of women in the industry was clearly a problem, one of many related to an even wider issue of diversity, and I think the misogyny that occasionally surfaced was something that would have been addressed if there had been more women in the office. As it was, we behaved like a high school math club that reunited ten years later. Bright but terribly, embarrassingly immature. Egged on by one of our more outgoing programmers, we ordered a dot matrix LED panel sign for our office, hooked up a webcam to it, and created a simple website where people could type in short messages and see it scroll across the sign.

Anyone on the internet could drop in and make a comment. They did, too. Mostly dumb, innocuous stuff. But one day our office administrator, a short, motherly woman, came in to do some bookkeeping. She didn't know she was on camera. Neither did she see the message on the sign behind her: "HEY LADY, NICE TITS!"

We got rid of the sign.

But the topic of women in the industry would soon come up again.

n the summer of 2000, I was contacted by a writer from *PC Gamer* magazine who wanted to include me in a cover story headlined "The New Game Gods." The magazine had done a similar cover story the previous fall headlined "Game Gods," featuring id's John Carmack and legendary game designers Sid Meier and Richard Garriott. I had been envious of those guys as I read that issue. I wanted to be a game god, dammit. And now, apparently, I was making all the right moves, because here was the offer for such recognition.

I flew to Seattle for a group interview and photo shoot with the seven others in the article, among them American McGee, a Bono look-alike with a superhero's name who was forging his own path at Electronic Arts after a split with id; Alex Garden, the tall, handsome tech-bro responsible for Relic Entertainment's hit space strategy series *Homeworld*; Ken Levine, the founder of Irrational Games; and Stevie Case, who was at Romero's studio Ion Storm in Dallas and one of the few women in the industry, if not the most famous, too.

We set up in a conference room at the W Hotel and talked about all the major issues and questions people had about the industry, starting with the most basic of all: How do you get a job in gaming? In addition to sharing our personal stories, all of us mentioned the need for talent, the ability to code and program, the patience to work your way up from the bottom by answering phones, doing QA, or just running errands. I tried to further simplify. "Make cool shit," I said, quoting Tim.

It was the truth. Those three words summed up the entire industry. *Make cool shit.* What else did you need to know?

Nevertheless, we continued to share opinions on topics from PCs versus consoles to storytelling in games and the phenomenon of Valve's fantastic first-person shooter *Half-Life* to obscure facts about ourselves. "I have an unhealthy obsession with my happy childhood,"

I said sarcastically. When questioned about violence in games and potential censorship, all of us were adamant about the government staying out of our business and ceasing to blame video games for senseless acts of violence. "The average kid sees something like six thousand murders on TV by the time they're six years old," Levine said. "You're trying to tell me that we're desensitizing kids to violence by playing a game like *Quake* where you're running and blowing up demons? Give me a goddamn break."

The other hot-button issue was the lack of women in gaming. All of us had something to say on the subject, including me, when I earnestly said, "I honestly think by having more women playing games you're going to have more women making games." My generalization may have been right, but it was a big, earnest *duh* that glossed over the deeper issues. In hindsight, the good intentions are still cringeworthy. None of us noted that only one woman was in the room with us. We had seven dudes, not quite mansplaining, but still spouting off on a topic we weren't qualified to answer. It was indicative of the problem.

Stevie didn't call any of us out, as she easily could have, but when she did take her turn, she did so with the quiet, confident authority of knowing what it's like to be the only woman in the room—and at the company—and she believed change was needed. "I think at a very basic level, it comes down to how we are socialized as children," she said. "Growing up, I had great parents, but I still wasn't encouraged to examine technology and learn about computers. I think so many girls have that experience." Once on the job, she didn't want her gender to be an issue. "I am just one of the guys on the team working on the game," she said.

Except she wasn't just one of the guys. The twenty-four-year-old redhead had recently posed for *Playboy*. She was every gamer's fantasy girl, including mine, but not because of her blue eyes and obvious physical attributes. It was because she was brainy and talented and, as she said, just like us. Better than us, in fact. She had defeated Romero himself in an online *Quake* deathmatch. After that, Romero hired her to work at his studio in Dallas. And at the time of our interview, they were living together as boyfriend and girlfriend.

It gave me one more reason to root against him. A couple months earlier, Romero, through his new studio, Ion Storm, had released an elaborate first-person shooter called *Daikatana*. It was his first game since parting with Carmack, and, though hotly anticipated, it bombed. It was a critical and commercial failure. I was among those who embraced the schadenfreude of my hero's misstep. Later, I would wonder why—why cheer the failure of someone I admired, and what did that say about me other than I was naïve, immature, and caught up in my own ego and ambition.

Rooting against someone like him, one of the industry's most exciting innovators, was like guzzling a bottle of cheap wine—easy to do and sweet going down, but inevitably it was going to result in a crushing headache, which I would experience many years later when I opened my own studio.

At the photo shoot, all of us wore sunglasses, making us look like an underground rock band, or characters from *The Matrix*. I was self-conscious when the photographer gave me a box to stand on because, at five nine, I was the shortest guy in the room. I made up for it, however, by being the funniest guy in the bar when we all met up for drinks later that night. But my quips and bon mots were directed to an audience of one: Stevie. After all my talk about welcoming more women into the industry, I behaved like such a fanboy. I couldn't dial back the dude in me.

She was cool and clearly adept at handling overly chatty guys in bars. We hit it off, and at the end of the night, we traded emails and promised to keep in touch. I told myself there was nothing untoward about our interaction, and yet I knew where my mind had gone and the comparisons I had made to Marcy, who was going to be my lawfully wedded wife in another six months. I knew what I was think-ing. What was I doing?

When I got to my room, I took a shower and stood under the hot water until my skin burned. I didn't know whether I was trying to wash away the guilt I felt for mentally cheating in the bar or the doubts I had about marrying Marcy.

Those doubts crystalized a few months later in Los Angeles. It was now 2001, and I was at E3 in LA, speaking on a panel about the future of video games. I spent the day whirring through the conven-tion center, flashing my VIP pass, chatting with journalists, meeting fans, and carousing with colleagues and pals in the industry. It was late when I finally fell into bed, and I was exhausted. I couldn't wait to sleep. But as soon as I hit the pillow, my eyes popped wide open with fear. It was like I'd seen a ghost.

What I'd seen was myself in the future with Marcy, and it scared the shit out of me. It was my nightmare. We had recently moved into a house in a nice, well-tended suburb, and I pictured myself trapped there. I was too young to get married. I was also too inexperienced. Marcy was the only girl with whom I'd had sex, and all the other issues we had aside, I wanted to see what sex was like with other women. That was a powerful blinking red light.

If I'd been making a game and felt this kind of conflict, I would have gone with my gut. But for some reason, my life was different. In-vitations went out to family and friends. We met with a caterer. And we put a down payment on a venue.

The big day was August 25, 2001. After a two-year engagement and even more time spent cohabitating, most people thought we were already married. But we made it legal at Castle McCulloch, a wedding venue outside Greensboro, with the crews from Epic and Digital Extremes in attendance. The weather was perfect. Marcy was gorgeous. We read our vows amid the beautiful flower gardens, and then we partied hard. The only glitch came when I asked the DJ to play Dr. Dre. The hard-core beats of "Nuthin' but a 'G' Thang" cleared the dance floor, except for me. I kept going, enjoying my solo in the spotlight.

But note to future self: dancing alone at your own wedding is not a sign of a long and happy marriage.

I was happiest at the office, where my shelves were filled with my old Transformers and classic Kaiju "Shogun Warrior" die-cast figures, and I blasted Crystal Method, Kid Rock, and Rob Zombie into my headphones while beavering away in front of my computer. Without realizing it, I had turned my office into the cool bedroom I'd fantasized about as a teenager. The conditions were so cozy and comfortable that I turned down a job offer from Romero. It was a surprisingly easy call.

Romero initially reached out through email. When we spoke, he offered the position of lead level designer at his Ion Storm studios. I was flattered that this guy who I grew up loving and hating and wanting to emulate thought enough of me that he now wanted to bring me on board. But I had read the articles and heard the gossip about the troubles at his company, and I didn't want to be the guy rearranging the deck chairs on the *Titanic*.

At Epic, I had no such worries. I had negotiated a good contract, and with my old nemesis James Schmalz running his own company, I was the company's head designer. In Tim, I had a friend, a mentor, a big brother, and a colleague who was one of the industry's reigning geniuses truly coming into his own. Why would I leave?

Epic was on a roll. We had guessed right with *UT*. Multiplayer was the rage. Epic was making money, not fuck you money, but enough for Tim to hand out small bonuses and stock options. As we prepared for the next round of *Unreal* projects, we also got the green light to beef up the staff. Among the key people I recruited were two

Ion Storm alum, artist Chris Perna and gameplay designer Lee Perry. Both were integral to Epic's future.

Chris had worked on *Daikatana* and could do anything—paint, render, light, and create. We bonded over a passion for horror movies and New York pizza. Before leaving Ion, and obviously through Romero, Chris had seen a demo of id's upcoming *DOOM 3*. He gushed about the tech, which made us eager to see more with our own eyes, but also let us know what we could have guessed on our own: the graphics and tech were awesome.

Lee was an inspired and inventive designer who crafted top-notch 3D models. He was tall, pale, and shaved his head. It was a look that reminded me of the lead in the 1995 movie *Powder*. Lee had soaked up Romero's artistic ethos and brought his own vision to our party. Creative and driven, he was constantly delving into the process: how we could cram more polygons onto the screen, how our designers could fill in the environments more efficiently, how we could improve the detail in levels, and how we could work faster and better.

He took to using static meshes—a new geometric tool in the engine that enabled faster rendering of increasingly detailed worlds—and proposed the idea of modular architecture, a way for designers making environments to easily and quickly duplicate their static mesh building blocks, scale them up or down, rotate them to make them look different, and save precious RAM in the process. For those of us building levels, it was a game changer.

Both Chris and Lee joined Epic when it was still a scrappy, overly ambitious company on the rise with only a few more than twenty employees. They fit right in. We were the Little Engine of game makers; we didn't know what we couldn't do. Anything was possible. "Epic is in the business of pulling miracles out of its ass," Lee once observed. It was true. And Chris kept a prop cube from the movie *Hellraiser* on the top of his desk. One day I went into his office to talk and absent-mindedly picked up the cube. Chris recoiled in horror.

"Be careful," he said. "You can unleash hell itself."

He was joking, but we were preparing to unleash some of our own awesome hell on the world.

MORE, MORE, MORE

In November 2001, Tim and Mark sent me to South Korea to demo the Unreal Editor for Korean game developers. I was nervous about flying so soon after the 9/11 terrorist attacks, and I didn't mind sharing that with people or, failing someone to talk to, indulging in the drink cart to sooth my nerves on the long flight there.

In Seoul, I attended the first World Cyber Games, an esports event that was about twenty years ahead of the curve. Few if anyone in mainstream media knew of the event, and it has remained mostly unknown in the West, but over there it was treated like the Olympics. An opening ceremony included more than four hundred participants from thirty-six countries aligned behind flags from their respective nations. They competed in *Counter-Strike, Quake III, Unreal Tournament,* and *StarCraft: Brood War* for $300,000 in prize money.

I thought it was tacky until the intense level of play sucked me into the drama of the competition. A smart software executive had once told me to "look East" if I wanted to see the future—and as I stood there, I knew he was right. Eyeballs equals money!

Later, after demoing the editor for the team at Softmax, I went to the bar at my hotel and pounded Asahi beers. I was drinking more. I was also trying to make nice with the pretty Korean bartenders. Hey, I was a world traveler now. The scenery out the window—a dense urban forest of tall buildings, neon lights, overcrowded spaces—reminded me of the movie *Blade Runner*. A few more beers, and I might have gone hunting for replicants.

From Seoul, I went to Tokyo. I had a few meetings, but it was really one of those as-long-as-I'm-in-the-neighborhood things. I couldn't pass up the chance to see Japan.

My first night there I strolled through Akihabara, Tokyo's electronics district. The neon-lit storefronts and businesses gave off a bright, surreal glow that was neither nighttime nor daytime. I understood why it was called Electric Town. It had the artificial hue of a video game and it was easy to imagine myself inside one. I had no idea where I was walking when I heard someone shout my name: "CliffyB!" I turned and spotted the vaguely familiar face of a gaming journalist. He waved. I walked over to him.

"I saw your jacket and recognized you," he said.

I was wearing a leather jacket with a custom *Unreal* logo on the back, a promotional item Epic had made for VIPs.

The journalist knew the city and I accepted his offer to show me around while I was there.

"How about we start tonight?" I said.

He laughed. "Sure."

We darted in and out of arcades, electronics stores, and smoky pachinko parlors. I tripped out on the candy-colored neon. Hungry, we went downstairs into an underground Japanese comfort food restaurant and ordered spicy ramen, fried pork, and tempura. I washed it down with cold Asahi beer. The next night we went out again, visiting more stores and arcades and eating at an extremely pricey Kobe beef restaurant, where the Wagyu was delicious and the beer was poured from large individual bottles.

"All I know is we're not in Kansas anymore," I said.

"You're far away," he said. "You don't need to know anything more."

"The whole time I've been here I have felt like I was in the movie *Blade Runner*. I'm the replicant, except I don't know it yet."

"Instead of being bioengineered," he said, "you're biobuzzed."

After dinner, we walked, took a crowded subway, and walked more. We dodged drunken businessmen as they wobbled along the sidewalk on their way home. Some were passed out on the pavement. Apparently, that was a thing there. Everything about Tokyo interested me. I thought of the great video game developer Hideo Kojima. Kojima-san was the designer of the 1988 game *Metal Gear*, a military adventure for the PlayStation whose super gun, stealth gameplay, cinematic storytelling, and dark political themes raised both game tech and design to a breathtaking art form.

Kojima-san was among the first game designers to be given rockstar status in the press. I'd read everything I could about him. Although he was ten years older than me, it seemed like we had much in common and could have been friends. We came from large families. We grew up loving movies. Our fathers died when we were teenagers. We coped by playing video games. At a similar age to myself, twenty-five, he had made *Metal Gear*. Before I left Tokyo, the sixth game in the series, *Metal Gear Solid 2: Sons of Liberty*, was released. It was about terrorists threatening environmental disaster and loaded with Kojima's trademark cut scenes and social commentary. It served as an inspiring end to my trip.

When I returned to Raleigh, we had three *Unreal*-related projects in the works—*Unreal Tournament 2003*, a sequel to *Unreal*, and *Unreal Championship*, which was a port of *UT 2003* for Microsoft's new Xbox console. We contracted Legend Entertainment to make the sequel, titled *Unreal II: The Awakening*, and we handed *Unreal Championship* to Digital Extremes.

Epic's own immediate resources were assigned to *UT 2003*. Mark and Jay wanted to annualize *UT* the way Electronic Arts had *Madden Football*. The strategy was smart, but my brain went numb when I thought about working on *Unreal* forever. Fortunately, we were co-developing *UT 2003* with Digital Extremes, which lightened the load. As a sequel to a very successful game, the objective was simple: don't fuck it up.

We set out to improve on what had worked in the original *UT*, fix the broken stuff, get rid of the boring parts, and add some cool new shit. In meetings, we sounded like weapons engineers devising new killing systems for the military, like our shock and sniper rifles and new shield gun. *We'll keep headshots and multi-kills . . . Deathmatch stays, Assault goes, and we'll add Bombing Run . . . it's like football with guns.*

It was crazy-sounding shit. But I knew in my bones I wanted to make something new and different. I felt that even more after seeing the demo for *DOOM 3* at E3 in Los Angeles. Chris Perna had given us a good verbal description, but seeing it in person and even more developed surpassed mine and everyone else's expectations. "Fuck, that's the future," I said to Tim and others from the company who had waited in the long line with me.

Carmack had again seemingly stretched the detail and tech beyond what we all believed was possible. Except for Tim, of course. Before we even left the convention center, I saw him begin calculating the updates he'd need to make to the Unreal Engine 3 to not only keep pace but also move a step or two ahead.

I had the same reaction. I was thinking about Kojima-san, as I did frequently since returning from Japan, and I wanted to respond with an entirely new game, something that would have my signature, like his *Metal Gear* games. I had notes for a large-scale, first-person multiplayer combat game that I had written at least six months before and referred to as *Apex War*, a name someone else had pitched that was a sort of inside joke inspired by the nearby suburb where so many Epic employees lived. I thought it captured the essence of what I was going for—peak war, the incendiary mayhem that could wreck a planet.

Eventually, I called it *Unreal Warfare*. Despite wanting to break away from the *Unreal* choo-choo, I knew that's where the money was.

The idea was one of those ripped-from-the-headlines things. War was in the air and on the airwaves. The country was dealing with fallout from the 9/11 attacks at home and abroad, including our invasion of Afghanistan, which dominated the nightly news. HBO's award-winning series *Band of Brothers* was also one of the biggest and most talked-about shows on television. I had watched and rewatched every episode.

When I explained this concept, I would say that I wanted to do something "beyond the cheap colored lights." That was a phrase from "One Song Glory," my favorite song from the hit Broadway musical *Rent*, and it described the direction I wanted to go. *Unreal* was known for its bright, gaudy lights, and I wanted to go somewhere *beyond the cheap colored lights*. It was the bleakness of war, I think.

But influences were everywhere. I'd hired a classically trained painter named John Mueller, a George Clooney–looking fella, who had made an Orwellian graphic novel called *Oink* about a pig-human hybrid slave. The logo for the book was a gear. John also had a tattoo of it on his forearm. That symbol planted a seed that would yield fruit down the road. For the time being, though, it was a powerful, iconic image that stayed with me.

Why did it have such a hold on me? I couldn't figure it out. I also knew that not everything had to make sense when trying to create.

Unreal Warfare had picked up heat around the office, starting back when it was *Apex War*. Even then, I could see everyone was like me, hungry for something other than *Unreal*. That's what happens when you put together a young, talented team who all come into their own around the same time. I pitched it in a meeting with Microsoft execs who came to the office while making the rounds in search of IP for their new Xbox.

In retrospect, I should have kept my mouth shut.

Unreal Warfare was barely a kernel of an idea, on top of which there was nothing to demo, but I got on a riff about this war game idea, featuring a ton of cool vehicles, which I boasted was going to "out-*Halo Halo*." Of course, Microsoft had launched their Xbox with *Halo*. I wanted them to know *Unreal Warfare* would be even bigger. But I wasn't just preaching to the converted; I was spouting off in front of the twelve apostles; and I screwed up when I said, "We're going to have a ton of vehicles. *Halo* only has their Warthog buggy."

At that point Microsoft's legendary designer Ken Lobb politely raised his hand. I paused and looked at him. He apologized for interrupting, but he wanted to also mention his fondness for another *Halo* vehicle, emphasis on the word "another," and that was its Banshee.

Ken instantly knew I had only played a tiny bit of *Halo*. "The Banshee flies," he said, with a smile that let me know I'd better have my shit together before pitching another idea.

Lesson learned. No harm done.

When Digital Extremes fell behind schedule on their portions of *UT 2003*, we backburnered *Unreal Warfare* and helped get it to the finish line. Because the game was now envisioned as a yearly edition, I pushed the sporty aspect of the tournament even more. I still felt the same way about football that I did as a kid—I didn't give a crap—but I tried to channel some of that Madden vibe into the game, and we wound up making a glitzy introduction that looked more like pro wrestling than football. At least the music had a *Monday Night Football* vibe.

On September 24, 2002, *Unreal Championship* was released on the Xbox. Six days later, *UT 2003* shipped on the PC. "Its visceral intensity is off the charts—other shooters seem frail and timid in comparison," wrote *GamePro*. "Gorgeous, gib-filled excitement," said *PC Gamer*. The most important measure of success was at the cash register, and *UT 2003* looked like it might be the bestselling *Unreal* game to date. The esports crowd gave us traction in the marketplace. Within six months, more than 130,000 games had been sold, roughly $6 million worth. It was a solid win.

Even so, my enthusiasm for the game we put out was uncharacteristically muted. The game felt like a mash-up of styles due to the increased graphical fidelity and Epic's and Digital Extremes's contrasting styles. Digital Extremes had also made some decisions I didn't like, like replacing *UT*'s iconic sniper rifle with a sci-fi lightning gun, much to fans' dismay, and eliminating the popular Assault mode. Even innovative features somehow hurt the fun. For instance, we had "ragdoll" physics—if a character was killed, their body would go flying and properly collide with the world. But gibbing—exploding people into little bits—was hardly in the game now. I wanted more blood, more chunks. Just more, more, more.

I was also bothered when journalists asked me what was going on with *Unreal Warfare*. It happened a few times while I was promoting *UT 2003*. "It'll come up eventually," I snapped at a reporter from Shacknews. "The more I talk about *Warfare* and waste breath on it, the more I'm not talking about games that will be out soon and playable. So it makes no sense to talk about it."

It was a rare lapse of charm in the one place where I always enjoying being—in front of a camera. I was back to my old fun-loving, party-hardy self at a celeb-filled bash our PR team hosted in New York. I rocked a pinstripe pimp suit at the party, and Marcy looked like a fembot from *Austin Powers* with her teased hair and pink boots, which she vomited on while walking back to our hotel after drinking too much. I comforted her until she fell asleep, but it was also the last time I took Marcy to an out-of-town PR event. I went to these things to have fun, and I couldn't be myself with her there.

I was convinced it was being myself that worked. Our PR team agreed, and the year ended with a dream come true: *Entertainment Weekly* featured me in their special year-end issue Guide to 2003. It was like seeing my name in *Nintendo Power*, only times one hundred. This was real fame. I had read every issue of *Entertainment Weekly* since it began publication. To me, it was the Holy Grail of pop culture, and there I was, on page 84, with bright red hair, baggy camo pants, and a sleeveless Pac-Man shirt, above a headline that read, "*Unreal*'s Cliff Bleszinski Proves Why He's the Best in the Business."

In January 2003, as the magazine filled the racks in airport gift shops and newsstands everywhere, Marcy and I traveled to Edinburgh, Scotland, and London, England, for an overdue vacation. The weather was going to be dismal, and I suffered from seasonal affective disorder, but what the fuck! I'd worked unforgiving hours ever since our move to Raleigh and through this most recent holiday season. My career had not been kind to our relationship. I wanted to see if things might change if it was just the two of us with no distractions.

I booked the nicest hotels I could find, and we did reconnect a bit. We visited all the sights, including Saint Paul's cathedral in the heart of London. I'll never forget the feeling of climbing all 528 steps to the top, and feeling the cool London breeze hitting my face as the sun set over the city. Something deep inside me clicked with the architecture of that city, all of it built on top of centuries of ruins, like the church itself, which had started as a wooden structure in 604 AD followed by additions made by the Vikings and Romans, until it was finished in 1711.

The idea of so much architecture from the past that could be felt but not seen made an impression on me. I thought of it as "destroyed beauty," and as we stood atop that historic structure, I knew eventually I'd have to make a game that mimicked the look. We just had to get *UT 2004* out of the way and keep moving forward.

Then we were back home. Marcy and I fell back into the same old pattern of me working late, coming home for dinner and a couple hours of reality TV on the sofa before she went to bed and I returned to my computer, beer in hand, and the *Unreal* forums waiting for me. One great vacation wasn't going to change things. I was more interested in my career, nonstop. One night I came home from work, grabbed a beer, and stood on my back porch staring up at the full moon. Marcy was already in bed. The two Labs that we adopted were at my feet. The sky was quiet and still and almost fragile, as winter nights can be. I was reminded of a time after my father had died. He had been gone only a couple weeks, and my mother had finally slept in their bed again.

She told me and Tyler that she had woken up in the predawn darkness and seen the biggest, most beautiful moon she had ever seen, seemingly right outside the window. It lit up her room, and she swore she felt Dad reaching out from beyond the void and telling her that everything was going to be okay.

As I looked up at the moon from my porch, it was also big and beautiful, and mysterious, like a glowing orb a psychic might peer into to see both the past and the future. I wondered if my father was looking down on me, and if so, would he know that, although I was imperfect, I was working hard and trying my best and wanting him to be proud of where I'd gotten to thus far. I also had a premonition that my life at work and at home was going to change, and I hoped everything was going to be okay.

MAD WORLD

"What's next for you guys? *Unreal: The Musical?*"

That was my oldest brother, Greg. We were catching up on the phone. He was being facetious. But it was *the* question: What was next?

It was February, and *Unreal II: The Awakening* had come out to mixed reviews. *GamePro* loved it, Firing Squad called it "unmemorable," and IGN said it offered "little in the way of new gameplay." To me, it was the David Hasselhoff of video games—a hit in Germany but maybe nowhere else. It was a sign that we needed a fresh idea.

I dove back into my *Unreal Warfare* notebook. The idea of a large, sweeping battlefield game with tons of vehicles, soldiers, and monsters seemed even more timely than it did a year earlier. The war would soon expand into Iraq, with a quick takedown of Saddam Hussein's rule and a continued search for weapons of mass destruction, though I didn't buy the premise that Saddam had been hiding WMDs. The real reason for the invasion seemed obvious to me: we wanted the oil. Those of us watching the news and fretting about body count were merely tiny specks in the grinding gears of the military-industrial complex.

There was so much for my brain to chew on. My trip to London. My desire to make something bombastic that made a statement about the Iraq War and the Bush presidency. My rapidly collapsing marriage. *Band of Brothers.* One day in the office I flashed on the 1990 Kevin Bacon movie *Tremors*, which had subterranean monsters that fed on humans, and it reminded me of the underground cave I had explored with Robert Allen when I was making *Jazz* and he had pointed out a pile of calcified bones—reputed to be the remains of Native American children who'd failed in their attempt to jump over the opening at the top and fallen to their deaths.

I knew there was something to the picture I had of a hole in the ground. It was scary down there; it was another world. I described it to Lee Perry and Chris Perna, but with a twist, saying something like what if instead of people falling to their death, the baddies lived down there and climbed out of the hole?

There was no question we would make this game, whatever this game turned out to be. The question was when.

In mid-March, just before the Game Developers Conference in San Jose, Epic announced it was absorbing its subsidiary, Scion Studios, which was run by Mike Capps, a thirty-year-old computer science PhD who was, very much to my surprise, also named the new president of Epic Games, overseeing management of development and production. In other words, he was my new boss.

I was stunned. Only two months earlier Epic had announced it was helping to launch Scion, a start-up that was run by Capps and, not coincidentally, located in offices just down the hall from Epic's. According to Mark Rein, the plan was to fund Scion while they made at least two games and then turn over ownership of the company to its employees. Having a small, nimble subsidiary would help develop new projects, he said.

While that may have been true on paper, the reality was different. Quite different, in fact.

I walked around GDC in a daze. I knew Mike, having met him months before at a conference. He was a serious dude with what I called presidential timbre, and very bright. After graduating from the University of North Carolina, he'd earned his master's in computer science and electrical engineering from MIT and had gone on to get a PhD in computer science from the Naval Academy. His biggest achievement was the development of *America's Army*, a video game the U.S. Army used as a recruiting tool. It ran on Unreal Engine 2.

When I found out, I joked that the licensing fees were returning some of my tax dollars to me. Mike seemed amused—sort of. I had been doing many of the jobs that would now fall under him, like scouting talent, negotiating contracts, and running the creative. We had a long-running joke internally that there wasn't a deadline we couldn't miss, and if I was the reason for that, I didn't see it. Just as I didn't really see Tim and Mark as my bosses as much as they were like my boys, the guys I ran with.

Eventually I thought it wasn't my management style that led Tim and Mark to promote Mike so much as it was a lack of overall management at Epic. We were a great team full of talented players, but we needed a coach to reach our full potential. And Mike was the total package of intellect and education, organizational ability, leadership, and charisma. Exactly what we needed if Epic was going to remain independent and evolve into a major company like Activision or Electronic Arts.

Still.

Mike wasn't in his new role more than a week before we met in his office. I didn't like being summoned to his office that first time or any time thereafter. I always felt like there should be people in the background shouting, "Dead man walking." Mike and I had always gotten along, and he gave me a warm greeting that day, so there was no reason for me to be nervous or fearful. I just was. It was an allergy to authority.

"Gladwell," I said.

Mike was momentarily confused. I pointed up at the bookshelves behind him. A Malcolm Gladwell hardcover stood out among the many books he kept in his office.

"*The Tipping Point*," he said. "Good book."

"Yeah, I read it too," I said.

We had a cordial discussion about *UT 2003*, *Unreal Championship*, and *UC 2*, which the Scion team had already taken on, and the excitement he anticipated going forward. I brought up news that id had sublicensed their *Quake*-related tech and IP to the company that had made the hit multiplayer game *Quake Wars*. We agreed that we wanted to stay in the multiplayer space, having gotten adept at it, and I riffed briefly about making *Unreal Warfare* a class-based shooter. It was all good and normal. Then, just as I began to relax, he explained that we needed more structure and process in the office, especially as we took on more projects.

I agreed, of course, and found myself nodding in further obsequious agreement as Mike said he wanted me to lead a design meeting every Friday and maintain a weekly status update of works in progress.

"It'll allow everyone to know where we are and how we're doing," he said.

"Totally get it," I said.

After we shook hands, I left his office and walked outside and around the lake until I was as far from the building as I could get. When I was sure I was alone and no one was around to hear me, I shouted, "Fuuuuuck!" The idea of accountability caused me to panic. It shouldn't have. I had led countless status meetings over the years, though it was more on a less-formal basis, as was most everything at Epic. I had always found it easier to dart into someone's office when I wanted an update or had an idea to share. I had flourished within Epic's lack of structure, and so had the company. Why was he changing things? How many games had he designed compared to me?

In my mind, I went through the gamut of personal affronts. I assumed it was personal. As always, I made everything about me. Was Mike setting me up to fail? And what if I did? Did he want to push me out?

But when it came time for my first Friday morning meeting, I was fine. I had prepped like I was auditioning for the lead in *Macbeth*. The high school drama nerd in me showed up as it always did whenever I spoke in front of people, just like when I played Mercutio. I realized that no one in the world could possibly step into this role and do it better than me, because all Mike wanted me to do was be myself. As time went on, he gave me only one note: talk slower.

It was a good note, and I watched my caffeine intake on Fridays.

The decision was made to delay *Unreal Warfare* again until it could be developed with Unreal Engine 3, and done at the level of a tentpole like *Halo* or *DOOM*. We were at a midrange point in tech development for the stuff we were building or wanted to build. We worked on *UT 2004* instead.

It was the right move. Minor tech problems were fixed, like sticky static meshes that impeded player collision in *UT 2003*; basics were tended to, like a new user interface; and more than one hundred maps were created. The brainstorming we'd done about *Unreal Warfare*—who was fighting and why—inspired us to develop more of a story in *UT 2004*. We dropped the Bombing Run game mode, which I never liked, brought back Assault from the original—improved, of course—and we upgraded the most popular modes: Deathmatch, Team Deathmatch, and Capture the Flag.

The highlight was Onslaught, an entirely new large-scale, vehicle-based battle game mode that, as Tim very happily noted to us, brought *UT 2004* up to date. Named after the bad guy Decepticon Transformer of the same name, Onslaught benefited from some ideas that had been intended for *Unreal Warfare*, but the real magic came from programmer Dave Hagewood, who was responsible for the gun-toting tanks, hovercraft, and space vehicles that turned nasties into roadkill. I'd met Dave at GDC, where he was showing off a mod for *UT 2003* that featured vehicles able to rocket up off the ground and zip through the air, something we weren't able to figure out on our own, and I knew we needed him on *UT 2004*.

He and a few guys who worked with him moved to Raleigh temporarily and had their own Waterloo experience in our office, setting up shop in what we referred to as the *UT 2004* war room. Churchill had his underground war room, and we had ours. I alternated between building my own levels, though not as many as previously; giving feedback; and overseeing outside contractors working on Skaarj, robots, and other crazy critters. As busy as this kept me, inevitably I pushed all these responsibilities to the side at least once a day while I slipped into the *UT 2004* war room to butt-stomp foes with Dave's zippy hovercraft, prompting *UT 2004*'s voice-of-Satan announcer to bellow, "PAAAAANCAKE!"

The feature was an instant classic. It's still irresistible fun today. *PAAAAANCAKE.*

I was twenty-eight years old but still learning how to manage adulthood without training wheels. A perfect example: I represented Epic at an *Unreal Tournament* esport competition in Dallas, where, during the trophy presentation, I nearly upstaged the winner, Johnathan "Fatal1ty" Wendel, by wearing a faux fur coat and a giant rapper-style brass necklace with the game's logo. Hey, MTV was shooting a *True Life* documentary on the pro gaming pioneer; dressed like that, I thought I might get my own MTV special. When I showed up at the office in the same getup, Mark Rein grumbled, "Too much."

Dennis Rodman got away with it, I argued.

"Don't be Rodman," he said. "Be Michael Jordan."

I was just being myself. The latest iteration included long stringy blond hair and a tiny patch of beard on my chin that made me look like I was moonlighting with a surf punk band. I bought toys and gadgets to spice up the home front, including old-fashioned *Ms. Pac-Man* and *Mortal Kombat 2* arcade games for our game room and a hot tub for the backyard that I hoped would heat up my love life with the wife. (Sadly, it didn't.)

At E3 in Los Angeles, Tim fell in love with an orange Lamborghini Diablo on display and bought it right off the convention center floor. No one is weirder than a nerd with money. Back in Raleigh, I splurged on a blue Dodge Viper convertible roadster. As I waited for delivery, Tim offered me stick shift driving lessons in his Lambo. I borrowed it once to drive around downtown Raleigh looking cool; after bottoming out on a couple of steep inclines, I gave it back. The Viper wasn't in the same league as Tim's super sports car, but it was an upgrade from my Lexus sedan, and when I drove through town, people knew it was CliffyB.

The only part of my life not working the way I wanted was my marriage. (See hot tub reference above.) We had two cats, two yellow Labs named Charlie and Toby, and a chinchilla, which I bought for Marcy when she wanted a new critter to love. There was no shortage of affection in our house. Just very little between the two of us. When Marcy had knee surgery, I slept in her hospital room at Duke and nursed her at home, but as I changed the bedpan and bandages, my resentment built ("Hey, I'm a hard-working guy, why am I doing this bullshit?"), and after she was able to hobble around on crutches, we got into a massive argument and I kicked her out of the house.

Not a pretty picture of me.

Our separation lasted a week. Epic had a company field trip to a special screening of *X-Men 2*, and Marcy arrived with Lee Perry and his wife. Seeing her limp up to the theater on crutches made me feel like a callous, uncaring, selfish piece of shit, which I was, and the two of us reconciled that night. Instead of the long talks we needed to address our problems and understand each other better, we had clunky make-up sex. It felt wrong.

A couple months later, we hosted a Fourth of July party for all our friends. It was an ambitious effort to keep the fireworks going. During the party, I met a guy who showed me there could be more to my life than coming home from work, watching TV with my wife until she went to bed, and then playing games and drinking until late at night when I finally conked out. His name was Ron, but everyone called him Vegas, after where he had grown up. He had once worked as a Flying Elvis. Now he was a cancer researcher in Raleigh.

A Dwayne "The Rock" Johnson look-alike, he had come to the party with a friend who worked at Epic. I was manning the grill when he mentioned having read about me in *Entertainment Weekly*. I liked him immediately—ha!—and more so when he admitted that he wasn't a gamer. We started meeting for dollar sushi roll dinners on Thursday nights. On Fridays, he watched TV with me and Marcy until my wife yawned and gave me permission to go out with him and have some fun.

Vegas was like my Morpheus in *The Matrix*. He showed me around the bars downtown, teaching me not to snap my fingers to get the bartender's attention ("He knows you're here. He's busy."), how much to tip ("Do you want a good experience next time?"), and the difference between the barback and the bartender ("Be patient."). When he saw me lighten up after a couple of cocktails and flirt with girls at the bar, he advised me to slow down. "You don't have to try that hard," he said. "They'll see you're a good guy. Just have fun."

I was an eager student. I befriended a guy in a coffee shop who had a cool power button tattoo on his arm. He turned out to be a designer at another tech company, and we met up regularly for coffee. Another guy who made tech that we licensed scooped me up at my house in his Porsche Boxster a couple times a month and we went to a downtown beer bar called the Flying Saucer that was known for having beautiful female servers who wore tacky schoolgirl-style outfits. They were poison to a guy like me in a sinking marriage.

The Flying Saucer was also known for having three hundred varieties of beer. If you drank all three hundred, they acknowledged the sudsy achievement by putting a plate with your name on it on the wall. I got mine two years later. It said, "CliffyB—Beers of War—2005." The challenge literally tapped into my high-score mentality. I was drinking more than ever, as do many people who deal with an unhappy relationship by posting themselves on a barstool and calling that fun. I'd learned to balance the booze with Claritin-D in the morning and NoDoz at night. It didn't always help.

One morning, after a long night of drinking too much, I woke up late for a meeting, hopped in my Viper, and barreled out of the driveway. When I walked into my office, I got a crazed phone call from Marcy, who said I had narrowly missed hitting a little old lady on her morning walk down the street. "She had to dive out of the way!" Marcy said. "You almost fucking killed her! I had to invite her in for tea and apologize. Who are you? Who did I marry?" I probably needed to put my training wheels back on.

Vegas usually drove when we went out, but one night I insisted on taking my car. It was a nice summer night, and I removed the top. He punched the button on the radio, expecting to hear something loud and hard. But the night air was pierced by the melancholy piano of the Gary Jules remake of "Mad World," which I played incessantly ("... the dreams in which I'm dying are the best I've ever had"). My friend winced in mock pain and hit eject, popping out the mix CD I'd made. I had titled the CD *Wallow*, hastily scrawled on it with a blue Sharpie.

"Dude, should we just stop and end it all right here?" he said.

I heard the pity in his voice. I had no response.

"It's not funny," he said. "This is sad shit. We need to get you help."

———

Her name was Emily. I ran into her at multiple video game conferences and we always vibed at industry parties. She was a writer. She was clever, brilliant, bubbly, bright-eyed, and beautiful. We always found ourselves chatting about games and tech and peeling off to shoot the shit. She was married, but not happily, which was something else we had in common, and we commiserated about not being thrilled with our situations.

We emailed back and forth, geeking out about video game stuff and pop culture. Marcy would play the occasional video game with me, but she wasn't truly in the thick of it. Not like Emily. Not even close to Emily.

One night I played through the classic video game *Silent Hill 2*, and something clicked in me. That game was in many ways like the Russian book and later the movie *Solaris*, the sci-fi classic about a researcher who visits a planet that manifests an idealized version of his wife. In *SH2*, the main character James gets a letter from his late wife that tells him to "come to Silent Hill, it was our happy place." When James arrives, he encounters monsters of all sorts, which are revealed to be manifestations of the fears and memories the planet's inhabitants pulled out of his head. This includes Maria, a woman he meets who looks exactly like his late wife, Mary, except she's different. She's flirty and sexy—everything he's missed.

There was much speculation about the themes and symbolism of this game and its array of influences from filmmaker David Cronenberg to writer Fyodor Dostoevsky to painter Francis Bacon. And this one night I played, it all suddenly made sense to me. Everything boiled down to the warring desires of libido, anger, and ego, an ongoing conflict that I knew well. I felt like I was James in *Silent Hill 2*, and Emily was my Maria.

I wanted that Disney-style romance that I imagined my parents had, and here was Emily, as if she had appeared straight out of the movie *Aladdin*. "Well, there's this . . . girl. She's smart and fun. She's got these eyes that just—and this hair, wow, and her smile!" Except I was married, and she was married. It was a "Mad World," and "the dreams in which I'm dying are the best I've ever had."

She matched wits and nerdy knowledge with me, trading mental dork paint via email and being available, interested, fun, flirty, and brilliant. I loved having someone to talk to about my world. That fall, she listened to me groan about missing the Christmas release of *UT 2004* and understood why it was imperative to get it right, not just out. Around that same time, Epic announced a partnership with Microsoft to make an unspecified number of games exclusively for Xbox, and she knew the seismic meaning of the deal. We discussed all the ramifications, including what this meant for my dream to make *Unreal Warfare*.

Microsoft was hungry for new IP, and not just any IP. They needed big, buzzy titles that would sell their consoles. *Halo 2* was slated for Christmas 2004. Then what?

"Then it's you," she said. "*Unreal Warfare. Apex War*. Whatever you end up calling it. You're next."

GEARS

She was right.

In March 2004, just a week before GDC, *Unreal Tournament 2004* finally shipped. It was praised by critics and ranked as one of the best games of the year. "This is the one, folks," G4 TV told viewers. "It may just be the best arcade-style online shooter ever made," gushed the review in GameZilla. And GameSpy called it "a fantastic mix of the fresh and familiar, and with enough content to make this the only game you need for the next few months."

I couldn't have felt any better as I traveled to San Jose for GDC. The whole team from Epic was riding on the high of another successful release, the strength of the improvements Tim and the team were making to Unreal Engine 3, and the pivot we had started to make to *Unreal Warfare*. But that wasn't all that had buoyed my spirits. Emily was also going to be at GDC, and through another friend in the industry based in LA, I heard that she was at that point in her marriage.

"What do you mean *that* point?" I asked.

"Cliff, do I have to spell it out?" he said. "She's at that point. She's ready."

Oh, I understood. Then I had to ask myself whether I was ready, whether I was willing to risk my marriage and everything else I'd worked so hard for, to be with this cute, nerdy girl with whom I traded multiple emails every day.

It turned out I was ready.

We met up at one of the nighttime soirees that happened to be at my hotel, got a couple drinks, settled onto a couch off in a corner, and proceeded to nerd out about the games we loved, the movies we'd seen or wanted to see, and stuff we'd read. She listened and laughed at my jokes and loved my childlike sensibilities. It was the opposite of the conversations I had at home. She caught me staring at her. I couldn't help it. She was a manic pixie dream girl before that became a thing. She got me, calling me a late bloomer, which I was and still am. Everything happens to me about fifteen years after it should on a normal timeline.

After a few drinks, I felt confident enough to say, "Wanna get out of here?" She nodded, mid-sip. We went to the elevator to go back to my room, and I immediately kissed her, passionately, in the elevator. Sparks flew, as did an initial pang of guilt. But I didn't care. I was tipsy, frustrated, and eager to get the love that I wasn't getting at home. I felt like I deserved this. I needed to get out of Silent Hill.

We went back to my room and drunkenly made love. Emily was literally the second person I had slept with. It was like an out-of-body experience. I'd had a crush on her for so long, and finally it was happening, and happening again, and I didn't care about the ramifications. You know how they say during times of crisis or war people often connect in odd ways? It was like that. A bond had been cemented between us, and I recall waking up the next day, looking at her curled up in bed, beautiful, and thinking, *Did that just happen?*

It did—and it was only the start of the two of us mixing business with pleasure. We met up again in May at E3 in LA. By this time, we had cobbled together a demo of the new technology of Unreal Engine 3 that showcased things like high- and low-resolution meshes, higher frame rates, increased polygon counts, and other mechanics that went into rendering next-generation graphics. It was breathtaking stuff. But there was more. Included in the demo were some early renderings of war-ravaged environments, along with the soon-to-be-infamous *Gears of War* monster, the Berserker, bursting through the wall to come after the player, as well as some other vignettes, all made in real-time 3D, in a distinctly muted palette of colors.

We didn't draw attention to this new work, as it was all about the engine. Watching it years later, though, was like spotting an ingenue in the background of a music video before she became a huge movie star. People seeing it again realized it wasn't just the engine on display. As one person wrote, "a legend [was] born."

I had the demo on my laptop, and during a break in the conference, Emily and I snuck off to my hotel room, where I fired up my laptop and showed her the demo. She was overjoyed and jumped up and down on the bed and clapped. It felt great to be appreciated. And then of course we had sex and watched the demo again.

I was searching for trademarks one day and the phrase "gears of war" popped into my head, and I immediately knew that this would be the title of our new game: *Gears of War*.

Not only that, as soon as I said it, the subtitle or tagline rolled off my tongue as if it had been sitting there my entire life, waiting for me to say it: *Gears of War—lubricated by the blood of soldiers*.

It worked. It just worked.

Development got off to a similarly inspired start. Perhaps that was because we had already talked about the idea and tinkered with it for so long that major pieces fell into place relatively fast. It was also because we had the right people in place; there was an instant chemistry and vision, starting with our new art director, Jerry O'Flaherty, who arrived in the merger with Scion. I didn't know what an art director did exactly, but Jerry had a cinematic sensibility and an amazing eye that made him an interesting sounding board.

As I got to know him, I frequently corralled him for in-depth discussions about the look and feel that I imagined for the game. I told him about the impression my trip to London had made, the regal beauty of Hampton Court and Westminster Abbey, and the climb to the top of St. Paul's Cathedral, where I pictured the centuries of ruins that had surrounded the building since its pre-Norman inception.

"Like I see shades of gray and smoke rising from the carnage and the dank feel of rain and humidity," I said.

Jerry nodded and began the thought process that would take me away from the damned colored lights and influence of a generation of console games.

I started contracting conceptual artists to paint the world I had forming in my head. The more they started to create, the less I had to reference *Band of Brothers*. But I kept talking about the vision to Jerry and Chris Perna and Lee Perry until I sensed they were able to see what I was seeing in my head. It caught on, this drab, dreary depiction of Europe under siege. The game wasn't going to be set on giant terrain; it would take place in bombed-out locations. More important, it wouldn't be on Earth. It would be on a mysterious planet known as Sera—Ares, the god of war, spelled backward.

That was important. I was jealous of the realistic vibe in *Counter-Strike*, one of the most airtight first-person shooters ever created. But I wanted us to stay in the sci-fi space, except I didn't want us to have plasma guns or any of the over-the-top, crazy laser weapons found in most sci-fi games. I was blending genres and styles. This game was about war, but we weren't going to storm the beaches in Normandy or fight the Battle of Stalingrad. We were going to be on another planet, in our own world, with our own fiction.

I felt the influence of Kojima-san. I wanted great characters, a realistic depiction of war, and emotion. Our straight-edge coder Brandon

Reinhart was a huge fan of the tabletop game series *Warhammer 40K*, and he and John Mueller, the artist with the gear tattoo, had long ago come up with the theme for the game that was beginning to form. It was order versus chaos. The Coalition of Ordered Governments, or COG, versus a race of mysterious baddies who we called "Geist"— that is until Nintendo published a game called *Geist* for their Game-Cube and we had to hunt for a new, more original name.

Not a problem, though. At this point, John's gear iconography was more crucial than a name. We were fitting pieces together, relying on inspiration, and the image of that gear was a talisman that I repeatedly turned to for direction. The COG was a military machine of human soldiers, in my mind like the British Empire, and our nameless baddies were chaotic beasts who swooped in guerilla warfare–style and shocked and killed.

I've always loved "survival horror" games—and the horror genre specifically. Few devices in entertainment are as compelling: run from the monster; turn and face the monster; eventually, hopefully kill the monster. It's basic. It's about gaining power over our fears. It's all the boss fights inherent in life. Run from the zombies, keep running from the zombies, get a hold of a big shotgun but discover there are now hordes of zombies, then say fuck it and fire like hell. The previously mentioned *Silent Hill 2* was among my favorite games of all time.

The *Resident Evil* series was another favorite of mine, and in 2005 *Resident Evil 4* came out and broke the mold, though I previewed it before then and was impressed. The player viewed the game in third person, over the shoulder of the protagonist, and could then stop, aim, and shoot charging zombies. It was gorgeous, horrifying, and gloriously paced. And as was my tendency, I told everyone about it.

Gears was coming together: the look, the location, the warring sides. There was no Big Bang moment—not until I was in Lee Perry's office one day and he showed me an interesting little third-person combat game that didn't get much traction on Xbox called *Kill.Switch*. It had cool ideas—as a soldier you could take cover behind walls and objects and then "blindfire" around corners without aiming at all. Third-person perspective, again.

"Great game, terrible execution," I said. "But you're right, the cover system is fucking genius."

Then came the Big Bang.

I suggested adopting both *Resident Evil*'s over-the-shoulder perspective and *Kill.Switch*'s ability to take cover. Most shooters consisted of what I called the *combat dance*: players ran around at high speeds and jumped like jackrabbits while shooting as fast and frequently as possible. *Unreal Tournament* and *Halo* were two examples. A blind-fire feature, though, would take the dance out of combat; cover would add strategy; and an over-the-shoulder perspective would give us, as storytellers, more control over the tempo.

A player seeing their avatar in 3D actually touching the world would not only be drawn in, but they would also *feel* the action. And the detail we could show. Close-ups of the art. The cinematics. It could be amazing.

Something valuable I'd learned about world creation, especially with action games, is that there must be something everyone is fighting over. In *Unreal*, the main resource was Tarydium, a glowing blue crystal that the all-powerful Skaarj aliens needed to power their mega spaceships. For *Gears*, the Bush administration's thinly veiled war for oil in Iraq inspired the idea of Imulsion, a glowing, hot, yellow lava-like fluid that powered the world of Sera. It worked. Even better, it popped onscreen in the rapidly forming Unreal Engine 3.

I traveled to Redmond, Washington, to pitch the game, hell, the entire intellectual property, to Microsoft. I downed a couple of vodka cranberries at the bar to quell my nerves and slept surprisingly well.

In the morning, I did as many push-ups as I could while listening to Eminem's "Lose Yourself," the classic pregame, get-pumped song. I traded emails with Emily, who said she knew I was going to kill it, and stepped into my meeting attire: Affliction shirt, designer jeans, bracelets and cuffs on my wrist.

An hour later, I walked into the conference room to the desired effect, like a young Keith Richards, edgy, cool, and about to preview for them *Exile on Main St.* Our partnership was already a sure thing, as was our partnership on *Gears*, and I needn't have been as nervous as I made myself, but I wanted to make up for the way I'd embarrassed myself the last time I was in front of this group.

Once the Microsoft team took their places around the table, a calm came over me when I saw an unexpectedly familiar face. He didn't know me, but two-thirds of the way down the long conference room table sat Howard Phillips, the bow-tied guru of all things Nintendo, whom I worshipped when I was growing up. He was consulting for Microsoft. I felt my childhood rushing into the present. It was perfect. Like this was all meant to be. Excitement and congratulations followed. I returned to Raleigh having attained a new personal best.

Game development is fluid, organic, mysterious, constant, and collaborative. It involves many people working simultaneously, often independently, before coming together to share their creations and figure out how to stitch it all together in a way that grips and dazzles and demands repeated play. So much was happening at the same time. I was head cheerleader as much as lead designer. I had the art department create propaganda posters that I posted all over the office. "Imulsion—The New Gold Rush!" and "Join the Coalition!"

I kept scratching my head on ways to differentiate *Gears* from the juggernaut that was *Halo*, including the just-released *Halo 2* in November. One of the features I kept returning to was the idea that our enemies would be from the planet's underground instead of space aliens. The name Wyrm came to me. One of Tim's genius young programmers was the first person I ran into after selling myself on this must-have idea. I pitched it to him, and he shrugged with that standard indifference I'd seen a million times from stoic coders.

"I don't get it," he said. "Why are they underground?"

"Because they are," I said.

"How'd they get there?" he asked.

How come he didn't get it? Typical coder. Flustered and frustrated, I took a step back before putting on a shit-eating grin.

"That's just part of the fucking mystery," I said.

I could have explained further. *DOOM 3* had come out months earlier and was maligned for having what were called "monster closets." Basically, every time a player encountered a demon and killed it, they would retrace its steps and find it had been sitting the whole time behind a door, waiting to burst out. It made zero sense. But we could have these underground lizard men burst from the surface of Sera anytime we needed. If they resided underground, they'd obviously mastered the ability to emerge whenever they wanted, right? All we needed was the fiction that explained why they broke through to the surface in the first place, that seminal moment, and that would come to us in time.

The bigger task was to keep building. Lee Perry and I agreed the main design challenge would be to make sure players actually used our cover system instead of doing the dance. Our solution? We made the enemies 30 percent or so more accurate with their weapons if you weren't in cover.

Our animation programmer, Laurent Delayen, was a big fan of that trickery. A short Frenchman who couldn't help but look French even in Raleigh, he was one of the most easygoing coders I'd ever encountered. The two of us were in the office late one night around the time our cover system and third-person over-the-shoulder camera system was coming online, and I had a eureka moment about how to take passive gameplay and make it active.

I'd been playing *Counter-Strike* in my office—hey, it really was work—and it dawned on me that reloading a weapon could dramatically affect the pacing, flow, and tension of a game. Not *could* change it. It *did* change it. And it changed my mind. *Unreal* and the *Unreal Tournament* games never had reloading; not that it hadn't been brought up. But I argued that it slowed the game down. I was wrong. It wasn't hard to implement. But I had questions. How could we make reloading interactive? Could we place a little meter on the screen that would make a mini game out of putting a fresh magazine in your weapon?

I burst into Laurent's office like Kramer on *Seinfeld*, arms and legs akimbo, brandishing a satisfied smile. "This is it," I said. "What if you timed that little game right by hitting the right bumper on the controller? You could shave precious seconds off your reload and get juiced-up bullets. If you screwed up the timing, your gun would jam, delaying your bullet spraying ever further as your bloodthirsty foes closed in. It's *active reload*."

It was so crystal clear to me. As I said above, getting to reload a weapon could dramatically affect the pacing, flow, and tension of the game.

"I can't think of a game that's allowed players to interact while reloading a weapon," I said.

Laurent put his hand on his chin, looked down at his desk as if trying to solve a crossword puzzle, and thought about it. I stood in front of him, counting the seconds. Finally, he looked up at me with the same puzzled expression as before. Then he grinned.

"It just might work."

Jerry, the art director, had his hands full with Chris Perna's strong-willed vision of monsters and vehicles. The two of them once had it out, some corny Joe Rogan–type shit, but occasionally that kind of alpha-male headbutting had to happen in order to clear paths and understand roles, and that was one of those times. Then they moved on.

Jerry nudged the team, and Chris worked shoulder to shoulder with the other artists, Kevin Lanning and James Hawkins, creating our underground creatures (now called Locust), COG fighters, vehicles, and weapons. James—or JayHawk, as he was known—was an interesting guy. Tall and handsome, as shy as he was talented, he hid under a baseball cap. Jerry and Chris instructed me and Lee Perry to avoid shoulder surfing with Jay because he was so sensitive. I suspected they feared we might undermine his artistic vision.

We didn't. I worked with JayHawk on two of the game's most iconic features. One was the main character, Marcus Fenix. I sat down with him one day, handed him a document I'd written describing Marcus as a legendary war hero who led the COG army in their endless battle against the Locust. I didn't have a ton of detail or backstory. But I provided him with the vibe I imagined: big, tough as fuck, cool, with a soul patch and a do-rag. Also one of those guys like Bruce Willis in *Die Hard*. Everything he touches turns to shit.

"Like my personal life," I said.

JayHawk barely cracked a smile.

"I'm serious," I added.

JayHawk was my favorite kind of artist. He went away for a few days and came back with six or seven different takes on the concept. Options were always better than no options. I was able to point to elements I liked in each of the different renderings. But he'd nailed the look and the vibe. We went through the same exercise with Marcus Fenix's gun. JayHawk's first draft of his Mark 2 Lancer Assault Rifle didn't include the now-infamous chain saw at the end, something I'd imagined since I'd scoured Home Depot with my digital camera, looking for textures, and imagined the tool section like a weapons depot.

I still loved his take. The gun was large and chunky, a mean mother of a killing tool that would do serious damage to the Locust springing up from underground. I got excited. Nothing was more thrilling than seeing ideas brought to life and then perfected. Which was the essence of development—and exactly what we were doing with *Gears*. When *Resident Evil 4*—the inspiration for our close-up, third-person perspective—finally came out in January 2005, it reminded us that *Gears* was about one thing—combat. And combat was fought close-up, and it was physical, strategic, scary, and subject to a rhythm that was all its own.

Then level designer Grayson Edge brought almost everything we had done up till that point together in a test map called "Street Fight." It was up-close combat on a short street . . . and it didn't just work, it blew us the fuck away.

LEVEL

5

DELTA SQUAD

Mike Capps sent a note: he wanted to see me in his office. It was the summons I hated more than anything. He shut the door. I stared at the placard on his desk that said, "If you want to grow your audience, defy expectations." What if I wasn't defying or even meeting expectations? I didn't feel that was the case, but my level of personal insecurity was sufficient to fuel an unhealthy paranoia.

It turned out Mike was concerned about my performance. "You don't seem in the right headspace," he said.

I bowed my head and softly said that was true. I wasn't good. I confessed that I had started the process of divorcing my wife.

He cut me some slack, but our conversation was a wake-up call. I had to roll up my sleeves and force myself to shut out the distraction when I was at work. I needed to leverage my anger and angst creatively. My best games came during periods when I was miserable. The classic tortured artist. I told myself to use my pain and anger and try to not cut off my ear in an absinthe binge. I meant it, too.

I had spent the end of the year trying to make things work with Marcy. One last go of it, I told myself. But I was concerned that might truly end up being the last go. I was mainlining Southern Comfort 100 proof like Meg Ryan in the alcoholic movie *When a Man Loves a Woman*. At night, I inevitably landed in our living room, drunk, lying on the carpet beneath the large-screen TV and the bronze sun sculpture Marcy and I had bought moons ago at the farmer's market, listening to my *Wallow* CD and playing the songs "My Immortal" and "Mad World" on repeat while sobbing uncontrollably.

After the first of the year, I realized I was on a road to self-destruction and needed to dial back my booze intake. My doctor prescribed Ambien to help me sleep and deal with the stress of what was coming. I left his office, turned on the stereo in my Mercedes—I'd sold the Viper, which was a deathtrap—and heard David Byrne of the Talking Heads singing, "And you may find . . . with a beautiful wife . . . well, how did I get here?"

It's always interesting when the universe talks to you, when the Matrix pushes back. I knew how I got there, thanks, David.

I needed to get out.

In early February, a week before my thirtieth birthday, I finally reached the point of no return. Literally. It was a weird day. Marcy and I stopped for coffee while out doing errands. While I was inside getting our order, she got into a verbal altercation with a woman in the parking lot. I came outside and immediately jumped to her defense. It was as if we were as tight as ever, and I spent the rest of the afternoon second-guessing the bombshell I was about to drop. But that night we went out for sushi, and after dinner, I told her that I wanted to move out for a while. She was shocked, which surprised me, because we were far from okay in our marriage.

We drove home in silence. I packed my bags and my laptop, said goodbye to the dogs, and checked into the Holiday Inn in nearby Cary. I had brought some candles from home and did my best to make my shitty hotel room feel a little cozy despite it being a fire hazard.

Never had a February night felt as cold and lonely. When Emily and I were in the thick of things, we'd often talk about leaving our spouses, maybe even for each other, and we referred to it as standing on the ledge and jumping off. One foot, then the other. In the morning, I called her on my cell phone, bleary eyed from Ambien, and told her that I was staring across a crappy hotel room about two miles from my house.

"The sun's pouring through the drapes like it did when we woke up together in that hotel in LA," I said.

"Wait, why are you in a hotel near your home?"

"Emily . . . I did it," I said. "I jumped."

She was overjoyed. She mentioned no plans to leave her own marriage—and she never did—but she immediately sent me links to songs she liked and thought would help me through this difficult emotional time. I had my own cringe-worthy playlist, including Dido's "White Flag," which I listened to on repeat like I was a high schooler breaking up with my girlfriend, which I sort of was, just fifteen years late.

I moved into a one-bedroom apartment across the street from Epic. It was $550 a month, with rented furniture. The carpet and the sofa had the creepy, crusty texture of stain-resistant indestructibility, like it had been manufactured so that the worst of human experiences could be easily vacuumed or wiped away. My cats went to friends; Marcy kept the dogs. The only item I took from the house was our second TV, an enormous, fat, pre-flat-screen lent to me by *Men's Health* magazine for a "show off your gear" bit. Vegas and another guy carried that monstrosity up three flights of stairs and then made a quick exit, as if they feared getting trapped there with me. "Well, good luck, buddy," they said.

I sat in that apartment and sobbed. This was my life now. I felt like I was back in my first apartment in California. I was starting over.

A new beginning was exactly what I needed. Who doesn't at one or more points in their life? I had been so busy creating and presenting an image of myself to the public and colleagues at work and in the industry that I lost the sense of who I really was away from the microphones and cameras. What was I about? What did I want? What was going to make me happy? In the icky, sterile starkness of that apartment, I began to search for answers. I covered the fridge with pictures of my friends. I brought in new furniture.

Without Marcy, the training wheels were off for good. I was thirty years old. Adulthood had arrived. I can't say that I looked in the mirror and now suddenly saw myself as a grown-up. I can't say that's ever happened. But I did see what I wanted in my life, what I thought would make me happy, and it was a tall order. I wanted my father back, or, failing that impossibility, I wanted the hurt of losing him so unexpectedly, suddenly, and young to go away. I wanted a home of my own. And I wanted to find love, the kind of storybook love that was forever.

I watched Zach Braff's sad-sack movie *Garden State* and shook with recognition when his character talked about his childhood home and all it meant. "You'll see when you move out," he said. "It just sort of happens. One day it's gone. And you can never get it back. It's like you get homesick for a place that doesn't exist. I mean it's like this rite of passage, you know. You won't have this feeling again until you create a new idea of home for yourself."

And so I began that next level.

In March 2005, we demoed the latest Unreal Engine 3 technology at GDC. The room was packed, and the buzz was everything we wanted. As always, we did things our own way, which was a little different. This time we slipped in a portion of Grayson Edge's test map, "Street Fight." There was no fanfare, no labeling it *Gears of War*, no explanations. It was simply layered in with confident understatement as part of the demo of the engine.

But it didn't go unnoticed. IGN writer Dan Adams compared his reaction to the thrill of seeing *DOOM 3* or *Half-Life* for the first time.

"It rocked," he wrote. "Textures were unbelievably crisp. Animation was excellent. Lighting was ridiculous. Architecture was well designed. The gameplay focused around a soldier ambushed by some aliens from within an abandoned structure. The level was played from the third-person perspective, giving an awesome view at the back of this superb model. Light effects from enemy weapons simply *looked* dangerous. The character dived behind cover, bumped up against it, peeked out and fired from around it with an over-the-shoulder view while firing."

He gave high marks to the engine, too. "Features such as pulley systems, particle-driven physics (such as splashing water driving a waterwheel), improved ragdoll, and support for soft objects should make any level designer snort with glee," he wrote, adding that Epic was providing a bright future for gaming and noting that Microsoft was among the most enthusiastic of new licensees.

That last bit about Microsoft was not just noteworthy, it was also crucial to both Epic and the Washington-based software giant. I flew to Redmond to give them a progress report and assure them we were in good shape. I might as well have been doing the same thing on my own life. The night before the meeting, I sat in the hotel lobby bar, talking on the phone with Emily, as I had done often in the past, except this time our back and forth felt perfunctory, futile, and a little like what I imagined cutting must be like—minus the pleasure and the pain. It was nothing.

"I don't think we should talk anymore," I said.

"What?" she said.

She started to say something but stopped.

"I just can't do it anymore," I said.

"I get it," she said.

"I don't know what more to say," I said. "I mean, I wish you good luck and a good life in everything. And . . ."

"Yeah," she said, cutting me off, and that was it for the two of us, me and my convention girlfriend.

Afterward, something unexpected happened. I felt lighter, upbeat, and optimistic. Marcy had sold our house and I knew that I was going to lose most of everything I had earned in our divorce, but suddenly, I was free. This new buoyancy was reflected in my demeanor at the next day's meeting with executives at Microsoft. They complimented the work I showed, but they wanted more accountability. In other words, a schedule that was more fact than fiction, along with detailed progress reports.

Microsoft needed a structured and regularly updated road map they could count on for taking *Gears* to market and selling their Xbox 360, which was the whole point of their investment in Epic. *Halo 2* had finally come out the previous November; *Counter-Strike* for Xbox had shipped in January. The House of Gates wanted to slot *Gears* into its 2006 lineup. We had a standout game in the works, plus leading engine technology that was going to sell the new console system. It was exciting stuff. Everything they'd hoped. Except they had very little proof—or faith—that we could hit a deadline.

That's when I found myself working in lockstep with a man who had been involved with *Gears* since the start of 2005. Rod Fergusson was Microsoft's top program manager, a simple title that didn't begin to explain his role as executive producer, chief project wrangler, and game whisperer. Assigned to *Gears* in January 2005, his job was to get *Gears* to the finish line. Nicknamed "the Viking" after his red hair and beard and no-nonsense attitude, we had no doubt he would. He came to Raleigh and covered his eyes the first time he saw our whiteboard. He saw the way we worked—everyone doing their own thing. He asked if we had a Gnatt flowchart. The response was silence. He stepped into the storm with reassuring calm.

We hit it off. JayHawk had finished work on Marcus's chainsaw-tipped gun, and all the principals involved in design agreed it was one of those things that didn't make sense in real life but was so gnarly and badass that it would soon be iconic. We were right, of course. And Rod dug it, too. He also thought renderings of Marcus Fenix were brilliant. "He's a hero," he said. "What's his story?" Hearing that I didn't have one yet, Rod arranged for us to have lunch with writer Eric Nylund the next time I was in Redmond. Eric had written the *Halo* novels and had a smart, college professor vibe. He suggested starting *Gears* with Marcus in prison to amplify his hero's journey. If you open with him at the bottom, he said, he can only go up.

Of course. Marcus was the reluctant hero—again, like Bruce Willis in *Die Hard*. He and his squad of fighters were part of the Coalition of Ordered Governments, or COG, battling the Locust for control of Sera. I scribbled more in my notebook: the fighting began on Emergence Day, the historic moment when the Locust first emerged in coordinated hordes from their underground lair and attacked the planet's human population, intent on wiping out civilization. Why did the Locust attack the humans on Sera? That was still TBD.

But it was enough. At GDC, Rod showed me a logo that Microsoft's advertising agency had created for the game. It was a red gear with a red skull spray-painted inside. I named it the Crimson Omen. It was an ominous warning: Locust ahead. I liked it. Rod called it iconic. He was just as decisive when he came to Raleigh and I showed him the work being done on Marcus's team of battle-weary fighters, a group of underdogs I called Delta Squad.

"Delta stands for D-list," I said. "Marcus is the fallen hero. He's leading a group of similar D-listers."

When I introduced Rod to my thoughts on the rest of Marcus's team, he had comments, starting with best friend Dominic Glynn.

"The name sounds weak," he said.

"Dom?"

"Glynn."

He turned and glanced around at my toy-filled shelves. Then he spotted a box of Santiago cigars on my desk that had been given to me as a gift.

"Santiago," he said. "Dominic Santiago."

That impressed me. I wanted to round out the squad with a former pro athlete and a snarky engineer—brawn and brains—but I wanted to avoid the cliché of a charismatic Black athlete, and so I pitched a David Beckham–type and a snarky Black engineer. Rod shook his head; he didn't feel it. Later that day he showed up in my office.

"I think we should go with the stereotypes you're trying to avoid," he said. "The angry white engineer and the charismatic Black athlete."

"Why?" I asked.

"Because they work," he said.

I wasn't completely sold. But a short time later, I was in my office with a few people, watching a video of Reebok shoes' Super Bowl commercial titled *Terry Tate: Office Linebacker*. It featured a charismatic Black football player tackling stiff corporate office workers who'd stepped out of line. "I want to go to war with *that* guy," I said, and he became the inspiration for Augustus "Cole Train" Cole. We rounded out the squad with scientist Damon Baird, a cocky, jaded engineer whose last name came from a friend of my brother's who we played hockey with as kids. Baird also wound up with goggles on his forehead as a wink to the earliest versions of *Jazz* when the rabbit had goggles instead of his signature bandana.

Not everything I suggested went over with Rod. We were prepping a new demo for E3 that showed, in part, Marcus entering Embry Square, the bombed-out landscape that would be featured at the start of the game. I didn't mention Embry was the last name of a pretty blond beer-slinger at the Flying Saucer; it was a rare moment of restraint. But I did pitch adding a stray dog to the scene. I liked the way dogs sniffed out robots in the first *Terminator* movie. I also missed my old dogs, which of course I shared with Rod and everyone else.

Rod was sympathetic but still responded no. "It's hard enough to make a character with two legs much less four," he said. "And it's a one-off. Not worth the time or effort." I didn't take the rejection personally. At the same time, it was all personal and I didn't hesitate to share my life or get emotional. One day, as several of us were talking about Delta Squad being the last hope for humanity, I went on a tangent about Marcus wanting the same thing every soldier wanted—an end to the fighting, peace, and to go home, wherever that was for him.

My voice cracked as I said that, because I wanted the same thing. I was going home at night to a shitty apartment across the street. I had lost my home and hoped to find a new one, as well as someone to share it with, and hopefully peace within myself. I saw recognition in my colleagues, especially Rod and Lee, both of whom had lost their fathers when they were young, like me. This game was personal for all of us. It couldn't be any other way.

Days prior to E3 in Los Angeles, Microsoft revealed their new Xbox 360 with an MTV special. It was inspired marketing. We gave them a few seconds of *Gears* for the show, but saved the bulk of our demo for those who stopped by our meeting room inside Microsoft's massive station on the convention center floor. Microsoft made up do-rags like the one Marcus Fenix wore, for us to hand out as giveaways and wear ourselves. I refused. Rod, being the good soldier himself, complied, and though sweat poured down his forehead from being stuck in the cramped, hot confines of our little meeting room, I admired his commitment.

The sample of *Gears* that we showed, billed as "Mankind's Last Battle," generated the kind of hype and excitement we all hoped it would ("the first potential megahit for the Xbox 360," said IGN), and gave me the excuse I needed for a few days of partying in LA. The previous year I had signed with an agent at one of the fancy Hollywood talent agencies who occasionally sent me scripts and shared industry gossip with me. This trip he hooked me up with a VIP dinner at the House of Blues on the Sunset Strip. Marcy had always accused me of having a "Hollywood hard-on," as if there was something wrong with wanting fame and fortune. I was unapologetic about it and totally in my comfort zone at dinner when *Saturday Night Live* original cast member Dan Aykroyd stopped by our table, and screenwriters Dan Weiss and David Benioff, who would later adapt *Game of Thrones* for HBO, chatted me up about *Gears*. They came to E3 the next day to check out our demo and pronounced it "amazing."

The blast of Hollywood glam was just the medicine I needed to jump-start my social life back in Raleigh. Newly single but not yet legally divorced—in North Carolina, it takes a year from the filing date for a divorce to be finalized—I wanted to plunge into the dating arena. I'd never dated much before, but I was good at playing games and thought the skill might transfer. My first date was with a woman I referred to as Joanne the Train Wreck. I got her number one night while I was out drinking with my friend Vegas at a basement bar called Stool Pigeons.

We went out a few nights later. I picked her up at her place and before we got to the restaurant, I learned that she was divorced, had lost custody of her kid, and had done so much coke that she had a hole in her nose. Later, as she pounded Jäger at the Ale House, she looked me in the eyes and whooped, "I just want to make it a blockbuster night!" It wasn't. As I told Vegas, I needed to start slower.

Dates with other women followed, including one with Suzanne, a blonde who worked at one of Raleigh's other game studios and was friendly with Vegas. We had a so-so first date, but I thought it might be my fault, so I arranged with her to go out again. Before catching a movie, we met Vegas and his roommate, Jess, at a bar. Jess showed up with her younger sister, Amy, who had a vivacious personality and slightly awkward manner that caused me to think about her long after we said goodbye. Two hours later, I texted Jess from inside the movie theater, asking for her sister's number. She sent it, along with a note that said, "Have fun."

We did. We met at a coffee shop near the North Carolina State campus and blended as easily as cream and sugar. That was both a good thing and a bad thing. The good part was we clicked even more every time we met up. The downside was our age difference. I was thirty, and she was nineteen and still attending NC State. One night she showed me her dorm, which was a dump. Clothes and papers and coffee cups were strewn everywhere. It smelled like a refugee camp. She blamed her roommate. I blamed my mother and father for most of my faults, so I could see the benefit of a roommate as an extra option.

She took me to a college party near State one night, which put the kibosh on the college experience I'd always dreamed about, because I stood out like a sore thumb among the kids. I had nothing in common with these southern college kids. I'd been surrounded by the misfit toys of developers since I was seventeen. What was with the backward baseball caps they wore? And why did southern girls swoon over that? Not that my hair was thinning, but show off your hair while you've fucking got it, boys!

By the keg, I sparked up a chat with one of the "bros" wearing a backward hat. Both of us held our red Solo party cups, which was all we had in common. I cajoled him into asking me what I did and proudly responded, "I make video games at Epic. Ever hear of *Unreal*

Tournament 2004?" He said, "Uh, yeah. I guess I like the mode with the nodes." He meant Onslaught. He was unimpressed, and I walked away. Once a misfit at school, always a misfit.

Our age difference made me wary of getting too involved, and because we weren't exclusive, I cast a wide net. Through regular Thursday night meetups with game developers, I met a skinny, bald dude named Don whose gift of small talk made him a magician at bars. He scooped me up one night and drove me to a sports bar near the small game studio where he worked. There we met a couple of rambunctious southern girls. All of us were drinking too much vodka and Red Bull entirely too fast, but it gave me the courage to chat them up, which was a huge step for a nerd like me.

Suddenly I could barely see straight. I was hammered. "Feel Good Inc." by the Gorillaz came on the jukebox. I turned to Don, who saw the color of my face turn from pasty white to sickening green. He drove me home.

I was in that horrible state that booze mixed with energy drinks puts you, an awake drunk. I popped an Ambien, brushed my teeth, and the next thing I knew, I was on the floor of my bathroom with warm fluid running down my face. I had passed out, and my face had hit the counter on the way down. A laceration beneath my right eye was pouring blood all over the bathmat. I said to myself, "Shit, there goes my security deposit."

I wound up with a black eye and told everyone at work that I'd slipped in my kitchen and hit the dishwasher. I ended up with a nasty scar. Without explaining why, I asked JayHawk to add scars to Marcus Fenix's face.

Amy moved in. I couldn't help it; we had fallen madly in love. Apparently, I didn't need to "sow my oats" as I had thought and friends had convinced me. Still, our age gap was an issue. I had to go to bars without her. One day I wore a vintage T-shirt with the Soviet hammer and sickle on the front and, in spite of Amy's family putting her in great private schools, she looked at the image and asked, "What's that?" During the weekends, we soaked in the apartment building's communal hot tub as the sun went down, then stayed up late watching *Lost in Translation*, *Eternal Sunshine of the Spotless Mind*, and other favorite movies of mine that she'd never seen.

Her family had done well for themselves, and their house in one of Raleigh's best suburbs had Roman-style columns in it—the most gauche and gaudy of symbols of the nouveau riche, if you ask me. And one night, during dinner at her parents' house, her mother did. She pointed to one of the columns and asked me if I knew what type it was. "Doric," I replied. She was impressed. "Smart young man," she said. I laughed to myself and thought, "Lady, I'm making a game that has this kind of architecture *everywhere*!"

Amy got a job at a local pet store where I frequently visited. What was more relaxing than playing with puppies? I bought a beautiful red merle Australian shepherd, whom I named Teddy because he looked like a teddy bear. I called him my divorce dog. After he tore up my apartment, I called him Trouble. But all was kind of good and calm for a change. Sleepy downtown Raleigh was perking up, like a mini Austin, Texas, with hip bars and businesses; I bought a newly constructed condo that I saw advertised in a free indie newspaper. The condo was only twenty minutes from Epic. Amy moved in, too.

"It cost as much as my first house," I told her. "But fuck it. This game is going to be big, and I'm going to bet Tim and Mark will take care of me."

EMERGENCE DAY

On one of his first visits to Raleigh, Rod Fergusson had stood in front of the whiteboard that held all our ideas for *Gears* and stared in deep thought. After a while, he sat down and continued to stare. Our ideas were written on multicolored Post-its and arranged in a giant circle from which various lines jutted out on their own. It was a classic hub-spoke model, like a bicycle wheel, with the circle representing the main hub and the spokes indicating alternative avenues away from it. Finally, Rod stood up and rearranged the Post-its into a straight line. Everything flowed linearly. There was, he explained later, a beginning and an end. It was the kind of adjustment that made Rod an exceptional producer. He saw the things that needed to be done to move projects forward, and he did them. That's why he was the Viking.

But it took six months of working on *Gears* before he made his boldest move. In July 2005 he left Microsoft and joined Epic as a full-time employee. He made the move with Microsoft's blessing, he said, knowing it was necessary if he was ever going to wrestle the game to the finish line, which, at the time, was still nowhere in sight. I think that was only part of his reason—and maybe not the main one. You don't leave a company like Microsoft for a lesser title at a much smaller, indie company and take a cut in pay unless something else is

My older brother Tyler and me in my crib. Oddly enough I remember this picture being taken as my very first memory.

My parents always went out of their way to make sure Christmas was special for their five boys. I'll always love Transformers. Just not the Michael Bay ones.

Clearly dorkiness is a genetic quality. My father was strict and had a temper but he was loving and had a great sense of humor.

Myself, my brother Tyler, and our neighbors. Growing up in New England in the eighties was pretty magical.

There it is, my name at the top of the high-score section in the first issue of *Nintendo Power*. My thirst for nerd fame began at this moment.

PLAYER'S FORUM

SUPER MARIO BROS.

Cliff Blezinski ▶	North Andover, MA ▶	9,999,950
Jayson Burkel ▶	Allen, TX ▶	9,999,950
Leon Darst ▶	Springfield, OH ▶	9,999,950
Alan Frank ▶	Medford, MN ▶	9,999,950
Jeff Hacker ▶	Columbus, OH ▶	9,999,950
Jason Harens ▶	Hamilton, IL ▶	9,999,950
Erik Haynie ▶	Hood River, OR ▶	9,999,950
Jeremy Klarner ▶	Shawnee, KS ▶	9,999,950
David Madden ▶	Rockford, IL ▶	9,999,950
Ellen Majewski ▶	Stratford, CT ▶	9,999,950
Jeff Marsden ▶	Pekin,IL ▶	9,999,950
Ricardo Morales ▶	Springfield, NJ ▶	9,999,950
Jon Pfendler ▶	Indianapolis, IN ▶	9,999,950
Mary Phong ▶	Baltimore, MD ▶	9,999,950
Jason Reynolds ▶	Chesterfield, MO ▶	9,999,950
Stephen Richardson ▶	Irvine, KT ▶	9,999,950
Dave Stayner ▶	Niagra Falls, NY ▶	9,999,950
Mark Wilkinson ▶	Salisbury, MA ▶	9,999,950
John Yochim ▶	Sterling, VA ▶	9,999,950
Andrew Yocum ▶	Mishawaka,IN ▶	9,999,950

Tyler and me on our bikes, ready to go full *Stranger Things*.

Visiting Robert Allen in Northern California looking like Eddie Vedder.

Developing the first *Unreal* game (and the engine) took a lot of caffeine. Note the pager.

Robert Allen and me in Moaning Caverns going caving. Deep down a seed was planted that the Locust monsters should come from below.

Circa 1995, myself and Tim and another coder in Rockville, Maryland, as the earliest versions of the Unreal Engine emerge.

My late Aussie, Teddy. He was there for me at the highest and lowest parts of my adult life. I still miss you, buddy bear.

My desk at Epic Games. Filled with Transformers and other giant robots. Arrested development, much?

Halloween at Epic was fun. We'd all dress up and the employees would bring their kiddos around for a trick or treat.

The seminal moment that would change my life and career: demonstrating *Gears* in front of a crowd at Grauman's Chinese Theatre in Hollywood.

The iconic picture of me holding the *Gears* Lancer chainsaw gun prop that would be used countless times on nearly every video game blog.

Pressing the very soft hands of Bill Gates. No pressure, right?

Gears won the *Wired* "Rave Awards," which is a big honor. Tim and me at the event. One of these people would go on to become a multimillionaire. The other? A multibillionaire.

Checking out one of the very first Oculus virtual reality prototypes. Immediately after seeing it I said, "I want in." Best investment of my entire life.

With Ice-T and Coco at a Microsoft party at E3. Coco was sweet and smelled of sunless tanner.

Lauren and I all cleaned up, ready for a video game awards show. The moment when I realized we'd become a power couple.

Lauren and I on the *Guardians of the Galaxy* ride at Disneyland. This picture encapsulates our relationship. I dive into adventure whereas she often remains hesitant and nervous.

At the Tonys with Anaïs Mitchell, the writer and creator of *Hadestown*. A much-needed win for us to produce a Broadway hit after Boss Key folded.

At one point I had two Lamborghinis. Having cars like that is no big deal in LA or Miami, but in Raleigh? Everyone loses their minds.

With Hideo Kojima and Guillermo del Toro at San Diego Comic-Con. Guillermo didn't know who I was.

Our Save the Date, lovingly drawn by the good folks from the hit web comic *Penny Arcade*. *Mike Krahulik*

Photo booth at our wedding with Tim and Mark. I was about to attempt to renegotiate my contract after the Tencent investment, and deep down I suspected this would be the last picture taken of the three of us together, possibly ever.

At our wedding. I took the brunt of the cake and didn't smear it on her face. That stylist was pricey, dammit. *Matt & Molly Snelson, Mathieu Photography*

I never knew true happiness until I married this beautiful dork. *Matt & Molly Snelson, Mathieu Photography*

Doing a lecture in Montreal right after my studio started.

First picture of Arjan and me right after we founded Boss Key.

Onstage at the *PC Gamer* show when I infamously said, "None of that sixty-dollar multiplayer-only bullshit!"

Lauren in front of the *LawBreakers* E3 banner at the LA Convention Center. In spite of the game failing, I'm still proud of what we achieved.

going on—and I think what was going on with Rod was that he fell in love with the game, the people making it, and the passion we all shared.

I saw the glint in his eye the first time he heard me say, "*Gears of War*—lubricated by the blood of soldiers."

Every Friday afternoon, art director Jerry O'Flaherty met with his team to show renders of what had been done that week. I loved attending them and seeing the world come into view before my eyes. The gentle push and pull between the two of us over the sepia tone he added to the game was behind us. We got to where both of us were pleased with the moody interpretation of destroyed beauty. Gamers would call the look "the Browns of War." I referred to it as the Zack Snyder *300* movie look. Chris Perna's monsters and creatures had grown beyond the original Locust Berserker to include Lambent, Brumak, and Drone. We also had gorgeous environments like Embry Square, the city of Ephyra, and Aspho Fields. We printed a banner of Marcus battling the evil lizard-like Locust, which covered the entire wall of the conference room. Thanks to Unreal Engine 3 being worked on simultaneously, the look was so striking that Microsoft offered to produce a special-edition book of *Gears* artwork.

One day I was in Chris Perna's office, talking with him and Jerry and Lee Perry about ways to emphasize the weight and bulk of Marcus and the others when they slammed into walls and took cover. My eye went to the incredible detail on Dominic Santiago's boots, and I cracked up.

"What's so funny?" Jerry asked.

"It just hit me," I said. "Where in this postapocalyptic world are these guys finding enough calories to stay so huge?"

Enter Susan O'Connor to fill out the story and write dialogue for Marcus and the rest of Delta Squad in our cut scenes. She was short, with red hair and a kind face. Rod brought her on, having met her a couple years earlier at Microsoft, and she began seven months of commuting between Raleigh and her home in Austin. She set up shop in an office near mine and became an expert at decoding my verbal shorthand and my scribble-filled notebooks explaining locations and battles and emotional tones that I wanted to inform *Gears*.

She was the only woman at Epic besides our receptionist, and we had several conversations about the failure within our company and the entire industry to hire women and provide them with the same opportunities men had to realize their dreams. The conversation was Stevie Case 2.0—a problem that would take time to rectify.

I loved the irony that this classic bro game was being written by a woman. Susan often joked and said in interviews that she was living the life of a twelve-year-old boy, which was a funny line, but again something that made me and others cringe for the way it led back to the lack of women in our world. Why couldn't a twelve-year-old girl like this stuff as much as any boy? Why did we even think of it in terms of boy-girl? Why couldn't it just be a great fucking game for everyone?

Ultimately, that's what Susan brought. In one of our first conversations, she introduced me to the concept of mirror neurons as the source of relative experiences and empathy, which essentially explained why I might wince when seeing someone get hit in a movie or why I might feel pain or shut my eyes when watching a scene where an animal was shot. I would actually feel the impact. The concept made even more sense, and also explained Susan's brilliance, when she applied it to the process of writing games. She helped create the story, of course, working to stitch the pieces of the game—pieces that were made independently of each other—together in ways that made sense.

But she took it a step further. She understood that she also had to write to the experience of the game, to what my childhood gaming friend Ralph Barbagallo had first taught me was the feel of the game, something that can't be forgotten or underestimated. How did the game feel while playing it? Why was the shotgun in *DOOM* so fun? Why did gibbing or exploding foes like they were a piñata feel so damn gratifying?

Susan explained it herself in an interview with her hometown paper, the *Austin Chronicle*, when she said, "I have to understand the story, the script, and in between the two is how the player is going to experience the story in the game."

That right there is the whole thing, the difference between good and great. And it can and should be applied to food, sex, and video games—all the important things in life. *How does it feel?*

To that end, one day Rod, Lee, Jerry, Mike Capps, a few other team leads, and I met to discuss putting a multiplayer in the game. We were perfecting our co-op, which we all agreed added an important emotional component to the game, but we were still debating whether to include a versus multiplayer gameplay mode. Mike made the case that many of the games produced by Midway did fine without it. I insisted that we needed it for longevity for the game and, potentially, a franchise. If you have a game where you can shoot baddies, players are going to want to virtually shoot one another, dammit!

Furthermore, Microsoft's online gaming initiative, Xbox Live, was getting a big push at the time, and one of the best ways to remain cozy with our partner was to produce features that furthered their agenda. Mike gave us a couple weeks to see if we could make it work. Lee Perry spearheaded the effort with his designers; first trying porous maps similar to those in *Counter-Strike*, but then going back to the basics of cover. If somebody was going to flank you, they had to earn it. People had to provide cover fire. You had to sneak around and use cover to get the drop on someone. Like in real combat.

As it came together, we referred to anyone who got extra good at sneaking around this way as Dr. Flankenstein. Finally, we got the team leads back together in the lab and played the damn thing. This time Mark Rein was there, and he was laughing as he played and having a good time. Mike Capps flashed the okay sign and said, "I think we got something here."

The clock was ticking. We had flipped our calendars to 2006 and delivered the news to our friends in Redmond that we weren't going to make a summer release. Microsoft, their patience already dwindling, sent a friendly ultimatum. Their new Xbox 360 was coming out at the end of 2005, and they knew *Gears of War* would drive sales. They wanted both under as many Christmas trees as possible.

More news followed. Microsoft was producing another special for MTV, this one about the making of *Gears of War* and the behind-the-scenes push to debut it at E3 in May. The documentary already had a title: *Gears of War: The Race to E3*. I didn't let the fact that it was probably bought and paid for as marketing, or that Tim, Mark, Mike, Rod, and everyone else at Epic would be featured. In my eyes, it was all about me. I finally had my own MTV special, and I was jubilant!

The documentary's crew swooped into Raleigh, spearheaded by director-producer Lee Brownstein. Lee wore glasses and had carefully groomed LA stubble on his face; he looked like a young version of Carl from the Pixar hit *Up*. Stern and efficient, he set up his own war room in a spare office. I noticed he gave it a personal touch by putting up pictures of his wife, the hilarious actress Jennifer Elise Cox, who played Jan in *The Brady Bunch* movies. Suddenly, we had cameras in our meetings and tailing some of us for nights out, including an after-hours foray to the Flying Saucer, where my Beers of War plate hung on the wall.

Microsoft's marketing team also descended on Raleigh. They came to pitch us their idea for a commercial that would preview the game and run after it went on sale. Their presentation took place in our conference room with the documentary crew recording the whole thing as if we had come to a crucial plot point on a reality TV show, which I suppose we had. I sat at the head of the table and their head guy, a charismatic marketing type with a slick, contemporary *Mad Men* vibe, played us a trailer they had cut.

The animatic showed Marcus and the ruins of the world where we were meeting him: destroyed, dangerous, and hopeless. Then the background music kicked in, and I heard the opening notes, delicate and haunting, and immediately familiar. Almost too familiar. It was Gary Jules's remake of "Mad World"—the song I had played thousands of times as my marriage to Marcy was circling the drain. How did they know? It fit the video on the screen as if we had designed *Gears* to the song. Who knows, maybe I had. I'd leave that for my future shrink to figure out.

With a camera pointed at me, I sat there in complete awe of the filmmaking: the music added depth and feeling to the look we had created, and provided a window into Marcus. We could feel all the sadness in his eyes, in his entire being. I became emotional, too. I choked back tears, and I wonder if I would have let myself cry if the documentary crew had not been there. Then the lights came on, and everyone at the table shared their thoughts, especially me. I loved it.

Tim had one comment: the commercial had to be rendered in Unreal Engine 3. We were tired of pre-baked ads for games that looked three times better than the actual product. We also had an engine to sell. As next steps were discussed, my phone buzzed on the table. Trying to be discreet—tough when everything in the room is being recorded—I looked down and saw it was from Amy. "I'm bored," she wrote. "Entertain me."

What? I was furious. I was in a meeting. I had poured my entire life into this game. I was trying to bounce back fiscally and emotionally from my disastrous marriage and divorce. Amy came from money, but I still had to hustle and make ends meet, especially now that I had my fancy new condo on which I had two mortgages, including one which was a five-year ARM that had started to soar along with my blood pressure.

She didn't get it—or me.

Maybe it was the age difference. I didn't know and didn't have the time to think about it. My career came first, so I broke up with her right in the middle of filming my MTV special and focused on what I thought was most important.

Most E3 demos are total fake, bullshit walk-throughs. Typically, they're a hastily cobbled-together vision of what the team *thinks* the game is going to be, most of it to be tossed aside after the Big Show. Not *Gears of War*. Not us. Rod "the Viking" Fergusson had been through high-pressure, all-or-nothing E3 presentations before, and he had a keen sense of knowing how to, as he said, put money on the screen. It had to do with what was at stake for Epic and Microsoft. The industry was more competitive than ever. So was media. If we were going to create buzz and get the level of coverage we wanted, we had to hit people over the head with a digital sledgehammer. We had to not only show them this visceral, violent yet beautiful wrecked world by way of the Unreal Engine 3 but we had to make them feel the pain of having to wait several more months before they could play it themselves.

So as we put together our presentation for E3, we decided to do something different and daring. We decided to demo the game live. I would play it live onstage in front of thousands of people—more if we counted those who'd watch it online.

Our first level was perfect for it.

It showed Marcus busting out of a prison with the help of his best friend, Dom, after it was overrun by the evil Locust Horde. Dashing through ruins, they escape on a helicopter as a Corpser—a Locust monster with giant knobby fingers and legs—digs its way up from the ground beneath the chopper as it peels off and up into the sky, barely escaping what would have most certainly been their demise. There was action and atmosphere, shooting, close combat, explosions, and blood courtesy of Marcus's chainsaw-tipped Lancer.

It was a cinematic, action-packed nail-biter unlike any other game demo I'd seen at E3, and after watching it through with Rod and several others, I could only think of one thing to say: "Fuuuuuuuuuck."

I began rehearsing several weeks before the convention. I worked tirelessly with Rod and Susan and the Microsoft PR rep who had come to town to keep an eye on our preparations and brief us on the press they'd lined up. The only hiccup occurred shortly before the Epic team flew out west. Mike Capps called me into his office and criticized me for monopolizing too much of the Microsoft publicist's time. He accused me of being more interested in promoting myself as opposed to the game.

"I have concerns you're spending too much time with the Microsoft people," he said.

"What do you mean?" I asked.

"I heard you went out to dinner with their publicist."

"I did," I said. "Did he complain?"

"No."

"So what's the problem? They're our partners. We should be close to them, and they should know who we are."

For once, I didn't back down. I knew Mike was wrong, and I told him so. "Let me do my thing," I said. To his credit, he heard me and did, indeed, let me do my thing, and we were fine after that exchange.

Before leaving town, I also repaired things with Amy and brought her on the trip with me. I loved her, and I was better with her close by.

Though nerves were jangly as the Epic crew decamped in LA, I was surprisingly calm and feeling in my element. Amy and I checked into the Hollywood Roosevelt Hotel, which was across the street and only a few blocks from Grauman's Chinese Theatre, the site of our presentation. The night before the demo, Amy and I mingled with Paris Hilton and other celebrities at a private party Microsoft threw in the hotel's pool area. "Be a good boy," Rod said as he cruised by in the crowd of beautiful people.

After an early bedtime, I woke up the next morning refreshed and excited. It was the biggest day of my career—no, my entire life— and I was ready for it. Our presentation at Grauman's was the kick-off event the night before E3 officially opened across the city at the convention center, and everyone who mattered in the industry, along with agents, journalists, and fans, would be in the theater. "No problem, right?" I said to Amy before I left our hotel room and walked to the theater for rehearsal.

Strolling down the block, I let myself relax in the late morning sunshine and soak up the energy of Hollywood Boulevard: sidewalks crowded with people, the street clogged with cars and buses, tourists taking photos of Marilyn Monroe, Wonder Woman, and Darth Vader look-alikes, and hip-hop music pulsing from storefronts. It was uplifting, the way Hollywood was supposed to be: alive! At the corner, I decided to cross the street, and as I did, I found myself walking straight toward the first billionaire I had ever seen in person—Bill Gates. I did a double take, then saw the security flanking him, and I knew it was really him.

"Hi, Bill," I said.

It was ridiculous, surreal, and if I hadn't been quick to explain who I was, that we were in some odd and nearly unbelievable way colleagues, my incursion into his space probably could have resulted in the voice of Satan bellowing, "PANCAKE!" Instead, after a polite handshake, I made my way to the theater. There I connected with Lee and his MTV documentary crew, Rod and the Epic team, and the theater's stage and production managers. Rehearsal went smooth. I found my mark, knew my lines, and played the game without any snafus. As I walked offstage, someone even complimented my hair.

A couple hours later, with the MTV crew still following me, director Lee Brownstein got word that Bill Gates had returned to the theater, and being the confident fucker that he was, he chased down Bill in his trailer, with me in tow behind him, for a meetup on camera. Just two computer nerds shooting the shit about Bill's new console.

Lee was ecstatic. "If we don't shoot it, it might as well never have happened," he said, repeating an oft-told adage of television news.

From there, things unfolded according to plan. Amy got to the theater and found her way backstage. I was given a ten-minute warning and a final dusting in makeup. Rod told me to break a leg and handed me the controller. I made sure it was turned on. Then I got my cue, took a deep breath, and walked to the center of the stage. After introducing myself and the game, I had Marcus fighting his way out of prison, taking cover, and blowing away attacking Locust. The audience was whooping and hollering their approval of the next-generation graphics Unreal Engine 3 was displaying on the theater's forty-by-one-hundred-foot screen, especially as blood splattered at the end when Marcus chainsawed a baddie. That was the money shot, the only one I had been thinking about having to nail, and I did. It was pure rock and roll.

Then it was over. Everything had worked perfectly. The stage vibrated from the applause. Offstage, I received hugs and high fives.

"We are all just cogs in Epic's brilliant, beautiful machine," raved IGN's reviewer. "From now until the game is actually in my hands, the only thing we care about is *Gears of War*."

In August, Microsoft announced a release date for *Gears of War*: November 7, 2006. It was the one-year anniversary of their Xbox 360. They called it Emergence Day.

Life in Raleigh was singularly focused on finishing the game. I would show people the scene in the movie *Glengarry Glen Ross* where Alec Baldwin barks into a room of salesmen, "A.B.C.—Always be closing!" Our joke was, "A.B.S.—Always be shipping!" The game was tight and beautiful, with cinematic set pieces that wove a very human story into our otherwise bombastic game. Back when we first talked about our cover system and keeping the fighting close, no long-distance pixel shooting, I'd said to the guys, "I want this to be a game that makes players scream *and* cry." We'd made that game.

It was magnificently conveyed in the commercial for *Gears*. I watched a final cut in the office. It opened amid the smoky ruins of a once-great city with "Mad World" playing in the background. A tear dropped into a pool of water. It belonged to armor-clad warrior Marcus Fenix, who turned over a piece of broken statue, a face cracked in half. Suddenly, the ground quaked and fissured behind him: it was the Locust emerging from underground. Marcus sprinted through the dark rubble of Embry Square. Looking up at the sky, he saw what he thought were stars. They turned out to be hordes of baddies closing in. He opened fire. The song ended and the Crimson Omen logo took over the screen: *Gears of War*.

It was a masterpiece. I still get emotional watching it.

I lost track of how many times I played different levels, and even the entire game, during this long QA process, but one day, as we closed in on our shipping date, I played *Gears* from start to finish. I wanted to experience the game fresh, as if I were playing for the first time. I wanted to feel it. It took me all day, maybe eight hours, maybe a little longer, and it was worth every minute. The prison break was thrilling. I loved the way the King Raven helicopter took out the Locust, saving my ass. The opening offered a taste of everything—the characters, the Locust, the firepower, the graphics.

If I'd been playing for the first time, I would have known I was in for a special time. As it was, the game, even at that early phase, struck me as remarkable. It was tight, beautiful, compact, kinetic.

Then I started down the road with Marcus, Dom, Minh Young Kim, and the rest of Delta Squad to find Alpha Squad. I picked up my Lancer. I obliterated a few Locust. I was into it. Maybe too into it. As the Locust began streaming out of Emergence holes, I grew very emotional. The whole creative and collaborative process came rushing back at me. I had repeatedly told people to make the game personal, and it was. I saw so much of me on the screen. And when Marcus thought his scientist father, Adam Fenix, might still be alive, and battled a mass of Locust while trying to get to his childhood home, tears filled my eyes.

"How was it?" Rod asked the next day.

I shook my head. "I'm still recovering."

BIGGER, BETTER, MORE BADASS

I lost track of how many times I have wished I could go back in time and stand next to my fifteen-year-old self as I looked at my acne-filled face in the bathroom mirror before school, full of insecurity and existential fragility, and say, "Don't worry as much. It's going to get better. A lot better." The November release of *Gears* was one of those times. A midnight launch party in LA drew hundreds of fans. Rod and I signed autographs in a VIP section. Unable to sit still, I hopped over the velvet ropes and ran down the queue, high-fiving people. "CliffyB!" some yelled. "Dude, I waited so long for this game."

The next night was another party, this one celeb-packed. I was impressed so many Hollywood stars were gamers. A random Microsoft publicist spun me around while I was talking to actor Mekhi Phifer and asked if I wanted to meet Britney Spears's husband, Kevin Federline. As a devoted reader of *Entertainment Weekly*, I knew she had just filed for divorce, so I declined out of loyalty. "Nope," I said. "That guy messed up my girl Britney."

I read every review on my way back to Raleigh. "I'm smitten with *Gears of War* and all its glorious, horrific violence, blood and anarchy," wrote GameSpy. "If you're a graphics whore, you absolutely, positively need to pick up this game," said TeamXbox. *Entertainment Weekly* added, "We'll just come out and say it: *Gears of War* is better than *Halo* . . . It's a fantastic-looking, riveting, fire-first-ask-questions-never third-person shooter that manages to show you things that you've never seen before on a console."

The best kind of review came one day when I was walking into the local Subway to grab lunch. A car packed with kids from NC State slowed down next to me and two guys leaned out the back window and shouted, "*Gears of War* rules!"

And it did. Games are about high scores, and *Gears* killed it where it counted: at retail. In its first two weeks, it sold one million copies, becoming the fastest-selling Xbox 360 game to date. By January, the game had rocketed past three million copies. *Gears* went on to sell over six million copies and set a record for the fastest-selling new game IP ever until Ubisoft's *Assassin's Creed* needed only a few months to break that record. Those impressive numbers gave those of us in key positions reason to wonder if and how Tim and Mark might share the wealth. It was as nerve-rattling as the march to get the game out.

In one of our weekly Friday meetings, Tim assured us that the spoils would be shared. But that didn't answer the question we all asked ourselves: How much? Tim was a funny dude when it came to money. He was hard to read. The MTV documentary showed him opening the front door of his mansion like he was a baller on *Cribs*, except he was Tim Sweeney, super brain and super nerd. "I don't know why I have a big house," he said. "I don't use much of the space. But I figured I have the money, why not."

Then I got to the office one day and heard whispers that Microsoft had delivered us a nice fat check. Mike Capps called a meeting with all the team leads in the conference room. When I walked in, I saw bottles of champagne and sparkling cider set up on both sides of the long table, with clear plastic cups. I poured a little bubbly, but my hands were shaking so hard that I put the cup down and waited. Mike gave a short speech about how well the game was selling, and then wrote a huge number on the whiteboard. It was the amount of money that was going into the bonus pool.

All of us already had our own magic number that corresponded to a percentage of whatever went into the bonus pool, so I quickly did the math. After taxes, I wasn't going to be a millionaire, not yet, but I would be able to pay off my mortgages and have a tidy six-figure sum left, and the game was still selling! *So this is it, this is happening,* I thought. I knew how it felt when life changed suddenly in a tragic way. *But this,* I told myself, *this is what it feels like when life changes in an incredible way.*

I closed my eyes, savoring the moment, and when I opened them again, I picked up my champagne and joined in the toast. It was Biggie Smalls time: "Condo paid for (uh-huh), no car payment (uh-huh) . . ."

In the days and weeks that followed, being in the office felt like the scene in *Scarface* when the success montage kicks in and Tony and his crew scramble to meet demand and scale their operations as fast as possible. After lunch one day, Lee Perry and I darted into our local GameStop and saw only two copies of *Gears* on the shelf. "Can't keep 'em in stock," the manager told us. If only the good news could have warded off the post-project depression that knocked me on my ass while I resurfaced from the intensity of developing the game. My seasonal affective disorder also kicked in. And because I was a glutton for self-punishment, I convinced myself that Mike Capps wanted to fire me.

Luckily, a couple trips out west saved me. In February, Mark Rein and I attended the D.I.C.E. (Design. Innovate. Communicate. Entertain.) Summit, an industry conference highlighted by the Academy of Interactive Arts and Sciences Awards, where we left with eight awards, including the coveted Game of the Year. The next month, I was at GDC in San Jose with the usual crew from Epic, collecting more honors. During the awards banquet, Mark leaned in close to me and gestured to a nearby table. "Did you see? Miyamoto is there."

He was right. It was the legendary Nintendo game designer—my childhood hero! How had I not noticed? Before I could digest my proximity to this godlike figure, I was onstage accepting the Game of the Year award for *Gears*. It was a career-defining moment, but rather than bask in the spotlight, I paid my respects to the legend. "Shigeru Miyamoto, you, sir, are the reason I got into this business and you're the reason I do what I do. Thank you." The packed ballroom erupted in applause. They knew his contributions, and most probably felt the way I did. Miyamoto nodded his appreciation. I was thrilled. Senpai had noticed me. It was as if my own father were there, saying he was proud of me.

By then, I was ready to get back to work. And it was time. Rod and I flew to Redmond to meet with Microsoft. *Gears* was still flying off the shelves, but everyone there wanted to know what was next, what did we have in mind for *Gears 2*. It was like the old showbiz cliché, where the grizzled label head says to the young rocker, "So that was great. What else you got?"

Rod was their guy, the former company man who had switched teams to tame the wild beast that was Epic and bring in *Gears*. He had done the job and deserved all the respect and accolades that came his way, yet all eyes in the conference room were on me. Since the New Year, I had been working out in Epic's gym a few times a week, and one of our more athletic artists had recently complimented me on the weight I was curling. "Yeah, I need to be bigger, better, more badass," I had quipped. Never one to waste a good line, I said that same thing to the folks at Microsoft. "*Gears 2* is going to be bigger, better, more badass."

The truth was—and I'd already said it to Rod—I wanted to go full-on Michael Bay in the next one. Turn it up to eleven. Rod agreed, as did the team leads, including stalwarts Chris Perna, who was promoted to art director after Jerry O'Flaherty left for Hollywood, and Lee Perry, level designer Dave Nash, and multiplayer lead Jim Brown. We had a lot of strong voices around the table, which was good and necessary, as Rod always began meetings with his own variation of my mantra: *What's new? What's going to be better? What's going to be more?* The round robin of ideas that always ensued was not for the meek.

"What if an enemy gets wounded and, as they tried to crawl to safety, you used them as a human shield?" I said.

"Then you're *meatbaggin'* them," Lee said.

"What if you chainsawed someone? Could you split them from perineum to shoulder?"

Rod grinned. "That's *chainsodomy*," he said.

The first *Gears* was about Marcus and Delta Squad fighting Locust to save humanity from being obliterated. It ended with the Locust Queen saying, "They do not understand. They do not know why we wage this war. Why we cannot stop. Why we will not stop. Why we will fight and fight and fight . . . until we die . . . and we are not dead yet." In *Gears 2*, we rejoined Marcus and Delta Squad on Sera six months later. The planet was even deadlier. The Locust were sinking entire cities, and Marcus and company had to stop them before civilization, already hanging by a thread, disappeared for good.

That was the game—an all-out attack on the Locust Horde. Questions arose: Why were the Locust sinking cities? What was going on underground?

To help answer these and other questions, we brought in Seattle-based writer Josh Ortega. Susan O'Connor had done an excellent job on the original *Gears*, but we wanted a fresh perspective at the table, and Josh brought it. We met at lunch in Redmond. He was a former music journalist-turned-novelist and pop culture junkie who unleashed torrents of words when he spoke. He rocked a tight leather jacket like Tyler Durden's from *Fight Club*, a look that took confidence to pull off, and as a guy who'd worn a woman's fur coat to an esport competition, I was impressed.

I compared *Gears* to the movie *Alien* and said we wanted *Gears 2* to be nothing less than the equivalent of James Cameron's sequel, *Aliens*. In other words, a masterpiece. "Give me a story they'll teach in college one day," I told him. He embraced the challenge, but more so, he opened my eyes with a riff on the similarities between video games and literature. The second you put the controller down, the action stopped. Reading a book was similar. As soon as you stopped reading, the story paused, too. Both required total engagement. That's why the experiences were so immersive.

With *Gears*, we had developed characters and a story that drew players in not only through action but also through complex, relatable emotions. The discussion about what a game at its best could be had evolved from whether it was fun to play repeatedly to include whether it could make players cheer and cry and think and wonder. Could it make political statements and issue philosophic warnings not just like Kojima's *Metal Gear* series but also like *Nineteen Eighty-Four*, *The Man in the High Castle*, *The Handmaid's Tale*, and other sci-fi and dystopian fiction that had influenced so many of us making games?

Hollywood was also checking out games as source material for new movies and TV series. New Line Cinema had recently optioned the film rights to *Gears*, and other studios and production companies had *Metal Gear Solid*, *World of Warcraft*, and *Halo* in development. Our little industry looked at those big screens as new avenues for marketing our IP. We didn't see ourselves as second cousins to traditional entertainment. We were the upstart that was going to be even bigger. Apple's Steve Jobs released the first iPhone in summer 2007.

It was obvious that video games with easy internet connections and high-quality graphics would soon be in people's pockets.

But, as I told Josh and others, in addition to making *Gears 2* an even bloodier gut-stomp than the original, I also wanted a two-hankie heart-wrencher. It was an impossibly high bar, but one we set about trying to achieve. In the original, Dominic Santiago—or Dom—alluded that he was searching for someone. In *Gears 2*, we revealed that someone was his wife, Maria, who had been abducted by the Locust on Emergence Day. In a meeting, I asked, "What do they do with the people they've taken hostage?" Josh added, "What do they do *to* them?"

Perfect. At the time, the CIA was being quizzed about waterboarding and other so-called enhanced interrogation techniques they used when interrogating prisoners at Guantánamo Bay. I wanted to address the issue. Josh took it a step further. It wasn't the only hot topic that made its way onto our whiteboard.

One of the new characters we introduced was Tai Kaliso, Sera's version of a Pacific Island Maori warrior. Why a Maori warrior? We needed someone with a distinctive look, someone who'd be memorable. Tai had a reputation for being unkillable. However, early in the game, he is captured by the Locust. One of the objectives is to find and rescue him from deep underground, what we had called the Hollow. But when Delta Squad finds him, Tai is locked in a coffin like an iron maiden. He stumbles out with a thousand-yard stare on his face, and before anyone can react, he grabs a shotgun and blows his head off.

When this was first proposed, level designer Dave Nash took exception. Among the most religious of those of us working on the game, he thought seeing Tai off himself in front of Delta Squad was too brutal. "Can't he just grab a grenade and jump off a ledge or something?" he asked. We discussed the options, and ultimately, I said no, I wanted him to shoot himself. I had followed the heartbreaking story of Terri Schiavo, a woman who wound up in a vegetative state after a massive heart attack. Her husband wanted to pull the plug and let her go, but her parents sued to keep her alive, at least technically, on machines. It became an important right-to-life legal case. Tai's death was my chance to make a statement about my belief in right to death. Who would want to live as a zombie shell of themselves? Could you even call that living?

Tai didn't think so. He'd been beaten and tortured to the point where he wanted out, and taking his own life was his last, boldest, and bravest act of living on his own terms. It was the kind of independence and reverence for life that I wanted communicated. And it foreshadowed what was going to happen when Dom finally found his wife, Maria.

We set up their relationship through a flashback Dom had while Delta Squad was carving their way through the guts of a ten-mile-long Riftworm that had swallowed them whole. It was an admittedly strange and gross circumstance; they had to avoid drowning in blood as the red goo collected in the beast's chest cavity. The perfect time for a soldier to think back to his wife making him breakfast on a more pleasant day in the past.

Then Dom and the squad found where Maria was located in the Hollow. When he freed her from the iron maiden cabinet where she'd been held prisoner, she looked exactly as he remembered, a dark-haired beauty. Only when the point of view changed to Marcus's perspective did the player see that Dom was delusional. Maria was a shell of her former self, tortured and malnourished beyond recognition, and in a near-vegetative state. He stared straight into her lifeless eyes and knew the action he had to take. The action of his gun firing a single bullet was off-screen. There was no need to see it. You could feel it.

Our cinematics editor spent weeks perfecting that scene. We brought in my high school drama class crush Courtney Ford, now a successful actress, to record the voice of Maria. The scene would become one of the most heartbreaking moments in video game history, ranking alongside Aeris getting killed in *Final Fantasy VII*. After I saw the finished cut, I thought, "Maybe one day this game *will* be taught in college classes."

As work was being done on the next phase of multiplayer versus, we zeroed in on an element we had wanted from the first days of *Gears*: cooperative play, or co-op. Player 1 was Marcus, player 2 was Dom, and they worked together. Lee and Rod came up with the idea of reconfiguring sections of the single-player campaign into a co-op mode in which players would face wave after wave of foes. I dubbed it Horde mode. When the hack of the single player didn't work, the multiplayer team cooked up customized maps, and Horde mode turned into a beautiful thing that was so fucking fun to play.

We didn't invent the wave-after-wave-of-enemies-coming-for-you game type. Hell, old shooters like *Robotron* and *Galaga* did it decades before. But we improved it and reintroduced it to a new generation of gamers.

Actually, it was a bonding experience in our playtest lab. Guys were nose-to-screen, but instead of being in a versus mode of death-matching and saying, "Fuck you, I'm going to kill you," they were rushing over to pick each other up. It wasn't quite emergent game-play, but it was a happy accident that promoted teamwork. I imagined many of those who would play the game enjoying the camaraderie. Instead of killing each other, you had each other's backs as you took on the baddies.

I took my friend Vegas back to the office one night after he joined a few of us for a pint at the Flying Saucer and he saw guys testing Horde mode. "This is work?" He laughed. I knew what he meant. It was my dream come true. Tim wasn't much of a gamer, so he was seldom in the playtests. It was more often Mark Rein who would bark out and complain about elements that were broken or not good enough, his classic grizzly style rattling the lab and making all of us thank God we had headphones.

Occasionally real life intruded on this high-pressure but relatively happy and insular world. I was in Rod's office one day when producer Tanya Jessen walked in, shut the door, and burst into tears. Tanya was a tough-as-nails, type-A Microsoft refugee whom Rod had brought in to help on production. She had just learned her good friend, Melissa Batten, had been murdered by her estranged husband.

We were shocked. Melissa was a friend of ours, too. A Harvard Law School graduate, she had worked at Microsoft and helped out in the early days of *Gears* as a tester. I'd last seen her at the W Hotel in San Francisco, where, grinning broadly, she'd asked, "Do you notice anything different about me?" She had lost a lot of weight. She had also split with her dude and was starting fresh. Except her ex was stalking her. And one morning, he shot her in the parking lot outside her apartment. Then he took his own life.

We consoled Tanya as best we could and sat together in silence, and though what happened to Melissa was not a game, I was reminded of the one we had in the works. Suddenly, I felt the way Marcus did after he heard Dom's gunshot: resigned to the fact that sometimes life sucked. The only option was to keep going.

Fortunately, I didn't have to take life too seriously too often. More bonus money came in and was divvied up among us. I used only a portion of my share to buy a 2005 maroon Lamborghini Gallardo Spyder. I paid for it with a cashier's check. The ability to do that blew my mind. I put the top down and cruised past the local bars, revving the engine until the ground shook like Locust were about to rip through the pavement and devour every establishment on Glenwood South. People ran outside to see what was shaking—literally. Half looked like they wanted a ride. The other half were asking, "Who's that asshole?"

The universe quickly put me in my place. As I navigated the narrow entry to my condo's parking lot, I ran the rims against the curb.

My new millionaire status didn't change anything at the office. One morning I found a lanky programmer in sweatpants waiting for me with a look of annoyance painted all over his face. "No more magic numbers!" he snapped. In the original *Gears*, I'd implemented various hacks, like making players temporarily invincible when chainsawing a baddie. Those were magic numbers. And I was pushing for more of the same in *Gears 2*. But I knew this guy was right—players wanted their games transparent and readable—and he had more important things to do than coding my behind-the-scenes trickery.

Still, his blunt manner bothered me enough to complain to his boss, who listened with a Zen-like calmness, then leaned back in his chair, put his hands behind his head, and laughed. "Don't sweat it, dude," he said. "By the time this game comes out, you'll be shopping for another Lambo!"

In February 2008 I made the annual pilgrimage to GDC, this time being held in San Francisco. Microsoft wanted to announce *Gears 2*. The problem with announcing *Gears 2* at this GDC was that we were so busy building the game, art assets, levels—shit, every facet of it—that we really didn't have the time or resources to produce a proper trailer. We couldn't do anything as memorable as our memorable "Mad World" trailer. We weren't even working with a marketing agency yet.

Microsoft didn't care. They wanted to get news of the sequel out and, more important, they wanted us on record promising a Christmastime release.

Rod and Chris decided to go with a minimalistic, highly stylized approach. The trailer opened with a long shot of Marcus's iconic armor silhouetted and bathed in a bloodred filter. "Sometimes death is all you can see," he says. "So you have to look it in the eye and . . . bare your teeth." Cue the sound of a chain saw and enter a Locust holding its own Lancer chainsaw gun. Marcus and the Locust lock weapons in a duel. After a brief struggle, Marcus gains the upper hand and gives the world its first look at chainsodomy. "It never ends," he sighs.

As the lights went up, I used a large Lancer chainsaw rifle to cut my way through a paper wall and walked to the front of the stage. "*Gears of War* was only a warm-up," I said. "*Gears 2* is going to be bigger, better, and more badass in every way." I let the message sink in. After turning to walk offstage, I paused and casually looked back over my shoulder. "Now I'm going to go kill some Locust!"

Backstage, I complained that the reception felt lukewarm, that developers were a cynical bunch, not like the enthusiastic press or die-hard gamer fans, but Mark and Rod said our demo had gone well and reminded me that this wasn't all about me or *Gears 2*. I'd been half of a successful double feature.

Earlier, Tim had previewed updates to the engine, captivating the audience of nerdy developers with talk of ambient occlusion technology (more realistic shadows), advanced character lighting (greater contrast and detail), real-time cinematics (movie-class control), and the ability to render more characters in a scene (hundreds of Locust were seen massing). "We never stop working on [the engine] or adding new features," he said.

It was a proud boast and a truthful admission that described life for all of us at Epic. Even Marcus Fenix, in his battle-weary voice, had said, "It never ends."

With cash rolling in, a rock-climbing wall, an office gym, free snacks, a comfortable environment, and work we loved, burnout was not a concern. In July, we took the *Gears 2* promo show to LA for E3.

With more time, we produced a dramatic trailer showing the COG staging a massive counteroffensive against the Locust in their underground cities. Giant transport trucks were assembled with digging pods that could inject hundreds of troops into the belly of Sera and confront the beasts where they lived. Marcus and his squad rode on a truck piloted by Dizzy, a redneck with a cowboy hat who I named after a member of Guns N' Roses.

These lumbering trucks were under assault from piles of Locust, including giant dinosaur-like beasts called "Brumaks" and flying Locust squid we called "Reavers." The programmers threw in thousands of Locust swarming in the distance, just because the engine's upgraded particle system gave them the opportunity for such wizardry. It achieved the look and effect I had wanted at the outset: it was full-on Michael Bay.

For the live demo, I stood onstage and played the co-op as Marcus, with Rod backstage playing as Dom. We traversed a Locust sinkhole filled with nasties, followed by six minutes of shooting, explosions, destruction, and flames. At the end, Dom and Marcus were still standing, but everyone knew there was more mayhem and fighting ahead. Something else was looming in the future: a release date.

Grinning, I announced *Gears 2* was going to be available November 7. The room filled with wild applause. I didn't know if people could wait.

Some apparently couldn't. While on my way to an interview with G4, a young woman grabbed my arm and said, "Hey, I have a *Gears* tattoo." Intrigued, I stopped. She pulled up her shirt and pointed to a spot on her rib cage where there was, indeed, a tattoo of the *Gears* logo, the Crimson Omen. I'd seen that before; but she'd gone further. Beneath it, in a clear script, was part of the Coalition oath: "Steadfast, I shall hold my place in the machine and acknowledge my place in the Coalition. I am a Gear."

"That's crazy," I said. "Very cool."

"I love *Gears of War*," she said. "And I love you."

Now in my early thirties, with my hair its natural color and my need for attention not completely tamed but seemingly under control, I was happy to go home at the end of the day to a good relationship. I loved Amy, but I knew that work had caused me to be neglectful. So had the carousing I'd done with *Gears 2* writer Josh Ortega, who had my same weakness for flirting with women and basking in the potential opportunities of those inebriated interactions. For me—and it might be the same for most guys—those nights out were akin to pulling my low self-esteem into a filling station.

Anyway, to recuperate from the long hours and to reconnect with Amy, we ventured out to the Carolina shore. We did it on the regular, driving the hour forty-five it took to get there, and solidifying our relationship along the way. At the beach, we listened to music, drank beer, and danced in the waves. I felt like I was smelling the roses, what I termed "emotionally inhaling." I remember sipping a Bud Lite and sounding like I had watched too many *Oprah* episodes as I told Amy that happiness wasn't a destination. It was a journey.

That said, I was extremely upset when she talked about wanting to study abroad in Thailand. I couldn't bear the thought of her being gone, and I conflated it with her leaving me. Months before, I had told Amy I would buy her diamond earrings if she quit her job. I wanted her to be available if I ditched work early or whenever else I wanted to play. It was a dick move. And now that Amy wanted her own adventure, as she was entitled to, I broke up with her. Instead of trying to understand her, it was easier to break up.

I thought I wanted my freedom anyway, and I returned to the dating pool eager to exercise it. Josh and my friend Vegas were enthusiastic wingmen. Soon I was going out with a beautiful Thai waitress at one of my favorite sushi restaurants. They had a sushi roll called The Screaming O, and Natalie always gave me a cheeky smile when she served it. Over coffee one day she asked, "You're not one of those guys who fetishizes Asian women, are you?" Was that really a thing? "Uh, no, you're cool, brilliant, nerdy, and gorgeous," I said.

And she was. Natalie loved anime and video games more than Amy did, and even dabbled in cosplay. One Saturday night she texted me that she was in the nightclub across the street from my condo. I met up with her, and after a couple drinks she said, "Let's get out of here." I took her home, and for a while it seemed like I had a new girlfriend, though the reproving look my dog, Teddy, gave me when I ushered Natalie through the front door filled me with guilt and shame, and if he hadn't been a dog, he would've said, "Dude, what are you doing? I know you. Is this really what you're looking for?"

He was right. That fall, as the Epic team tied up loose ends on *Gears 2*, I went to Europe on a whirlwind press tour. The fact that I was sent overseas to promote the game illustrated how truly popular the *Gears* franchise was not only in the U.S. but also internationally, and how important it was to Microsoft. I did five cities in five days: Milan, Madrid, Paris, London, and Munich. A lovely British PR person who resembled Baby Spice and had a quick, biting wit coordinated all my flights, hotels, and marching orders with the press in each spot.

Milan was the final stop. Exhausted, I settled into my hotel room, popped open my laptop, and found Emily online. Broken up with Amy, keeping a distance from my cute PR woman, I guess I didn't want to be alone. I hadn't spoken to Emily for a long time, and I was nervous but curious if she would respond when I typed, "Hey," and hit send. She did.

"Hey you."

"How've you been?"

"Good. Nice to hear from you. And you?"

"*Gears* craziness. *Gears 2.* I'm in Milan."

"Wow. Very cool. Congratulations."

"You happy? Anything changed with you?"

"I'm thinking of getting into game development. But still the same. You know how it is with me."

"I do."

I didn't expect or want anything from our exchange other than to hear that Emily was okay and doing well. It brought a satisfying closure to our friendship. After a relaxing bath, I ate dinner in the hotel's restaurant, where I sat by myself at a corner table and mulled my relationships with Marcy, Emily, and Amy, wondering about the lessons I was supposed to take from them. Were there always lessons? Had I just failed? Were they bad matches? How could I find what continued to elude me? Love.

Later that night, as I enjoyed a drink at the hotel bar, a British gentleman struck up a conversation with me. He worked in fashion and traveled frequently. He was in Milan for business. He hoped I didn't think him nosy, but he said he'd met all sorts of fascinating individuals in hotel bars, and I struck him as someone who had a lot on his mind. Without going into detail, I didn't dispute his assumption, and I explained why I was in town and what I did for a living. After I answered several questions about game development and *Gears* specifically, he asked if I had read Joseph Campbell's book *The Hero with a Thousand Faces.*

"No," I said. "I haven't heard of Joseph Campbell."

"He writes about the hero in classic mythology in a way that the rest of us can relate to," he explained, adding a slight chuckle at the end.

"Like the hero in my video game," I said, though as soon as those words left my mouth, I realized this stranger had just seen straight inside me and it was more than the hero in my game. Since my midteens I had been creating games, and through them, I had been writing my own story, my own journey, trying to figure out what it was, where it was headed, who I was, who I wanted to be, and who I was supposed to be.

He nodded. "We face trials and challenges in our life. Our lives are a quest to learn things and hopefully make something of ourselves that we can share with others. All of us—you and me—we are on our own hero's journey. That's Campbell."

"I'll get the book," I said.

LEVEL

6

A JOURNEY BEGINS

It was almost too good to be true. Sales of *Gears of War 2* were explosive—two million copies on release weekend, and a total of four million copies sold in the first two months. The marketing campaign, dubbed prop-a-game-da for the way it saturated Spike, X-Play, Xbox Live, the Sci-Fi channel, and MTV, was fantastic. Everything seemed perfect until I tried to play the multiplayer versus online and I got the eternally spinning wheel, the icon that lets you know your Xbox is not responding and that you are fucked.

I flashed back to the first *Unreal*. When I walked into lead level designer Dave Nash's office, I found him staring at the same thing on his screen. "Not good, dude," he said without looking up at me.

"So you got it too?" I asked.

"Not good."

This one mistake wasn't going to ruin the game, but I marveled at how we could be sitting atop an enormous office building enjoying the gratification of having made and shipped a product for distribution all over the world, and suddenly the focus of our entire lives at that moment was a tiny spinning wheel on a computer screen. So small and so consuming. The fix, which began immediately, took longer than we would have liked. Fortunately, the issue didn't impact reaction to the game. "The only thing bad about *Gears 2* is that it's almost too good," said one review. Another added, "If Miyamoto designed a shooter, this would be it."

There would be time to celebrate and indulge, but not just yet. We had already set up the final game in the *Gears* trilogy. At the end of *Gears 2*, Marcus and Delta Squad fight their way out of the Locust underworld and escape on helicopters as it floods. With Dom looking at an old, handwritten note from his beloved Maria, the Locust Queen warns, "Your world can end in the blink of an eye. One event, one unexpected twist of fate, and suddenly the world as you knew it is gone forever." Then Marcus tries unsuccessfully to reach his COG dispatcher Anya Stroud on the radio. The Locust Queen continues: "All that you held dear, all that you held close is washed away into the sea of distant memory." Fade to a black background with the title of the game and the Crimson Omen. And over that, we hear a radio crackle and a voice: "This is Adam Fenix. Can you hear me? What have you done?"

It was January 2009, and the heavy, gray skies of winter kept us indoors and at our desks, as did Microsoft's release schedule. They wanted *Gears* and *Halo* to alternate every other Christmas, giving each of us a two-year production window. Those plans would go the same way the Lambent Brumak did at the end of *Gears 2*, basically up in flames. But that was yet to happen. I walked into Rod's office one day, pushed up my sleeves, and said, "It's time." He smiled, ready. "Once more into the fray, my friend."

The whole team was ready to head back into the maelstrom. Chris Perna wanted to shed the "Grays of War" legacy and let color bleed into the franchise. I was tired of the desaturated thing, too. A generation of shooters had adopted our look; it was time to zig while others zagged. Lee Perry pushed for new baddies other than Locust, whom we had drowned at the end of *Gears 2*. I countered that Locust were resilient as hell, and I imagined them adapting into aquatic versions of themselves. "They would've evolved and adapted," I said.

I compared them to Freddy Krueger coming back for more *Nightmare on Elm Street* movies. No one bought it. "We need a new threat," Rod said.

We settled on our infected Locust, the Lambent, the strongest and most violent creatures who'd initially poisoned the Locust and instigated Emergence Day, beginning the nightmare that engulfed Sera. We also agreed on using AI for our boss creatures instead of making every monster a one-off. This enabled us to reuse the monsters in the campaign as well as in Horde mode. As that was discussed, Lee also brought up making changes to the cover system. Despite the popularity of the game's four-player co-op, players still wanted to roll around and gib each other. I did not disagree. It was basic game-playing instinct. I listened to fans in the online forums, what they liked and didn't like; incorporating such feedback was a balancing act. Their comments were essential to our understanding of the game, but we also weighed that against the data we saw, where we were with the tech, our timeline, the cost of making changes, and finally and most important, our instincts as creators. You didn't want to be swayed by a vocal minority. Neither did you want to lose your decision-making confidence. At the same time, you didn't want to dismiss a good idea.

Lee and I were resistant to too much change. To us, *Gears* was still about the close-up combat that made the chainsaw Lancer such an iconic component of the game. But we recognized that those playing *Gears 2* online saw a different game. I went into Lee's office one day, ready to capitulate to popular demand. Might as well give them what they want, I said. Lee agreed. "How about a sawed-off shotgun?"

I pretended to fire one and fall backward from the recoil.

"Super-short range," he added. "But if you get multiple foes in your radius, you can insta-kill them all at once!"

I liked it. "The ultimate multi-kill!"

This was always the most fun part of development or preproduction, this phase when ideas fly freely and there's no fear of being laughed out of the room because everyone is laughing at themselves. I was reminded of times during my childhood when my friends and I sat in our fort, trading outlandish what-ifs. Like: *What would you do if we were attacked by a bear? What if aliens landed? What if Miss August was your teacher?* When we were brainstorming *Gears 2*, I shared a crazy suggestion: "Why not have the player encounter worms in the underground of Sera? They're impervious to bullets and you can take cover behind them while dropping fruit from the ceiling to goad them into advancing your front line?" The response? "Fruit from the ceiling? Bleszinski, you're a freak."

I had a kindred spirit in our new writer, Karen Traviss, a brilliant British woman who had written several of the novels based on the franchise. She spoke with the spit-spot exactitude of Mary Poppins and rejoiced in the apocalyptic obsessions of Margaret Atwood. In a meeting, she wryly quipped, "No matter what's going on, humanity is only three meals away from total annihilation." Hearing such a dire pronouncement delivered so sweetly made it seem like something to look forward to. But I also knew she was frighteningly correct.

She took over the writer's desk next to mine and, except for inhibiting us from farting in the office, she handled the chore of wrestling a narrative with deceptive ease. She and Rod suggested starting *Gears 3* with the COG adrift at sea. We'd figure out a way the Lambent could ambush them. Lee Perry walked us through his idea of "stalks"—giant, coiled tentacles that could burst out of anywhere, including water. The stalks had pods that grew. If they were shot fast, the threat inside could be negated. If not, a heinous infected Lambent spilled out and sprayed white-hot Imulsion projectiles.

You get the idea. We were figuring it out. Karen knew we were going to have to deal with Marcus Fenix's father, Adam Fenix. We knew he was alive somewhere and wondering if anyone could hear him. The two of us spent days discussing this. I thought at some point Marcus should look for his father at East Barricade Academy, the institution where he resided and worked as a researcher and lecturer. I pictured Adam's home like my childhood home, set up on a hill and Marcus battling demons to get to it.

"It's like the nightmares I had as a kid," I told her. "I was always surrounded by monsters."

I also told her about the recurring dream I had after my father died, how I dreamed that he was in an apartment somewhere outside Boston, having faked his death for insurance reasons, and one day I would find him.

"Have you ever sought professional help for this?" she snickered.

"Yeah, I came to work here," I said.

It was such a cold, miserable Carolina winter, and seasonal depression was kicking my ass. I needed my beach—just like I knew Marcus did, too. Something away from the maelstrom. I bought a two-bedroom condo at the shore. Everything needed updating, except the view. It was always beautiful there, and some days it was spectacular, like that day Amy and I had danced in the waves. Missing the easy companionship we had, I got back together with Amy and tried to make it work. We made weekend jaunts to the beach with friends and by ourselves. "Let's have fun," we said.

Whether it was the age difference or the ups and downs and time apart we'd had, I knew deep down it wasn't going to work when I traded my burgundy Lamborghini for a lime-green model. I was still building my life, not our life, and trying to buy happiness, which is impossible. At the beach, she was glued to her phone. We were together but having two separate experiences. A friend once told me the only thing getting back together with an ex does is remind you of what your problems were in the first place, and though I was not quick to admit it, that was true with us.

Not that it bothered me the way it might have if I wasn't distracted—no, make that entranced—by a woman whose picture I noticed online after she won an all-female online gaming competition. Lauren Berggren had topped a field of three hundred women who were pitted against one another in a variety of games: *Mario Kart 64, Counter-Strike: Source, Guitar Hero III, Brain Age II,* and *NASCAR 2008.* She was the most beautiful woman I had ever seen. She had flaxen strawberry blond hair, a button nose, a smile that was slightly askew, and giant azure anime eyes that I imagined were looking at me.

I pored over her Myspace page until I had memorized every photo of her like a creepy-assed stalker. Her page was built in L33t speak, a coded gamer language; online, she called herself L337. I assumed she was a high-maintenance pain in the butt—in other words a snob—and I would have moved on if she hadn't looked like Buffy the Vampire Slayer and won a gaming tournament and made me wonder, "Is she the one? Could there be a girl out there who can play games as well as I can? Maybe better? Could she be my co-op buddy . . . for life?"

I tried to refrain from reaching out to Lauren until I ran out of self-control. At my desk one day and unable to concentrate, I emailed her. "What's up, cracker, how's things?!" It was a super-douchey one-liner, negging her with "cracker," and acting like she already knew me. Apparently, she didn't mind. I asked her what she was up to since winning the Miss Video Game gig, and she replied, "I actually live in Dallas and work at id Software as a tester/build manager."

Pleasantly surprised and amused, I replied, "They're our competition. We can't talk anymore!" I don't know how she took it, but three days went by without any correspondence before I emailed, "Just joshin.'" We started chatting again, sharing more personal details about our careers, hopes, and dreams, and of course the games we loved. It turned out she had been a professional *Counter-Strike* player for a while. As I confided to one of my friends, that didn't make her hot. It made her *hotter*.

My friend Randy Pitchford's Gearbox Studio was headquartered in Dallas, and I arranged a "business" trip to see him. During the latter stages of development on the original *Gears*, Randy had come to Raleigh and offered valuable feedback on the game. Now his studio was readying a first-person shooter called *Borderlands* for release that fall, and I offered to return the favor. At the end of June, I flew to Dallas, played Randy's game, and made a dinner reservation for me and Lauren at Nobu, the fanciest sushi restaurant in the city. I wanted to impress her. We had graduated from email and texts to talking constantly on the phone, and if she had asked, I would have admitted I was already in love.

I basically did that anyway. We met at the W Hotel. Lauren wore a red slip dress from Victoria's Secret and was more beautiful in person than I had imagined. She was also a little goofy and clumsy, which I found even more endearing. We got a drink at the bar and then went out for our fancy dinner, where we indulged in raw fish and lychee martinis. Afterward, we closed the hotel's nightclub and went up to my room. She offered to sleep on the sofa. Obviously, that didn't happen. We were already madly, hotly, and perfectly in love.

I cut ties with Amy, finally. We weren't living together, but I didn't want even a smattering of guilt that came with being a cheater. Been there. Done that. No thanks.

Lauren and I didn't see each other for a few weeks, and it was torture. Finally, in mid-July, we met up for Comic-Con in San Diego. It was my first time at the annual event, and as much as I enjoyed E3, GDC, and all the other industry conferences, Comic-Con encompassed everything that I loved outside of work: film, TV, action figures, comic books, cosplay, and video games. Lauren and I roamed the floor, bought nerdy swag, and went celeb-spotting at the *Entertainment Weekly* party, the hottest private soiree of the event. At one point, I texted my friend Vegas: "Wowowowow!" And it was. It was the best week of my life.

For the next nineteen weekends in a row (yes, I counted), we maintained our long-distance relationship. On Friday, after work, Lauren flew to Raleigh. When I took her to the airport on Monday morning, both of us cried. Something had to change—and it did. Lauren's boss informed her that they needed her to work weekends. It was crunch time on a project, and she wouldn't be able to travel. "Fuck that," I said. "Quit your job and move in with me." She did, and the two of us were never happier.

Besides being madly in love, one of the things I noticed about my relationship with Lauren that was different from those in the past was that I made time to be with her no matter my workload at Epic, which seemed to have doubled, even tripled. That was because it had. I regularly playtested the new first-person shooter *Bulletstorm* we had in the works. It was being built in partnership with Epic's Poland-based subsidiary, People Can Fly, a company we had invested in back in 2007, and Electronic Arts. Our superstar producer Tanya Jessen was put in charge, and her tenacity and willingness to spend her life on an airplane, traveling between Raleigh, Warsaw, and Redwood City, CA, was making that nutty game happen.

Bulletstorm featured a trash-talking protagonist named Grayson Hunt who'd crashed into an abandoned planet—"stranded in paradise" was the ironic message onscreen. The core idea? Kill with skill. Instead of just annihilating foes as fast as possible, as was the case in almost every shooter, the player was encouraged to toy with their victims, like a sadistic cat with a mouse, by stringing together cool combos that unlocked more cool shit. It was pure sci-fi madness, which made it ironic that NRA chief Wayne LaPierre would call it out by name years later as one of the causes of gun violence in the U.S.

Sure, Wayne, I thought at the time, *that laser lasso and kicking foes into cacti and all those wacky weapons like the energy leash are to blame. Right.* By contrast, I only got halfway through the prototype—kicking and impaling enemies, thumping them into walls—before I turned to Tanya and exclaimed, "Brilliant." It was, and later *TIME* magazine noted, "This time, the person in charge isn't a dude."

Then there was the not-so-little matter of the iPhone. It was barely on the market two years, maybe not even, before Tim and Mark wanted the engine on it. In its first weekend on the market back in 2007, Apple sold only two hundred seventy thousand devices. A year later, they sold one million 3G iPhones the first weekend and thirteen million for the year. One of my officemates built a little demo, a fly-through, that showed we could have high-quality graphics on an iPhone, and its success led to Epic acquiring Utah-based game maker Chair Entertainment. I had worked with them on *Shadow Complex*, a cool little 2D side-scroller.

Now in 2009, with Apple projected to ship twenty million iPhones, Tim and Mark wanted an iOS game. The potential they saw and their determination to make sure Unreal Engine was on every platform, and delivering the highest quality on every platform, led us to Chair to start work on *Infinity Blade*, a game that was basically *Mike Tyson's Punch-Out* with dungeons and swords. My days filled up with back-to-back meetings and nonstop playtesting for all these games in progress—*Gears 3, Bulletstorm,* and *Infinity Blade*—but that's not why I was one of the few who had trouble mustering enthusiasm for making a mobile game. They felt slight to me, the ugly side of free-to-play. I would be proven wrong. The game, released in 2010, would bring in upward of $23 million.

Among my better attributes, especially as one of the industry's most outspoken, opinionated personalities, is being able to admit I didn't always get it right. No one does—except maybe Tim. Decisions were being made in private about the company's future. At an all-hands meeting, Mike alluded to this when he asked us to start mulling ideas for new IP. "*Gears* might not always be cool," he said. Though correct, his comment was hard to believe. *Gears* and *Gears 2* were still top-selling titles at retail outlets, and still moving the Xbox 360, and we were deep into hammering out *Gears 3*. Fans still sent me photos of their *Gears* tattoos via email, Twitter, and every other social media platform.

A seed was planted. More like a question. What was next? For gaming. For the company. For me.

I got in the habit of popping into Tim's office and asking if he wanted to take a walk around the neighborhood. He usually did. I had no idea Apple co-founder Steve Jobs preferred taking walks in lieu of regular meetings. He thought it was the best way to have a conversation, and he regarded design as an ongoing conversation. He reportedly also liked walking barefoot. Tim and I both wore shoes, typically sneakers. I knew getting him out of the office for a stroll was the easiest way to hold his attention.

He seemed to enjoy getting away from all the demands on him in the office. In the old days, programming occupied more of his time than business. Now Epic was in growth mode and only a handful of years away from becoming a billion-dollar business, and Tim's calendar was filled with meetings much like mine that took him away from the simple pursuits of the early days when, as he'd said before, the goal was to not have to get a real job. Ironically, we had done so well over the years that we had created real jobs for ourselves.

On our walks, I was able to pick his brain about where the company and the industry were headed. For instance, it was while we were ambling around the building's parklike grounds that I learned the backstory behind Mike's comments. Tim explained the original *Gears* had cost $12 million to make and was estimated to make about ten times that in revenue. He estimated *Gears 3* was going to cost us $40–$50 million to make, without generating the same return on investment.

The business had changed, he said, and was only going to continue to evolve. Having been at Epic since the early days when we sold games on shareware for a few bucks, to our present focus on $60 games that were played on $250 consoles, I was aware of this reality. I lived it daily and said some of those same things to my team in our regular Friday meetings. But it felt good hearing it from the boss, who also happened to be one of the industry's driving forces and visionaries. And my friend. He teased me about dating younger women and always made sure to remind me to push for features that showed off the engine.

There was much to figure out. In *Gears 3*, humanity's desperation had forced women to enter the fray. Anya would have a significant role and a running mate, Samantha Byrne. We should've introduced them as fighters much sooner. It was an opportunity to inspire female gamers and future coders; this was the way to effect change. I was adamant about not sexualizing them. They could be pretty, but they couldn't be a fifteen-year-old boy's fantasy. "We're creating warriors, not centerfolds," I said.

And frankly, it was easier to give them maximum firepower and let 'em rip alongside Marcus and Delta Squad. This was war. There was no time for eye shadow and push-up bras. Chris Perna showed me a 3D model of Samantha. I stared at the picture, and for some reason the rapper Nelly popped into my head.

"Put a Band-Aid on her face," I suggested.

"All right," he said.

He flipped his Wacom tablet back around, painted it on her face, and showed me the result.

"Yes," I said.

Our biggest task was addressing the surprising status of Marcus Fenix's father, Adam Fenix. He was still alive. We had to figure out how that was possible and where he had been hiding. I wanted Marcus to try to rescue him. My notebook had pages of thoughts about this mystery. It was as if I had journaled about giving up my own fantasy of my father being alive back when I was a teenager and dreaming that he'd faked his death to get insurance money. Crazy, but now Marcus Fenix had to let go of his dad, too.

As part of that process, Adam Fenix would hold the solution for taking out the Locust at the end. I knew it would cost him his life. That was the letting-go part. But that's all I had. I took this vague idea to Rod and our writer Karen Traviss, and over time others joined the conversation, including Chris Perna and Lee Perry. We plotted that Marcus and his team would, at the end, have a knockdown with the Locust Queen Myrrah. It was time to shut her up for good. Not all the details were clear, but we had a map showing where to go.

One day head level designer Dave Nash came into my office with an idea for a new environment. In the fiction of *Gears*, the COG had used the Hammer of Dawn, a powerful orbital satellite laser, on themselves scorched-earth style to repel the Locust invasion. Dave was picturing the aftermath of this desperate act on a city like Hiroshima, a place hit so hard they forgot the name of it and simply called it Char. Everything there had been burned in the fighting.

"How about the Hammer strikes were so severe that people were frozen in ash, like the bodies in Pompeii?" I said.

Dave turned it into a spooky visual painted in shades of black and white that so perfectly captured the horrific toll of this sci-fi war, we chose to feature the environment in the initial reveal of *Gears 3* at GDC in April 2010. The new trailer was titled "Ashes to Ashes," and in it, set against the hypnotic melody of Sun Kil Moon's "Heron Blue," we showed Dom in Char, running from Locust. As he runs, dust people frozen in time are trampled and shattered into millions of particles. We didn't have to say the obvious: life is fragile.

As Locust bear down on him, he trips, and for a brief moment it appears he's giving up. Suddenly Marcus shows up off-screen with the sawed-off shotgun and wastes the Locust. The rest of Delta Squad is behind him, including Anya, the blond dispatcher from the first two games, who is now in combat and kicking ass right alongside the fellas. She drops a Lancer on Dom's chest. Suddenly a gigantic Lambent fills the sky, casting a menacing shadow over Delta right as the screen fades to black and the words appear, "Brothers To The End."

Lauren cried as she watched it on my laptop. I loved being able to share this with a partner who was knowledgeable and in tune with all that went into developing everything we saw onscreen, and to also understanding its deeper meaning. Karen Traviss would have been forgiven had she also cried. New material like this was the most grueling part of the writer's job because they weren't necessarily expecting it, and then they had to figure out how the hell to connect it to everything else. I knew one writer who got so stressed writing video games, he landed in the hospital. I shit you not.

But Karen delighted in dire, end-of-the-world situations, and when we dropped Char in her lap, as she did with the other game-playing scenarios we dumped in her lap, she assessed it with a librarian-like "Hmmm," and got to work.

After a rousing GDC presentation, I flew to New York to announce *Gears 3* to the public on *Late Night with Jimmy Fallon*. A gamer himself, Jimmy was breaking new ground in TV talk shows with a weeklong gaming theme. They even referred to it as Game Week on *Late Night*. I was prepared to announce both *Gears 3* and

Bulletstorm, but I was bumped for a new teen music sensation named Justin Bieber, and the honor of breaking news about *Bulletstorm's* April release went to *Game Informer* magazine.

While waiting to be rescheduled, which happened a few days later (and included a chat about the green-shell loophole in *Super Mario* that allowed me to get to that high number when I was fifteen and revealed Jimmy's nerd cred), I went on Twitter and gave updates on my whereabouts in New York City: Little Italy, Central Park, the Metropolitan Museum of Art, the Guggenheim, and the Museum of Modern Art, where I saw performance artist Marina Abramović in the middle of her famous *The Artist Is Present* piece. Inspired, I organized a meetup at the GameStop store in Union Square. I was like Adam Fenix. Is anyone out there? Can you hear me?

They could. A couple hundred *Gears* fans showed up. I spent an hour or so answering questions. But one of the traits I took pride in was knowing I was just like my fans, a gamer, and I treated them the same way I would have wanted to be treated, which meant soon I was asking them as many questions as they fired at me. I wanted to know what they were playing, what they liked and disliked about *Gears 2*, and what they thought was going to happen in *Gears 3*. A few people blurted out ideas. One guy's comment caught my attention.

"Dom's gotta die," he said.

"Why do you say that?" I asked.

He shrugged. "Shit's gotta happen."

He was right. Shit did indeed have to happen.

WE HAVE A TOMORROW

On the flight back to Raleigh, I thought about the placard on Mike Capps's desk: "If you want to increase your audience, defy expectations."

Yes. *Defy expectations.*

On Sunday Lauren and I had brunch at the Flying Biscuit. She had been in New York with me and knew what the fan had told me. She knew the way it had occupied my thoughts since we had gotten back—hell, since the guy had said it. He might as well have been the Locust Queen telling me that the world could change in an instant.

"We have to kill Dom," I said.

"That's what you're thinking now?" she said.

"Yeah, we have to off Dom. He's been through enough already."

"Yikes, that's pretty drastic," she said.

I texted Rod, who agreed with Lauren. It was pretty drastic. But he acknowledged that we had foreshadowed his demise in the "Ashes to Ashes" video. Karen recognized the power of this idea right away, but with a condition.

"Dom can't go in vain," she said. "He can't go without a fight."

In other words, it couldn't be like Tai offing himself with a shot-gun after being tortured. No, if we were going to bid goodbye to Dom, we needed to ratchet up the stakes. He was going to have to sacrifice himself to save the rest of Delta Squad as the baddies closed in on them. Karen shut her eyes. She was picturing the action.

"Dom needs closure," she said.

We talked through scenarios and Karen crafted a sequence where Delta Squad journeyed to Mercy, the hometown of Dom's wife, Maria. There he placed her beloved necklace at a shrine he had made for her. He was resigning himself to a similar fate. Indeed, soon after, Delta Squad was cornered and Dom hijacked a fuel truck, plowed it into enemy forces, and finished his own hero's journey while saving Delta Squad, his "brothers to the end."

Thinking about this sequence gave me chills. The emotion was the secret sauce of *Gears*. It was the reason so many goombahs had left screenings of *Rocky* shouting, "Adrian! Adrian!" We gave people permission to be tough and have a heart.

"What if we got 'Mad World' to play when Dom makes the call to sacrifice himself for everyone else?"

"This time the rights won't be cheap," Rod said.

"We don't need the Gary Jules version," I said. "We just need the instrumental track, and that probably won't be expensive."

It wasn't. We got the track, played it in the background, and Dom's sacrifice became one of the greatest scenes in gaming history. But that was just one scene, albeit a perfectly crafted scene, but we had an entire game to finish. As always, deadlines loomed and there was no stopping the march of time. We needed to "close the patient," as Rod said. Starting a game is easy. Finishing is a motherfucker.

For that reason, Rod shook his head when I came to him with the idea of putting hard-core rap superstar Ice-T in the game.

Video game personality Jace Hall had connected me and Ice-T on his internet talk show. The rapper was a notorious gamer, and he wanted to be in *Gears 3*. He'd told Jace, "Put Ice-T on the box and that'll be a million sales right there." After I persuaded Rod, we created the character Aaron Griffin, the former CEO of Imulsion Oil turned gangland-style boss of the ruined city of Char. Ice-T nailed the voice-over.

I had created a character for Jace in *Gears 2*, Jayson Stratton, aka Jace. His role was expanded in *Gears 3*, and we signed future superstar Drake, then on the cusp of releasing his first album, to provide Jace's voice. But his manager pulled him after one recording session. "All the yelling is going to mess with his voice," he told us. In his place, we landed up-and-comer Michael B. Jordan, who was red-hot from his work on HBO's *The Wire*. We were getting some heat online for Cole Train being a stereotype, and Michael had the chops to give Jace a mix of quasi-religious cool and hair-trigger badassness.

The last pieces of the puzzle we hammered out concerned Adam Fenix. We decided he had gone into hiding after a major battle to develop a solution to the infectious nature of Imulsion, which would finally put an end to the Lambent and Locust. Working in secret on the secluded island of Azura, he had experimented for years on himself, like the Curies did with radiation. Now Marcus and company arrive on that secure bunker of land, where they fight through what seems like a million odious creatures and find Adam Fenix, who activates his Imulsion Countermeasure Weapon as his son and Delta Squad face off in a final battle with the Locust Queen herself, Myrrah.

Defeated, the queen crawls off her fallen steed and approaches Marcus, talking shit about his father. Marcus stabs her, mid-rant, with Dom's knife. At the same time, Adam Fenix's Imulsion Countermeasure Weapon works, drying up the Lambent and causing the Locust and their war beasts to collapse. Sera is saved, and Marcus can finally be with his father.

Except the victory came at a price. As the Imulsion Countermeasure Weapon hit its peak power, Marcus sees his father turn to dust right in front of him. Adam Fenix is gone forever. After decades of suffering on this war-torn planet, though, the fighting is finally over. The victory is bittersweet. Beyond exhausted, Marcus sits down on the beach, drops his weapons, and begins removing his armor. He is joined by Anya.

"What do we have now, Anya?" he asks.

She gently puts her hand on top of his and says, "We have a tomorrow."

That ending and that line felt so perfect and good and, like everything else associated with *Gears*, so incredibly personal, and it motivated me to organize for my own tomorrow. In February 2011, Lauren and I hopped out to LA for a party celebrating the release of *Bulletstorm*. When we got back home, I purchased the condo next door to mine, punched a hole in the wall, and began making my place more comfortable for two people. A short time later, I bought a second Lamborghini. It wasn't the way most people showed they were serious about their relationships, but my girlfriend was different. She beat me in *Tetris* on the Nintendo DS regularly.

Lauren came home one day from doing errands and told me that a little girl had stopped her in the parking lot outside CVS as she was getting into the Lambo.

"Is that your car?" the girl asked.

"Yes, it is," Lauren said.

"I didn't know girls could drive cars like that," she said.

Lauren got in and revved the engine. "Girls can do anything they want."

I didn't know it was possible to fall even more in love with Lauren, but I did every single day. That spring, we spent weekends at the beach. One day I found a large piece of pink beach glass and gave it to Lauren. It was a practice run. In April, we traveled to New Orleans, where Lauren had grown up and where her twin brother, older brother, younger sister, and parents still lived, and I had a private conversation with her father, who gave me his blessing to take the next step with his daughter.

Back home, I managed to sneak out to a fancy jewelry store downtown and purchase a diamond ring. Not just any diamond, but a 3.5-karat sparkler that left no doubt about my feelings for Lauren. Then came the hard part. Finding the perfect time to give it to her. It was May, and we went to LA for E3. Ice-T joined me onstage to demo *Gears 3*. At that night's after-party, Lauren and I shared a table with Ice-T and his wife, Coco Marie, whose barely-there dress incurred a malfunction that bared one of her boobs. "Happens all the time," she laughed to Lauren. I rolled my eyes and quipped, "Toto, I have a feeling we aren't in Raleigh anymore."

For obvious reasons, the ring stayed in my pocket. After E3, we flew to New York where I made my second appearance on *Late Night with Jimmy Fallon*—more proof that gaming had truly hit the mainstream. By this time, I had booked a trip to Mexico, where a catamaran with a captain and crew awaited to take us on a romantic voyage during which I intended to ask Lauren to marry me. It would have been amazing if only I'd had the willpower to wait. On our first morning in New York City, we were walking in Central Park, and in the middle of the bridge spanning the park's lake, I got down on one knee and popped the question. Lauren jumped into my arms and screamed. I thought I heard her say yes, but I wasn't sure.

"Babe, I didn't hear you," I said. "Did you say yes you would marry my goofy ass?"

She nodded. "I did. I said yes!"

After resuming our walk, we picked up lunch from a street vendor and sat down on a park bench. We noticed a small tribute plaque on the bench. "Leonard, dear," it said, "meet me here . . . I love you . . . Janet." We had no idea who Leonard and Janet were, but the city was full of love stories like theirs, and Lauren and I had just added one more.

Gears 3 shipped on September 20, 2011, and sold three million copies its first week—faster than the previous two hit that same mark—and pushed revenue for the entire franchise over one billion dollars. *Wired* magazine called it "a triumphant threequel." "Quite easily the best *Gears of War* yet," claimed VideoGamer. Microsoft threw a launch party at the Best Buy Theater in Times Square. Big Sean performed. A line of eager gamers waiting to get in stretched around the block. Some had slept there all night. I ordered forty pizzas and handed out slices up and down the line as a thank-you to the fans.

The smell of weed from Big Sean and his entourage wafted outside, where the party-time atmosphere seemed to ratchet up a notch or two each time someone noticed my T-shirt, which boasted a headline of the recent Supreme Court decision stating that video games were forms of free expression protected by the First Amendment. The case was *Brown v. Entertainment Merchants Association*, and the court's ruling struck down a California law prohibiting minors from buying or renting violent games. It was really kids versus ignorant and out-of-touch politicians. The court got it right, and I was thrilled to celebrate with fellow gamers on the street. We were in it together. Gamers forever.

After the event, a bunch of us went to the Rum House bar at the Edison Hotel. Around four a.m., they booted us onto the sidewalk, and I stood in the chilly morning air looking up and down Forty-Seventh Street. Times Square was empty. It felt like the apocalypse had hit while we were inside drinking. Or else it was life presenting itself as a clean slate. "We have a tomorrow," someone said. "It's already tomorrow," another responded. It was one of those moments where time stopped and I saw my life in front of me, the hero's journey spread out like pictures in an album. I had met challenges, found my goddess, acquired wealth, and accomplished my goals. But damn Joseph Campbell. If he was right, I knew it wasn't over.

Rod was ahead of me, also taking in the quiet of the city, and perhaps having a moment like mine. I stepped up to his side and said, "What the fuck is next?"

"Besides sleep?" he said.

"Yeah."

"We'll see." He shrugged. "It might be time to shake things up."

IT COULD BE BIG

I was among the many at Epic who were craving a move onto the next thing. There was gratitude for *Gears*. But there was also burnout. We had ended the trilogy with Marcus on the beach, setting down his gun, removing his armor, and looking forward to a peaceful future with Anya. Except for Rod, we wanted our beach. Our tomorrow. Even Tim and Mark Rein were strategizing a next phase for Epic that rode the unceasing waves of change that ruled the industry and didn't include the new adventures of Delta Squad.

There was just one hitch in the plan: we still owed Microsoft one more *Gears*. Lee Perry and I put our heads together. Lee proposed a hub-based game in which players went on missions and returned to home base, which they had to defend from attack in a constant state of Horde mode. He even cobbled together a sweet demo.

It seemed like a role-playing game to me, along the lines of *The Elder Scrolls* series, where players' power and capabilities expanded as they accomplished increasingly difficult tasks. The world was open, as opposed to a linear progression, and you could go anywhere. It wasn't just aim and shoot. I thought RPGs were the future of shooters.

I proposed something like *Halo*'s spinoff *ODST* game—four Onyx Guard characters armed with all the super-high-tech equipment we denied Delta Squad in the first three games. "No Marcus or

Delta anywhere in sight," I said. "We can have all the cool toys—heat vision, night vision, EMP grenades, portable lasers . . . I think fans will love it."

Rod nixed it. Too pragmatic to mess with the status quo of where we'd left the franchise, he wanted to go the prequel route, which I understood but thought was risky. It seemed like a spinoff to me, and I knew that for every *Frasier* there were dozens of *Joeys*. The game was called *Gears of War: Judgment,* and because of the escalating costs and time it took for Epic to build a game, and the diminishing returns, *Judgment* was farmed out to People Can Fly, the Polish subsidiary that had built *Bulletstorm.*

I gave feedback on *Judgment*'s initial story, but it didn't come easily like it did before. I'd said what I had to say in the trilogy.

I took advantage of Epic's policy of offering long-term employees a sabbatical up to a month long. That fall Lauren and I jetted off to Barcelona, Spain, where I spoke at a gaming conference. Hideo Kojima was among the other speakers, and one night we met him for drinks in the hotel bar. Kojima-san brought his producer-translator Ken-Ichiro Imaizumi, and though he didn't speak much English, I knew he understood me when he laughed after I said my fiancée could kick my ass in *Counter-Strike* and *Tetris.*

Talking through a translator made conversation difficult, but I told the master about shipping *Gears 3* and the uncertainty I felt about what to do next. It was hard to explain, because I didn't feel conflicted or confused, and more nuanced attempts at explanation, like feeling empty, a little depressed, and in need of a recharge, got lost in translation. But Kojima-san looked in my eyes and seemed to see inside me. He repeated something I'd read in past interviews with him—that *Metal Gear* was both his biggest failure and biggest success.

The point was not lost on me. *Metal Gear* had brought Kojima prominence and wealth, but it had also locked him into a single title, like golden handcuffs, and as a creative person, a true artist, he wanted to and in fact needed to work on other ideas. He was more than *Metal Gear*, just as I was more than *Gears of War*. It was a profound thing to say. It was also scary. Do you play it safe? Or do you get back on the high wire? Because if I was more than *Gears of War*, what was I?

This was the conundrum of adulthood and the last part of my hero's journey. I'd confronted the demons of the past. Now what? As I'd said to Rod and Lauren and everyone else, including myself, what's next?

"You've created new worlds before," Kojima said. "Why not do it again?"

He smiled, and I recognized it was the smile of someone who knew the hellish task of what he'd just suggested. It was evil.

But he was right.

During my sabbatical, Mike Capps had addressed that same question. He had told Epic's leads to get their teams together and see what ideas they could come up with in a short period of time. In the industry, this is known as a game jam. Everyone jams on ideas until one or two ideas rise to the top and get even more attention. These free-for-all brainstorms are often romanticized as collaborative drum circles. Oh my God, how fun!

To be sure, your typical developer who spends years on the same game loves these opportunities to think outside the box. Then, inevitably, they suggest something with a steampunk theme and zombies. Always zombies, because you don't need a justification for shooting thousands of them. Nobody's going to get offended.

I felt a bit undermined, though, when I returned to the office and found out about the game jam. I'd always worried that Mike's endgame was to wrestle creative control from me, and this seemed to support that theory. Then again, Mike was just doing his job. As he'd said, *Gears* might not always be cool.

I had to admit, the games that came out of the jam showed promise, including a top-down tactical *Gears* strategy game, a bullet hell space shoot-'em-up, and several ideas built around exactly what I'd predicted, steampunk and zombies. I thought the most promising thing to come out of the jam was that a cluster of developers headed up by Lee Perry really clicked as a group. They started going to lunch every day, and Mike let them move into their own war room for six weeks to see what they could come up with.

Lee and his crew were fans of the "tower defense" genre—the player guards a main location from wave after wave of foes, like Horde mode—which was trending upward thanks to the hot games *Plants vs. Zombies* and *Monday Night Combat*. They wanted to make something similar, but with crafting, like *Minecraft*, which was also exploding in popularity at the time.

Lee ran their pitch by me. "What if you were in some sort of parallel world in which the zombie apocalypse had hit and you had to scavenge for resources, return to your tower, and try to fortify it before nightfall hit?"

"Honestly, that sounds really damned cool," I said. "Run with it."

Full confession: I always thought many of *Minecraft*'s systems were convoluted. *What? I have to punch a tree to get wood to build a bench to then do more stuff? Get the fuck out of here.* But Lee and his cohorts cobbled together a deceptively simple grid-based resource system that allowed the player to build things—to forge a ramp, a door, a wall, a ceiling, all the other fundamentals—and do it fast as hell and on the fly, which appealed to me.

They quickly got into the creative place where good things happen. I could feel the momentum every time I entered their war room or heard an update from Lee. Debate about the art direction was nonstop until an artist within Lee's group took it upon himself to slap together a cartoony art style, like a suburban neighborhood illustrated by Pixar, only a little simpler and sillier. I saw it in an email thread and replied, "THIS!"

As they began prototyping the game, they needed a name. Dozens of suggestions were floated. It was always hard coming up with that perfect name. Determined to meet the challenge, I sat down at my desk and wrote down the core features of the prototyped game, the most basic of which was the player built a fort. It was like my childhood fort minus the skin magazines. The fort also had to be defended from attacks that came at night—the time when all the bad stuff happened. A clock ticked inside the game.

I stared at everything I'd written until the obvious hit me. Put the two features together and call it *Fortnight*? Everyone liked it. But when our legal department reported the trademark wasn't available, we didn't go back to the drawing board. We followed standard practice: we kept the name but changed its spelling to *Fortnite*.

Fortnite.

It felt right.

I sensed tension from Rod. He was in the midst of developing and managing *Gears of War: Judgment*, and though we were outsourcing it, he still needed resources and he had a cagey way of pulling talent into his universe no matter how much anyone in the studio wanted to try other things. He wasn't the Viking for nothing. His stature within the company gave him veto power over projects, and he used it to try to thwart this promising new game when the team leads met with Tim, Mark Rein, and Mike Capps to decide whether it was a go or no-go.

"I like it," Rod said. "It could be big. Actually, it could be too big. Which is why we need to cancel it."

He was voting his loyalty to *Gears*. Lee and his crew were furious. It was uncomfortable in the room. Even though I saw huge potential in *Fortnite*, and I was actively helping them by playing it and providing notes, I bit my tongue. But Tim, Mark, and Mike saw its potential. We had to move on from *Gears* at some point, just like we'd moved on from the *Unreal* games. At the end of the meeting, *Fortnite* was a go.

Lauren and I spent Thanksgiving playing the prototype. It reminded her of the game *Plants vs. Zombies*. Bottom line: she liked it—more than the latter version the world would know.

In December 2011, I announced *Fortnite* at the Spike Video Game Awards in LA. "You may know me from such games as *Unreal Tournament* and *Gears of War*," I said. "At Epic Games, we always like working on new things, and this time we figured we'd switch it up a little." I felt guilty about taking the spotlight instead of Lee or one of the others working on the game, but Lauren reminded me that I had established myself as the face of Epic at events like this, and I was good at it. Still, something didn't feel right.

Judgment was languishing. The staff was obsessed with the strategy game *League of Legends*; shooters suddenly felt passé and none of my ideas were getting through. One day Mike said to me, "These games are huge, and they're based all on systems. That's not your forte, Cliff. You're more of a feel designer." I didn't know what that meant, but it stung. In June 2012, Rod and I promoted *Gears of War: Judgment* at E3, and when we returned to Raleigh, Lee and the five developers working with him announced they were leaving to form their own studio, BitMonster Games.

It was not an easy summer. The game jam had splintered loyalties at Epic. To my knowledge, this was the first time politics had reached such a serious level at the company. Lee and his crew had tired of fighting for talent within the studio to work on *Fortnite*. I was in Mike's office when Lee broke the news. They believed in the potential of *Fortnite*, but they were willing to give it up to be able to do their own thing. Mike tried to talk him into staying.

"I can't say what it is, but something might be happening that you may want to stick around for," he said.

"Nope," Lee said. "We gotta go. These guys are my brothers."

A few weeks later, Mike's cryptic comments made more sense when it was announced that mega Chinese game maker Tencent was purchasing a 40 percent interest in Epic for $330 million. It reflected a major shift in Tim's thinking about the company's future. He wanted to move away from partnerships with publishers and put *Fortnite* out independently. Indie games were the rage. What if *Fortnite* became a phenomenon like *Minecraft* and Epic didn't have to give a cut to a publisher? The Tencent deal gave him that opportunity. Lauren and I were eating dinner at Hibernian when Mark Rein called to confirm the news. He told me how much money I was going to make.

"Holy shit," I said.

"What are you going to do with the money?" he asked.

"I have no fucking idea," I said. "I'm eating dinner."

He chuckled. "Well, I hope you don't sing that old Steve Miller song and take the money and run."

A couple weeks later, Rod called me into his office and said he'd had it. Despite all its success, *Gears* no longer felt like the favorite of the company. He was mad, and now he was rich as hell—rich enough that he didn't have to take it anymore. He'd already lined up another gig shipping *BioShock: Infinite* at Irrational Games outside Boston. He had been essential to the success of *Gears*. He got the first trilogy out the door, and its success set up all the others that followed. I told him as much, too.

I hugged him, wished him well, and hoped we would remain

friends. After all, he and his wonderful wife, Sandy, were coming to my wedding in a few days.

Lauren and I were married on August 4, 2012, at San Diego's Safari Park, an eighteen-hundred-acre home to giraffes, buffalo, tigers, rhinos, and elephants. Our choice of venue was a message to our guests: we were wild about each other. Prior to the big event, Lauren and her mother and younger sister, Lacey, were featured on the popular TV series *Say Yes to the Dress.* They argued about how much cleavage to show. (Lauren won.) Our rehearsal dinner, held at a Mexican restaurant, included a celebrity drop-in from Crystal, the adorable monkey from the movie *The Hangover.*

The next day, our family and closest friends—including Tim, Mark, and Rod—watched Lauren and I recite vows we had written ourselves. "Today is the happiest day of my life," said Lauren, who looked picture-perfect in a white Kleinfeld gown and Jimmy Choo high heels. "You make my heart race. You balance me, challenge me, and encourage me. You believe in me even when I don't believe in myself." I had tears in my eyes. "One look from you melts me," I said. "One touch paralyzes me. You are my happy place. You are my angel, my love, and my best friend. You have been a princess to me. Now I'll be honored if you become my queen."

The party carried on past midnight. Lauren's garter was caught by Tim, who grinned as he showed off his prize to me. "Geez, Cliff, your wife has a lot of hot friends," he said. I agreed. "Go do something about it, dude," I said.

At the end of the night, my brother Tyler wrapped an arm around me and asked how I felt. I glanced at Lauren taking one last spin on the dance floor surrounded by her bridesmaids and girlfriends and gazed up at the star-filled sky. "I feel . . . like I finally found home," I said. What I meant was that I finally felt at peace. Career-wise, I had surpassed all my dreams. I had wealth and fame. I had also discovered how empty those two things can be without having someone you love to share it with.

But finding love is harder than making money or getting attention. In a world increasingly defined by science, logic, and ones and zeroes, love remains as mysterious as ever, defying all explanation and making sense only to poets. There are over seven billion people in the world. How do you find the one? I got lucky.

I returned from honeymooning in Hawaii to a different Epic Games. Rod and Lee were both gone, and it felt like the band was breaking up. *Fortnite* topped our to-do list, but I was out of my element. Sure, it had shooting and was third person, but what was the point of the whole game? Collect resources. Build. And defend. Was that enough? I set up a desk in the *Fortnite* war room and gave feedback but no real direction. Tanya Jessen, ever the workhorse, took over supervising development. I was out of steam.

For the first time in two decades at Epic, I didn't feel connected to the game the company was bringing to life. I wondered if the same was true about the company itself.

All my years in the business had taught me that one thing could always be counted on—change. One day Mark Rein called me into his office, where he was meeting with tech entrepreneur Brendan Iribe. Brendan was pitching Epic on making Unreal Engine viable for his fledgling VR company, Oculus VR. I'd met Brendan in LA at a dinner with Mark. "The guy dates models," Mark had told me. I saw why. He was a shrewd businessman who'd built and sold several companies. He looked like actor Christian Slater, and he was extremely articulate. But more than that, what he said was fascinating.

Brendan had gotten involved with a brilliant young garage tin-
kerer named Palmer Lucky and John Carmack in their red-hot project, the Oculus VR headset. Carmack had demoed it at the most
recent E3. VR had face-planted in the nineties, but I'd always been
enamored with the idea of technology that would allow me to escape
the crappy world of "actual reality." What if I could be transported to
another world, like lucid dreaming? I'd had lucid dreams many times
since childhood; each time it was the same—I was flying.

What if Brendan's tech let me fly? Especially now when I was
itching, aching to fly.

In Mark's office, Brendan handed me a crude headset held together with duct tape. I held it up to my face. The placeholder on the
other side was a 3D scene from id Software's game *Rage*. I chuckled.
My brilliant, beautiful wife had worked on that, I thought. When I
looked down into the chasm, though, I felt an incredibly real and
compelling sense of vertigo. I was sold. After a minute or two, I took
it off and said to Brendan that I wanted in. Personally.

"I have to invest," I said.

He smiled. "You want some skin in the game, eh?"

"Yup."

"We're going to need you to plug the hell out of this to the press."

"Happy to oblige."

It would turn out to be the best investment of my life after Facebook purchased Oculus for $2 billion. For now, it was a gamble and a
reason to ask myself whether it was my time to fly, not virtually, but in
real life. Tim was positioning Epic for change by bringing in Tencent,
moving away from reliance on Microsoft and other publishers, and
deciding to release *Fortnite* independently when the game was ready.
I didn't know if I wanted to leave the company or if I needed to have a
talk with Tim and Mark, as I had done in the past, to figure out where
Epic was going and how I fit in. Weren't those the same questions I'd
asked in high school? If not the same, they were similar enough.

And now here I was at thirty-seven years old—married, a millionaire, the owner of two Lamborghinis, a double-wide condo, and a place at the beach—and I was still asking where I was going and how I fit in.

I was at my desk the day the Tencent investment money hit mine and everyone else's bank account. My jaw hit the fucking floor. I turned to one of my officemates and chirped, "Dude!" He replied, "Sweet!" I'd been talking to my longtime agent, Ophir Lupu, about my feelings about the company and the work itself, using him as a trusted advisor-slash-therapist, and he said it was time to ask for a bump in salary and a larger bonus. He was an agent, after all. "You should be flying private, dude," he said. "You need some insight into the mysterious bonus plan they have. You're worth more. Now's the time."

That sounded good, but I didn't know if I was worth more or if I had the backbone to find out. I did know that I was tired of the long hours I worked. They were fun until they weren't. I was also tired of fighting for ideas and fighting in general. Arguing with an engineer is like wrestling with a pig in the mud. After a while, you realize the pig likes it. And I was exhausted, bored, disengaged, burned out. I really didn't know what I wanted, and when you don't know what you want, more money always sounds good.

"It's Tim's company," I told Ophir. "He can tell me as much or as little as he wants about the way they compensate me and other people."

"You have leverage," he said.

Did I? I hadn't negotiated with Tim since I'd moved with the company to Raleigh and asked for a six-figure salary. As Epic grew, I accepted whatever Tim and Mark gave me. They were generous, and I was grateful. But I bought into the idea Ophir planted in my head that I was underappreciated. "As generous as they've been, you don't get what you deserve," he said. "You get what you negotiate." It was mid-September, and I told Ophir to see what he could get for me. As I waited to hear back, I got Lauren a new dog, a half Australian shepherd/American Eskimo that we named "Eevee" after Lauren's favorite Pokémon. Like all puppies, she was a cute distraction. Even our older dog, Teddy, seemed appreciative.

At the end of the month, Ophir called with an update. They'd hit an impasse.

"What does that mean?" I asked. "What should I do?"

"Stop going into the office," he said.

Lauren and I ran off to the beach. I didn't tell HR. I didn't file for out-of-office time. I just fled, like I was the runaway bride. Lauren and I went for long walks and talked through the situation. Deep down I knew how this was going to play out. I was going to leave Epic. While that wasn't certain, Lauren gave me all the confidence and support to take whatever path was going to make me feel good. We were Marcus and Anya on the beach, only our world was not destroyed, it was just beginning, and we were certain we'd have our tomorrow. But damnit, I wanted to know what that tomorrow would be like.

For three days I stayed off email. Finally, Tim called and asked if we could go for a walk. I told him I was at the beach.

"I know," he said. "I drove down to see you."

"He actually drove all the way down here?" Lauren said, surprised and impressed. "He must really care."

"I think he does," I said, sounding hopeful.

It was October 2012, and we were having one of those lovely extended North Carolina summers, and it was a beautiful night. I gave Tim our address and showed him around our little beach condo, and then we took our shoes off and went for what would be our final walk and talk on the moonlit beach.

The two of us walked out into the warm, salty Indian summer

breeze of the Carolina shore. I had never thought of Tim, this lanky, childlike genius, as just my boss. He was a peer, a mentor, a friend, a fellow nerd, a father figure, a protector, and a guide. He was Zeus on my hero's journey. I loved him, and I had no doubt he shared similar feelings toward me. We had been through too much together for it to be any other way. And yet when we reached the wet sand near the water and stopped walking, I felt the chill of his Spock-like mannerisms.

"Unfortunately, the terms of your employment and what we've given you are set," he said. "There's not going to be a renegotiation. I need you to decide whether you want to be with us or not. We want you to stick around. I want you to stick around. But this whole not-coming-into-work thing looks bad. I need you to make a decision tomorrow."

"I understand," I said. "Let me sleep on it."

We shook hands and Tim sped away in his Corvette.

Back inside the condo, Lauren practically leapt across the room to give me a hug. "How did it go?" she asked.

"Apparently, Tim doesn't negotiate with terrorists." I looked down at the floor and then back up at her. "I think I'm done. I think it's time to pull the rip cord."

Tears were streaming down my face. I didn't know if was crying because I was happy, sad, or frightened. Maybe a little of all three.

Lauren held my face in her hands, looked at me with those beautiful giant blue eyes, and kissed my wet face.

"I'll support you in whatever you choose," she said.

"I'm going to send in my resignation in the morning," I said. "And then . . ."

I didn't know.

WHAT IF . . . ?

At Tim's request, I gave a goodbye speech at the next Friday meeting. Standing in the main lobby, with the giant slide and rock-climbing wall and twenty-foot statue of *Unreal*'s hulking fighter Malcolm as a backdrop, I thanked everyone at Epic for their hard work, friendship, trust, inspiration, and laughter.

I tried to hold back the emotion, and then I couldn't—and didn't care. My voice cracked as I called out Mark for being a good roommate in the hotel rooms we shared in the early days, and as I expressed my gratitude to Tim for opening the envelope I'd sent him containing *Dare to Dream*, and for welcoming me into the Epic family when it was only a few of us posting games on CompuServe and the thought of becoming a billion-dollar company would've sounded preposterous.

The scene was surreal, and for many, including myself, almost unbelievable considering the fixture I'd been at Epic.

"This has been my life since I was . . . hell, it's more accurate to say this has been my life," I said. "It's been great, too. More than I ever *dared to dream*." I paused briefly to control my emotions before adding, "I know Unreal Engine 4 is about to come online. Do me a favor and please, remaster the first *Unreal* in the new engine. So long and, as Douglas Adams wrote, thanks for all the fish. Hasta la vista, baby!"

And that was it. I hired a moving company to pick up all the toys and crap I'd accumulated in my office over twenty years. Then I had to call one of my officemates and ask him to delete some photos of Lauren that I'd forgotten to remove from my computer. They were flirty photos, PG-13 at worst. Then I was officially done and out the door.

Lauren and I bought a Tudor mansion outside the city. Despite its size, the house was cozy and warm, with lots of rooms, and a large backyard with a pool that was ideal for our two dogs. The place needed updating, but it had good bones and we had nothing but time to turn it into our dream house. After meeting with our contractor one day, I stood in the spacious entry thinking about the trauma I'd experienced in junior high, and suddenly I let loose a volley of loud, unrestrained, soul-quenching laughter. *Fuck you, kids on the school bus in middle school. Nintendo Boy won!*

Life was easy and laid-back. Lauren and I woke up around noon, grabbed coffee and breakfast, read the news, did our chores, rode our bikes to the nearby gym, and spent the rest of the afternoon reading. I pored through *The Fifth Wave, Ender's Game, Leviathan Wakes,* and other books. I remembered how much I loved carrying a stack of books home from the library. I had missed that. I made up for lost reading time. Dinner was usually at the local pub, where we had a pint or two, before going home and watching a movie.

I traded our green Lamborghini in for a pearl-white LP560 Spyder and ordered an orange Aventador. His-and-hers sports cars.

In December, Mike Capps announced his departure from Epic. The company man was no longer going to be at the company. The news would've shocked me a year earlier. But not now. Once a person has enough money to be comfortable for the rest of their life, it changes their perspective, as I knew firsthand. I still maintained a few ties to Epic. Every so often I had lunch with the designer who landed in charge of *Fortnite.* I had made my egress from Epic just after he was hired. He was brilliant, a little twitchy, and a great guy. One day I asked him what was up at the office.

"Work," he said.

"Where're you living now?" I asked.

"An apartment across from Epic," he said.

I knew the routine and recognized his tired stare into nowhere. I didn't go into it with him, but I was going through my own version of detox from work. I had stress-related nightmares of missing deadlines, blowing interviews, not coming up with ideas. I told Lauren that I never realized how stressful it all was when I was in the thick of it, but then I remembered all the Claritin-D and Red Bull I had guzzled to keep myself on the edge of brilliance, and all the booze I took in to come down at the end of the day. This really was detox, I supposed.

I visited Lee and his crew in their BitMonster Games studio and went out for a pint or two with them at the Raleigh Times. When I asked what it was like having their own studio, one of the guys said, "No bullshit." Another added, "We make whatever we want. No politics." They reminded me that I missed the banter with artists, designers, and programmers. I missed the road map, a slate of projects to develop. I missed seeing ideas come to life. I missed getting end-of-day build notes—coming in the next morning, seeing the new goodies the programmers had added, trying 'em out, giving them feedback. I even missed some of the pressure.

I knew that was hard to reconcile, but it boiled down to this: I was a creative person who wasn't creating.

I started a blog and ramped up my presence on social media. I ranted about the industry ("If you think EA is nickel-and-diming you, don't buy their games, it's that simple"), news and movies, TV shows and music. I even gave dating advice. But blogging wasn't a satisfying substitute for making something. I sounded like a crank. I put a leather-bound notebook on my nightstand to write down ideas, and before long I was waking up late at night or in the morning to jot down notes like "portable nuke cannon" and "an electricity zapper gun." Although they weren't connected to anything specific, by spring I was wondering if I had another game in me.

"Do you think I should get back into the biz?" I asked Lauren.

We were eating dinner.

"Are you missing it that much?" she asked.

"I don't know," I said. "I miss writing up a description of something and having an artist send me back exactly what was in my head."

I missed the glory days of *Unreal Tournament.* I missed the idea of a simple shooter with a few game modes. With *Gears,* I had wanted to make a game that could be taught in college classrooms, and we made that game. "It's Jay McInerney and Lorrie Moore territory," novelist Nathan Englander had told the *New Yorker* about *Gears.* But laid out end to end, *Gears* was complex, taxing, and expensive. It had consumed me for more than a decade, almost two. If I were going to dive back in, I thought, it would have to be with a simple arena shooter, like *UT.*

Not a lot of good new shooters had hit the market lately. Realistic war games like *Call of Duty* had taken over the space. Soon there would be an entire generation of younger gamers who didn't know about dodging, double jumping, low-gravity maps, instagib, and all of it. What if I could make a fun, small-arena-style shooter? What if I could find the right publisher to fund it? What if I started my own game studio here in Raleigh? What if I could attract talent from places like Seattle, San Francisco, and LA? What if I could poach a few folks from Epic to help? What if . . .

None of this happened overnight. By summer 2013, though, I took a baby step back toward the fire. I hired a freelance concept artist to work up a few images based on the concept I'd been mulling of a simple shooter set in a world where gravity reversed itself. "What if the Big One hits LA, wrecks everything, and the city gets rebuilt in a way that solves all of its problems—except for one, this issue with gravity. It's broken."

The idea came from a dream I'd had as a kid. I was playing in the front yard with my Transformers when suddenly they started floating in the air. Then I started floating. Gravity had reversed itself. I grabbed on to the lawn, trying not to get sucked up into the atmosphere and shot into space. But the grass wasn't strong enough. It gave way and . . . that's when I woke up.

When the artist finished, I tweeted the images out and the internet gobbled them up like a bag of Cool Ranch Doritos. Bloggers posted stories. My agent heard the buzz. *CliffyB is working on something.*

Ophir wanted to know what I was up to.

"I don't know if I was up to anything," I said. "Just noodling ideas. Throwing shit out there to see if anyone cares."

"Apparently they do," Ophir said. "What do you want to do?"

"Nothing," I said. "I'll wait for a sign that says otherwise."

Then a friend of mine from LA messaged me that he was in Charlotte, directing an episode of the Cinemax TV series *Banshee*, and invited me and Lauren to the set. "We're going to blow up a brickyard," he texted. "Huge explosion! You'll love it." Lauren and I booked Teddy and Eevee at doggie camp and zipped down to Charlotte in her white convertible Benz, top down, and checked into the Ritz. This life of ours was not hard. That night we had drinks with the cast, and the next night we showed up on the set for the fireworks.

It was August, and even at night it was still blistering hot and humid. But anticipating a huge, fiery explosion somehow made that immaterial. We stood in a dusty brickyard. The crew was poised and waiting for the money shot. The pyrotechnics specialist told everyone to hold, remain quiet immediately after the explosion because several of the actors had lines to say in reaction to it and they only had one chance to get everything right.

Moments before the explosion my phone buzzed. I pulled it out of my pocket and saw I had a text from Arjan Brussee, the guy with whom I'd made *Jazz Jackrabbit*. "Dude, what the fuck are you up to lately?!" he wrote. "I'm at EA and miserable. We should make another game together." I barely finished reading the last sentence before the ground shook and everything was engulfed by an enormous explosion. I'd never experienced anything like it or been as close to such a blast—and didn't know if I wanted to again. There was a blinding flash of light and heat, a deafening noise, and an invisible shock wave that shook every fucking thing from the ground up. I reached for Lauren.

"You okay, hon?" I whispered.

She looked like a wide-eyed kid who had just gotten off a roller coaster.

"Wow," she said, grinning.

Clearly, I wasn't as tough as my wife. I showed her the text from Arjan. She gave me one of those sideways looks that could've been interpreted in a dozen ways but seemed to be asking for a reaction from me.

"I think it's the sign I've been looking for," I said.

Ophir and I had each other on speed dial. We spoke often and fast and spun up various scenarios that would not only get me back in the game but also have me heading my own studio. We exchanged thoughts on prospective partners and publishers and what kind of deal we might be able to get. It was intoxicating stuff. Practically speaking, though, he said I'd need a killer right-hand person to be COO. I messaged that to Arjan.

"I'm not even considering leaving EA for your gig until you have a deal in place," he said. "I have a family. But let's keep chatting."

Ophir's nonstop calls were exhausting. He wanted me to give

him the okay to let people know I was getting back in the game, but I was hesitant to make that move without the support I'd need. My old partner would get me past that hump. I put Ophir in touch with Arjan. Thirty minutes later, Ophir called me back, excited.

"He's your guy!" he said. "He's your COO."

"Well then, get me a fucking deal so he can make a clean break," I said. "The dude has two kids to feed."

"I'll reach out to publishers," he said. "Let me see who nibbles."

I had no idea what, if any, reaction he was going to get. In the meantime, as Ophir called publishers, I worked up a formal pitch, building on the initial description I had given my concept artist. The game would be an arena shooter with unique weapons and various ways of modifying gravity, set in and around the American Southwest and West Coast, most likely this vision I had of a post-quake Los Angeles 2.0.

"It's a futuristic world with gangs, guns, and crazy gravity," I said to Ophir.

I wasn't thinking about the old *Gears 2* mantra, "bigger, better, more badass." I liked alliteration. It was an efficient way to snap an audience to attention and make an idea stick. Ophir asked a few questions, but he was sold and ready to try and sell it to others.

"I guess it's time for a bake sale," he said.

Lauren and I were still waiting for work on our house to be completed when Arjan called and said he had a handful of vacation days socked away and wanted to visit Raleigh. He hadn't been back for years. I invited him to stay with us at our condo downtown. He arrived the following week. When he walked in with that confident alpha programmer swagger of his, I felt a jolt of adrenaline. It was the same feeling I had when the first version of *Jazz* started coming together. All of a sudden I was thinking this crazy notion could really happen. We walked to a nearby Starbucks, and I pitched him the idea the whole way there.

"Calm the fuck down," he said as we sat down at a table. "Dude, I have to ship a new *Battlefield* game with EA before I can do shit."

"Okay. I understand."

"But don't get me wrong," he said. "I like Raleigh. It's affordable and sane. So go get a fucking publishing partner and then we can talk seriously."

Ophir filled up a calendar with meetings starting with all the big publishers on the West Coast, including Electronic Arts, Microsoft, and Take-Two. Up in the Bay Area, I had a terrible meeting with Zynga and their CEO, who cut me off mid-pitch and barked, "I want *World of Warcraft* for the iPad." He and his company went straight into the Life's Too Short file.

Beyond not letting one bad meeting deter me, I was surprised at how much I wanted someone to bite. After months of being so chill, I was suddenly feeling very competitive. At GDC, I had a secret meeting with Rod, who was shipping *BioShock Infinite* at 2K Games. We snuck out for a late lunch at a steakhouse, where I told him what was going on with me and he said, "I'd be interested in doing this thing with you. I can see it. But it would have to be you and me doing this. It has to be the Cliff and Rod thing. It can't just be the Cliff thing."

I looked down at the table. "I'm sorry, man," I said. "This has to be my gig."

In hindsight, you don't have to be a genius to see that I was blinded by my overinflated ego and should have at the very least continued the conversation. I look back on that as a mistake, the first of many. Rod and I had not only worked well together but we were also integral to each other's success with *Gears*. Our track record was beyond dispute and longer running and at a level that was much bigger than the work I'd done with Arjan. It would have been interesting to see what we might have accomplished. As it was, we remained friends.

I snapped up an invitation to meet with Ubisoft in Paris. They flew Lauren and me business class, put us up in a hotel near the Louvre, and arranged for a five-star dinner at La Tour d'Argent. The next day I met with Yves Guillemot, the CEO of Ubisoft. After I did my shtick, he said in his thick French accent, "Why do you want to work with us?" I tapped my notebook.

"I miss being creative," I said. "*Gears* was once the fastest-selling new IP in gaming history. Then your company shattered that record months later with *Assassin's Creed.*"

He chuckled.

"I think it would be fun to break new records together," I said.

"Let my people see what your agent wants," he said. "We'll see."

I left feeling we had made a connection. Unfortunately, the terms were unrealistic. I wasn't too disappointed. I had been warned that Ubisoft was stingy as hell and that unless you were French there would always be a limit to what they would do. Back home, at Ophir's urging, I flew to San Francisco for the annual Nite to Unite charity auction benefiting the ESA Foundation, which offered college scholarships to promising video game developers. Arjan, who lived in the Bay Area, joined me. Visibility was a part of creating buzz. As I worked the party, I ran into Min Kim, the U.S. president of powerhouse Korean gaming publisher Nexon. Min was a good guy—a long-haired eighties-pop-culture junkie who grew up playing NES and left Wall Street for gaming after 9/11. We shook hands.

"I'm in serious talks with Ophir," he said. "Nexon wants to make a Western game."

"You don't get more Western than me, dude," I said.

Then the lights flashed off and on and the auction started. Lauren wanted a metal prop sword from a recent *Legend of Zelda* commercial. Nintendo had donated it, and I decided I would go up to ten thousand dollars to please my wife. A bidding war erupted between me and a business guy from a gaming expo. As the dollar amount spiraled upward, Ophir's grin got bigger and brighter. He loved that nearly every important executive in the gaming industry was watching me hold up my bidding card. I won the sword for Lauren. I got a kiss from her and very nearly the same from my agent.

"Nexon is hot to trot, dude," he said. "I think they're going to be the ideal partner for you. They want to work with you so bad you don't even need to pitch them."

I was speechless. It was no longer what-if. I was going to return to the industry with my own gaming studio.

BOSS KEY

God bless Tim. It was good to be rich.

In the winter of 2013, Lauren and I moved into our new home. We had everything we'd ever wanted and dreamed of: a craft room for Lauren, an office for me, a gaming room upstairs, a speaker system through which we piped songs like Neighbourhood's "Sweater Weather" as we danced around the large kitchen, and a movie theater that was our sanctuary at night. On our first night there, I cranked the heater in the backyard pool and went for a dip.

I was an overgrown kid, and I didn't care who knew. Or how cold it was outside. I had to try the slide. It was fun and fast—and full of tiny chunks of gunite that had been haphazardly sprayed and not cleaned up when the pool was redone. As a result, I emerged from the water dripping blood down my back.

I hoped it wasn't an indication of rough waters ahead. Negotiations with Nexon stretched out for months before the Korean publisher and I agreed to terms. There was the standard milestone-based advance against future royalties to fund the studio. They also acquired a minority stake in the studio for an additional sum. I kept 52 percent and my title as owner, CEO, and chief creative officer. I also kept ownership of any IP we developed.

By the time we signed our deal, Epic had sold the *Gears of War* franchise to Microsoft for an undisclosed amount. (They also hired Rod Fergusson to oversee remastering of the games and new development.) It didn't come cheap; I knew that much. *Gears* had sold twenty-two million units and grossed more than $1 billion in the U.S. I didn't get an extra penny from the deal, even though *Gears* was my baby. If I created a universe in the future, I wanted to own it.

Microsoft had already bought the rights to *Halo*, and by the end of 2014 they would also acquire *Minecraft*. As Epic and other companies turned away from exclusives with them, Microsoft gobbled up franchises that would keep selling their consoles. For me, it looked like an auspicious time to be creating content.

Arjan nearly ran out of patience before I closed the Nexon deal. He hated politics and corporate life. If Electronic Arts hadn't been overflowing with both, he might not have stuck it out with me. I can't say I loved spending all day on conference calls with my lawyer and Ophir discussing terms. Relief for me came at night when I opened my PC and banged out ideas for the new game—characters, weapons, environments, and backstory that explained why gravity was acting so funky in this world. (After the Big One, the moon had exploded!)

When all was finally done, I gave Arjan a comfy salary and nice chunk of the company, while keeping the 52 percent controlling stake for myself, something I'd learned from Tim. Arjan gave his notice and emailed me: "Let's make sure this studio is a no-bullshit zone." I responded, "Absolutely." We were a go.

News of my return to making games after nearly two years away broke on July 4, 2014. The internet exploded. "Nexon Acquires Minority Stake in *Gears of War* Designer's New Company," headlined CNET. "The Asian Gaming Company Signs Some American Star Power," crowed Vox. Very little was left unsaid. I was making a free-to-play shooter. It was code-named *BlueStreak*. My new studio was called Boss Key. I was working with Arjan Brussee. I wasn't worried that this was my first free-to-play game after years of triple-A design.

I had already hired an assistant and an experienced producer to get things going. Then, as soon as the deal was announced, I heard from two Epic employees who were ready to bail—character artist Chris Wells and JayHawk, the guy who had done nearly all the concept art for the *Gears* franchise.

"Arjan, JayHawk's amazing, easy to work with, super chill, and he'd be an amazing score," I said, excited by his level of talent and experience. "And Chris is great."

"Better get them on board, then," Arjan said.

We found a historic space in the heart of downtown Raleigh for the Boss Key offices. It was on the second floor of a three-story building. The wood floors were creaky, and the walls were thin, but the vibe was cool, and I liked that we were going to be a high-tech company in a low-tech environment. We got it wired for high-end computers so we weren't constantly popping breakers. We also settled on a Boss Key logo—military-style wings pointing upward, a key-like shape running down the middle that formed the *K* in "key" and a keyhole in the *O* in "boss." Lauren made me a T-shirt with the logo on the front.

The actual first day of work came late that summer. I woke up before noon for the first time in a year and got a warm send-off from Lauren. The parking deck we'd reserved for Boss Key turned out not to be Lamborghini friendly. Cars sped out of the parking lot too fast, and trucks obscured the view around corners. The stairwell and elevator also smelled like piss. All were minor inconveniences and quickly forgotten as I walked into our new office with my backpack, feeling nervous, like it was the first day of school. My favorite part? The producer we'd hired was already at his desk. "We have a lot of résumés to sort through," he said by way of greeting me. God, I loved ambition.

That week we added chairs, desks, insurance, bank accounts, and high-end tower PCs. JayHawk came into the office. I typed up descriptions. I jokingly asked Arjan what engine we were going to use. He didn't see the humor. "You know, Unreal," he said. I laughed. "Of course." The final touch was a doormat with a quote printed on it from an Apple computer commercial: "Here's to the crazy ones, the misfits, the rebels, the troublemakers . . ." Every day we would walk into the office and be reminded that's who we were.

Arjan set up his desk across from mine. We sorted through résumés, endlessly it seemed. I saw one from art director Tramell Isaac, who I knew as T-Ray from having tried to hire him years earlier at Epic. One of the few Black guys in the industry at that time, he had worked at Interplay and Sony. I sent him the design documents and notes I had created—boiling oceans in a futuristic Santa Monica; a shattered moon; floating architecture; gangs and factions of escaped prisoners; futuristic law enforcement—and asked him to put together a mood board, a sequence of art that illustrated the new game's overall look and feel.

A few days later, T-Ray sent us his work. I thought he'd nailed it, and after JayHawk said he could work with that art, we signed our art director. By fall, we had the core team, including level designers, a lead programmer, and an ace animator. As a small shop, we had to work efficiently. We prototyped almost every idea the way we'd done in the early days of *Gears*. It made no sense to build something if we weren't going to use it in the game.

Work on *BlueStreak* got into a flow. I cracked open the Unreal Editor for the first time in a couple years and, after admiring Tim's devotion to its continual improvement—constantly making it bigger, better, and more badass—I cobbled together a map I called "Gravity Gym." I asked our coders to construct it in sections as opposed to one seamless environment, so that I could play around with manipulating the gravity in different areas. Increased gravity spots, decreased spots, and areas with none at all. I had a rocket launcher in the works, and the coders were able to modify its arc depending on which gravity zone it was fired in.

This was the fun part, and I wondered what else we could invent. A gravity-assisted slingshot, like *Apollo 13* going around the dark side of the moon? What about the ability to run on the walls or ceiling? How would the player move in zero gravity? How would their weapon work without gravity? Could the player propel themself faster through that environment by shooting backward, even?

I did an interview at the time with the gaming site Venture-Beat that got me thinking about the way my approach to design had changed over the years. In the beginning, starting with *Dare to Dream* and *Jazz Jackrabbit*, I was about trying anything and everything, whatever worked. During the *Unreal* days, it was all about the weapons and trying to be different and more outrageous than everyone else. That's when I started saying, "We need to zig when others zag." *Gears* was all about gameplay and being cinematic. And now with *BlueStreak*, as I told VB, it was "what kind of unique, YouTube game-winning moments can this yield?"

Not that the bottom line wasn't always the feeling I got in my gut that something was cool and fun. But I was noticing the coders offered lukewarm, perfunctory responses to my ideas—"Yeah, that could be cool"—and when finished with their work, they dove straight into the multiplayer, real-time strategy hit *League of Legends*, a genre I never liked and whose popularity I never understood. But that didn't necessarily negate our game. We had a few prototype levels of *BlueStreak*, in which we were able to jump around and play both free-for-all and team deathmatch, with everyone flying all over the place, and goddamnit if even the most jaded and disinterested of our hipster coders didn't hoot and holler as they played.

It was fun. Gravity surfing became a thing—jump into a particular zone and bob up and down while cruising through it, like riding giant waves. Rockets curved. There were chasms you could cross to get a better weapon, but you had to clear the jump, otherwise the inverted gravity would cause you to fall upward to your death. But I worried the game seemed thin, like we had built a clever gimmick and nothing more. I worried it might be a one-trick and lack the depth to keep players coming back.

Our lead coder shared my concern, and he came into my office one day to tell me the guys had been playing a ton of *League of Legends*, as if this was news.

"I know," I said, my jaw tightening. "I'm not really into it."

"Why?"

"I don't know," I said. "I've enjoyed *Command & Conquer* games. But for some reason, *League* doesn't grab me. Maybe it's the anime art style. Maybe it's that the community feels kind of toxic to me. Like if I don't select the right hero, the people online will just yell at me. I never got *World of Warcraft* either."

He scratched his chin while digesting my response. Then he shook it off.

"I think we need abilities," he said.

Abilities were powers that the player earned. But they were usually connected to a timer. When the timer was up, you could activate your powers, and then you had to build them up again. It required a balancing act of thought, finesse, and strategy, and contributed greatly to the success of *League* and games like it.

His suggestion caused me to cringe inside. I knew he was right. But we needed more than abilities to keep people playing *Blue-Streak* over other games. I wanted to build a little shooter. I could feel the pull away from that simple concept toward a hero shooter with MOBA (multiplayer online battle arena) elements, like *League*. I could feel the pain of compromise and change, and I didn't like it.

The moment you chase trends is the moment you start to lose your originality, the things that make you different from everyone else.

In August 2014, the video game world was rocked by an ugly incident. A game developer named Zoe Quinn had dated a guy named Eron Gjoni, who wrote a long, rambling diatribe against her after they split. In it, he alleged that she had slept with writer Nathan Greyson in exchange for a favorable review about her game *Depression Quest* on the website Kotaku. Eron later claimed that he misspoke. However, it was too late. Angry internet gamer trolls attacked Zoe, and the Salem-style stake burning spread to other women in the industry.

"Gamergate," as the situation was called, morphed into a culture war, with right-wingers claiming "social justice warriors" were trying to take away their large-breasted, scantily clad female characters and inject more diversity where they didn't feel it was wanted or necessary. I went public with my opinion on Twitter. "No one is trying to take your games from you," I tweeted. "Progress and representation are good things, dammit!" To me, assholes from the bowels of the internet were using this as an opportunity to harass and dox people they didn't like and ruin their lives. High school didn't end. It got meaner.

Video games were supposed to be for the misfits. They were the haven for the weirdos who did not want to play sports. They were the last refuge from the bullies of the outside world. But now the weirdos and nerds who'd been bullied had become the bullies. Why was I getting back into the business when I could lounge by my pool or watch movies in my home theater or escape to the beach with my wife?

We had a small, nimble, and vocal team. Personalities didn't always mesh. Arjan complained about one coder's incessant negativity. We had a designer who constantly battled coders for ownership of ideas. I heard them but I didn't want to deal with them. Management wasn't among my strengths. I was more comfortable in the role of head designer than the boss, which was a problem given that Boss Key was my company, and my job was to manage it.

On the plus side, I shared opinions easily. I didn't like the way MOBA strategy games were always described as heroes battling forces of evil when they really didn't battle evil; in reality, everyone attacked each other for no reason until somebody won. I wanted our game to have more structure. In this world where gravity had gone haywire, I wanted two sides—the law and the law breakers. It would make our game easily understandable. There were good guys, bad guys, and weirdness.

With the game taking shape, we needed a name for it. This was always a challenge. It seemed nearly every word or combination of them in the English language had already been trademarked. I tried to come up with something stemming from the fact we were breaking the law of gravity. Since we were a free-to-play game, I wrote down the name *Freebreakers*. I didn't realize it at the time, but the people in the office next to ours were shooting a video and playing Taylor Swift's "Shake It Off" throughout the day, and I kept hearing the line, "Heartbreakers gonna break, break, break" as "Breakers gonna break, break, break."

I went into T-Ray's office. "Hey, how about *Freebreakers*?"

He didn't like it. "Sounds like a cheap iPhone game," he said.

Then he put down his drawing pen and rubbed his face in thought. "What about *LawBreakers*?"

I repeated it to myself. I thought about the game. Good guys and bad guys. The law and the law breakers. Character models with variants: two abilities, two weapons with alternate fire on each, unique movements, and so on, with medium-sized teams.

"Shit, that works," I said.

I told Arjan. "Might work," he said, without looking up from his computer screen. "Hit up legal, dude."

T-Ray and his stable of artists put together an environmental flyby, a sample map that included a broken Grand Canyon with gravity anomalies that had been sold to the Japanese Yakuza after the events leading the moon to explode, what we called "the Shattering." Traditional temple-style architecture and beautiful cherry blossoms contrasted with high-tech bits and giant rocks floating in the distance. We brought several heroes online so we could test player size, environment scale, speed, and jump heights.

It looked solid enough that Nexon asked us to host a panel at the gamer convention Penny Arcade Expo in March 2015 and give the fans a taste of the work in progress. We said okay, and then went to the bar after work and drank.

I encouraged bonding among the team by taking anyone who wanted to go out for a drink after work to Raleigh Times. Because people wanted to get home early on Fridays, we went on Thursdays, and called it Thirstdays. At five thirty, someone grabbed a megaphone I bought for the studio and shouted, "It's Thirstday! Let's go, folks!"

Whatever differences the team had with each other seemed to fade. We put together a playtest lab in the back of the room—ten high-end PCs—five on one side, five on the other—and set aside time for all the developers to play the work they had done up to this time. "Make them eat their own dog food," Arjan said, using a rough-sounding phrase that was common among developers. Best-case scenario: the game looks cool, and everyone is excited. Worst-case scenario: the devs feel shame and rush back to their desk to fix whatever issues came up in order to feel vindicated the next day.

It was an effective strategy. I bought lab coats and clipboards as a gag for our two QA guys who would watch over the sessions as if they were doing real science. At the end of the day, everyone's reviews were positive. It didn't mean we were without problems. But we didn't want dog food. We needed steak, and I just didn't know if we had sirloin yet.

One Thirstday night in November 2014, a bunch of us went for our usual pint at Raleigh Times. We sat upstairs, lengthwise, half of us against the wall on a repurposed church pew, the other half on creaky chairs. Blizzard Games, the maker of *Diablo* and *World of Warcraft*, had been rumored to have been working on a supersecret project for some time (who wasn't?), and this was the day their trailer dropped. The game was called *Overwatch*. One of our artists had called it up on his phone. He stared at it slack-jawed. "We are soooooo fucked," he said as it finished.

All of us pulled out our phones and watched the trailer for ourselves. *Overwatch* was a first-person shooter game featuring a rogue's gallery of anime-looking heroes with two abilities apiece, all backed by Blizzard's famously talented cinematic department. I looked across the table and I said to everyone, "Relax, guys. Now we know what *not* to do. Let's keep an eye on their characters, abilities, and art style, and make sure we don't copy them. We can have our own spin on all these things."

I wasn't BS-ing. That strategy had worked for *Unreal* and *Quake*, and there had been room for both games in the market. I turned to T-Ray. "Let's keep going down our path. This anime style looks like it is for horny fourteen-year-old boys. Let's make *LawBreakers* the more realistic, gritty, sci-fi hero shooter!"

"We'll stay in our lane, dude," he said, stroking his chin.

Zigging when everyone else zagged had paid off for me in the past, and I prayed that it would work again. Driving home that cold November night, though, I couldn't stop thinking about how *Overwatch* looked incredibly polished and gorgeous, and I was worried sick that I would let down my troops and their families.

When I got home, Lauren was in the kitchen, making tacos for dinner.

"I assume you saw Blizzard's new game," she said. "It looks amazing! Did you see the beautiful blond hero named Mercy? And that cute British girl, Tracer?"

As a lifelong fan of all things Blizzard, Lauren was super excited. I wanted to share her enthusiasm, but I couldn't—and didn't. It made me even more agitated and anxious.

"I get that you're excited, hon, but my entire team is terrified right now," I said. "Blizzard and *Overwatch* is our number one competition. We need to find a way to carve out our own chunk of this hero-shooter market. It's going to get really crowded really soon."

OUT IN THE WILD

Shortly after launching Boss Key, I hired a young guy named Rohan Rivas to head up community engagement. Sharp, affable, and highly skilled in this area, he spent January and February 2015 planning our PAX East presentation. He crafted a slick Power-Point followed by a video capture of our fly-through, including concept art of environments and characters. We weren't quite ready to show actual gameplay; instead, Rohan's presentation highlighted the track record and gaming pedigrees of the key people involved.

I was disappointed when legal informed me they hadn't cleared the name *LawBreakers* yet, but I could gloss over that and emphasize the vision—gangs, guns, and gravity.

In 2015, GDC was in San Francisco from March 2 to 6, and PAX was March 6–8 in Boston. We attended both conferences, which was wearying, but we put on our big-boy pants and rallied for our moment in the spotlight. For me, going back to Boston felt poetic. I was previewing the work from my new studio only thirty minutes from my childhood home. As the plane made its approach, I looked out the window and saw the city was encased by a recent record-setting snowfall. Suddenly, my feet felt cold, like they used to during the winter when I had my paper route. The kid was back in town, but thank goodness only for a few days.

I reviewed the presentation and tried to think of every question I would be asked at our panel. The work we were bringing gave me confidence. While this kind of stuff can't be rushed, we had, by this time, some very cool assets to show: the Grand Canyon map had evolved around a harder, more competitive idea of seizing a power-enhancing battery; and we had modeled several new heroes, including a futuristic cop carrying an assault rifle with dual abilities and a female fighter with a built-in jet pack and a powerful Gatling gun that could launch a cluster of mini grenades while dive-bombing to the ground. Her name was Maverick, after Tom Cruise in the movie *Top Gun*. She was my middle finger response to Gamergate.

Besides the usual worries about the panel—would people like the game, would the presentation work—I had a new concern, one I'd never had to deal with in the past: Would anyone show up? I'd been out of the business for two-plus years. Would it matter that I was coming back with my own thing? Would they care?

I had always urged people to make their work personal. This preview of *LawBreakers* couldn't have been more personal to me. It wasn't just a game I'd designed. It was my friggin' company. What were people going to think? Were they hoping I'd succeed? Or did they want a car wreck? I remembered the way I had rooted against Romero when he started Ion Storm, and cheered the failure of his game *Daikatana*. It's never pleasant to meet the worst of yourself, even years later. What a jerk I was.

Our panel was in an upstairs conference room at four p.m. Rohan wanted me there a half hour early. At three thirty, we found ourselves in the back half of the Boston Convention Center, and I realized that we had to hoof it back if we were going to be on time. I'd never missed my call time, dammit, and I sure as shit was not going to miss this one. When we got there, I saw a line of people waiting to get in. Several people recognized me and shouted, "CliffyB!" I relaxed, smiled, and high-fived my way to the front, where I spotted a young woman dressed in homemade cosplay. I didn't recognize the character or the game.

"Has to be *League of Legends*," I said to Rohan.

"It is," he said.

"Cool," I said. "If she loves *League* and is interested enough to be here and see what we're doing, then we have a chance."

More than a chance, it seemed. The room was packed, and the panel was flawless. Lauren sat front and center and smiled throughout the presentation. At the end, people could see I was emotional. "Thank you so much," I said. "When you try something as crazy as this, you don't know if people will care, or even show up, and you all did, and we all truly appreciate it from the bottom of our hearts." That night, we celebrated at Regina Pizza, my childhood favorite, in the North End. I allowed myself a peek at the reaction online. "Great visuals," one person wrote. "Now don't fuck up the gameplay."

Back in Raleigh, the memory I had of rooting against Romero continued to bother me. Why had I been such a self-centered asshat? What happened to that line about a rising tide lifting all boats? My life was going so well, personally and professionally; only now, because of the way my brain seemed to drift toward any and all negative and irrational possibilities, I was fraught with worry that karma was going to wrap itself around my neck like a returning boomerang.

There were signs. Arjan and I started to see cliques beginning to form within the studio, and it worried us. Each department started to go to lunch together. The programmers ate with one another, as did the animators, the artists, etc. I tried to stop that by taking a mix of different people to lunch every week. At first it was fun, and then it was exhausting. One day Arjan and one of his main coders cornered me in my office with disappointing news. We weren't going to be able to do asymmetrical gameplay—creating character models with variants, two abilities, two weapons with alternate fire on each, unique movements, and so on.

"Dude, there's no way," Arjan said. "We can't handle that much work."

"We don't have the time or budget for it," his coder added. "Look how long it took to make four heroes!"

This was why I hated the MOBA strategy games. We were all going to be heroes somehow fighting evil. Except there wasn't any evil. It would be a salad of heroes pummeling one another. Even with my own studio I was having one of those dreaded conversations with developers shooting down my ideas. *It's been done . . . Just to play devil's advocate . . . Let's save that for down the line . . . I've never seen that done before . . . It's just too much work . . .* How was this happening again? Before I had an attack of PTSD, I got up and took a few steps around the office.

"Can we just make it cosmetic, then? Law versus Breakers, both play the exact same way, but they are visually different characters that play the same?"

"Fine," Arjan said. "But this is going to increase our art budget. T-Ray is going to have to outsource a ton."

I knew the look of frustration I saw on Arjan's face. He was biting his tongue. I swear I saw more of his hair turn gray right in front of my eyes.

Rohan started up a weekly live online stream to give eager fans a glimpse behind the curtain. Engage early, engage often, he said on a regular basis. In an empty area he called "the Boss Room," he set up a little soundstage with a desk, mics, and a backdrop filled with concept art. Some of the art had already been released online, but a lot of it had not, and we wanted those who tuned in to try to figure out what was going on behind us even though it was nearly impossible to see.

Rohan and I hosted, and we brought in someone from one of the teams to talk about their work. We never got *that* many people tuned in concurrently, maybe a dozen or so, but we had enough to keep the chat lively, and we always ended each session with a Q&A. Impressed, our rep at Nexon asked us to present a story trailer at PAX Prime, the West Coast version of the conference in Boston. This one was in Seattle. In addition to the story trailer, we would debut an actual gameplay video and a brief narrative video explaining how the Earth got so fucked up in the first place.

"You can't just dump a sci-fi world on players and expect them to care if they don't understand the context of it!" Nexon's rep said.

As we broke our backs getting all this together, Nexon's marketing department sent word that all the floor space at PAX had been booked, so our event would have to take place off-site. Arjan and I both had the same thought: red flag. *Danger, Will Robinson!* That said, in mid-August, we saw a final cut of our story announce trailer, which included our four heroes and rocket jumping, swinging with laser grappling hooks, and the ability to propel your body through low-gravity situations by shooting behind yourself, and we were ecstatic. Emotions rocketed up and down and across the board like errant pinballs. This was good. "Seeing something I made in the real world put on film never, ever gets old!" said JayHawk.

Then we were in September. The story trailer hit online right before PAX, and people dug it, though they weren't quite sure what to make of it. "We're post-postapocalyptic," I explained. "Humanity has rebuilt, and now violent roving gangs threaten to upend all of that." The gameplay trailer dropped a couple of days later and the reception wasn't as glowing, which caused us concern. Rohan got to Seattle ahead of us and warned of numerous fires: the computers were late, the venue had no mood lighting, and they couldn't figure out how to regulate the temperature in a room with ten high-end gaming rigs. Arjan was pissed at Nexon. "Are they going to be able to market this game?" he snapped.

By the time Arjan, Lauren, and I arrived in Seattle, our setup was in fine form, and we relaxed. Our room—more like an area—had two levels. On the main floor was a large HD monitor for showing gamers and journalists how to play the game, and a space arranged for interviews. Upstairs, we had ten PCs—five on each side—just like our playtest lab, where people could test-drive *LawBreakers*. Despite the inconvenience of fans having to ferry in vans from the convention center to our nearby venue, our debut was a smash. By three p.m. every day, we had to turn people away because we'd hit capacity.

Between interviews, I surveyed the gameplay upstairs and noticed a large skill gap between players. I could tell who hadn't played a lot of first-person shooters or only played them on consoles, because they struggled against the more experienced FPS players. "We've gotta make sure our player-to-player matchmaking is great or these sharks are going to destroy everyone," I told Arjan. He gave that knowing nod he always gave, because when it came to the guts of the game, he was always four steps ahead of me.

We announced *LawBreakers* would be ready in summer or fall of 2016. Everyone who attended got a T-shirt that said "BREAK FREE" and a card that guaranteed early access to an upcoming alpha test of the game. Fans who had played were excited. "Fucking bananas," one dude said. "Soiled myself," cooed another. "It was insane."

Shortly after PAX, I had dinner with Jay Wilbur from the early days at Epic. We sat outside at a local Lebanese spot. The crispness of fall was in the night air. "What you really should have done is spent some of that Tencent money on a small team of your own to do a prototype, which would have given you more leverage with publishers," he said.

I put down my chicken kebab and thought about it. "You're not wrong. However, that's a risk I wasn't willing to take. I didn't even know if anyone would sign up."

"You would have been fine," he replied.

Too late now. All that winter we marched toward the VIP alpha test. Interested players were sent a code to enter the online game store Steam, download the game, and play it for a weekend. In exchange, they gave us feedback. I asked our PR and marketing folks to target campaigns to MMA and pro sports fans, as well as the typical and traditional gaming outlets, and also to sponsor streams on Twitch, the live-streaming, interactive gaming platform that had sucked everything to do with gaming into its force field, like a black hole. Twitch streams. If your game wasn't among the top ten streams on Twitch, you were dead in the water.

Twitch produced its own stars, like Ninja and Lyrik. They were kids who made millions playing games and yammering about them on the platform. I told our PR team that we had to try to get those influencers on board. They responded, "Let's shoot for mid-tier influencers and hope it trickles up." I scratched my head. Did anything trickle up?

Well, maybe in an anti-gravity game . . .

At the same time, we were working to put the game on consoles as well. Without the resources to do both Xbox One and PlayStation 4, we had to make a choice. Arjan pushed for the PS4. It had a far larger install base, and Arjan still knew plenty of folks at Sony, where he had worked for years prior to his stint at EA. I reluctantly agreed that the PS4 would be fine; hedging our bets on the larger platform seemed to make sense.

When news of the game coming to PS4 broke, along with the fact that we weren't doing an Xbox port, the fans erupted in anger.

They were getting a new shooter from the *Gears* guy, but they saw it as a betrayal. I offered an olive branch on social. "If the game does well, we'll take a look at putting it on Xbox!" It failed to alleviate the negative sentiment. As I knew, hell hath no fury like a die-hard gamer scorned.

Work intensified. Anytime a bug caused the game to chug, I heard Arjan yell either from his desk or the playtest lab. The man had a temper that would flare up when easily remedied issues weren't resolved, and he could be very intense and intimidating. However, he had a gift for rallying the team, especially the programmers, because he still programmed himself, which garnered a ton of respect from them. No matter how intense Arjan could get, everyone was down for grabbing a beer with the guy after work.

One crucial problem we weren't able to solve was the free-to-play conundrum. Nearly every free-to-play, no matter how successful, like *League of Legends*, always felt to us like a shell game to the consumers. They knew it wasn't really free; down the line they'd have to pay. *League*'s success showed they didn't mind, but we couldn't find a way to properly put *LawBreakers* out for free. Selling character outfits felt like nickel-and-diming fans, and we didn't have enough heroes to monetize access to them.

"Dude, why don't we just charge a fee for the game?" Arjan said.

"Do you think Nexon would go for that?" I asked.

"What's the worst that could happen?" He laughed.

One of our developers, eavesdropping from nearby, chimed in. "I'd be shocked if they did."

"Don't you guys think players are getting tired of these sixty-dollar multiplayer games?" I countered. "Why not go in at a lower price with some sort of light microtransactions?!"

"Couldn't hurt to ask," Arjan said.

To my surprise, Nexon green-lit the change in strategy. When I announced that tidbit to the team in a company meeting, everyone was aflutter with the news and obsessed with what exactly people would be willing to pay for a fun multiplayer shooter like *LawBreakers.* I had no idea. None of us did. We would find out.

That spring the pre-alpha was shaping up well. Balancing work on the full game while also shaving off just enough to test in the wild was and always will be tricky, and with the PlayStation port also under construction, it was like we had three separate projects in the works. Days flew by as if we were stuck on fast-forward, and suddenly it was June 2016, and we were heading to LA for E3. *PC Gamer* had started sponsoring an annual PC Gaming Show, usually hosted off-site in an old theater in the outskirts of downtown Los Angeles, and we decided that was ideal for our closed test.

We had multiple combat arenas to show off, including my re-imagining Santa Monica after it was destroyed and rebuilt. We also cobbled together a solid montage of gameplay action for me to show journalists and fans. Backstage during rehearsal, I ran into Rod Fergusson, who was there to talk about the recently announced *Gears of War 4.* I gave him a hug and asked how things were going.

"Crazy," he said. "We're hiring left and right!"

"What I saw looks promising. Are you ever going to give the Locust the wings that I wanted?"

He offered a coy smile. "Some things you've gotta build up to."

Nexon rented us a room on the second story of the LA Convention Center instead of the conference center floor where people roamed and gathered. Arjan fumed. "What the fuck, dude? We're going through this shit again?" It worked out fine. The room was full when I gave my spiel about the game and boasted about the Twitch streamers who were on board to play in an upcoming matchup. I finished with the trailer. Reaction gave me reason to believe. Everyone who played *LawBreakers* at the PC Gaming Show loved it, and we even scored two award nominations, one for Best Action Game and the other for Best Multiplayer Game.

A few days later, our alpha test went live on Stream. I was already back in Raleigh. I will never forget the date, June 18. The game was out in the wild and being able to play it with random gamers felt amazing. We'd given out thousands of online codes as opposed to millions because online launches are often fraught with complications. Making sure the servers stay up, keeping players in the matches, keeping an eye out for cheaters; it's a dark art and one that our guy, who I called Billy the Wizard, did a fantastic job managing. No matter the season, he always wore flip-flops, and I suspected they were the source of his power.

I'd also reminded our Boss Key employees to take it easy on the public.

"You've been playing this game for a year," I said. "They're new. If they get slaughtered, they won't want to come back."

Midway through the test, we took a stab at making the alpha a living product by unlocking the Santa Monica map followed by our territory control mode called Turf War. Positive impressions on You-Tube gave me hope. However, I noticed many struggled with the way our abilities and weapons deviated from the standard stuff they knew in the rapidly growing hero-shooter genre. For instance, using the shift button for anything other than "run" threw them off. Our powerful melee swords frustrated those who wanted a gunfight. And I didn't see a lot of alternate fire modes deployed from our guns. Newbies flailed, and one player, before quitting, left a message in the chat: "Dis game trash!"

I was ready to use one of the melee swords on myself when Mark Rein called to congratulate me. He said he'd played the game but was terrible at it. I encouraged him to stick with it.

"It's a skill-based shooter," I said. "It takes practice."

"Cliffy, I feel like you out-*UT*'d *Unreal Tournament*," he said.

Even if he was blowing smoke up my butt, I suspected Mark wanted me to have success not only because of our shared history but also because it was yet another good-looking game to further Epic's agenda of selling that good ol' evergreen Unreal Engine. But hey, I was happy and eager for any and all support. What Mark didn't know, and I didn't share, were the comments coming back to us from the test. I tried to be philosophic and tell myself it was part of the journey: belief one day, despair another, and then, hopefully, ultimately success.

I had my doubts.

LEVEL

8

DON'T PANIC

On the surface, it didn't look good that our initial summer deadline for shipping *LawBreakers* came and went while I was with Lauren in San Diego, co-hosting a party at Comic-Con. We missed our Christmas deadline, too. It wasn't my fault. It wasn't Arjan's or anyone else's fault. The work was just hard and took time. The important thing, as I told everyone, was not to panic. I repeated it to myself, too. *Don't panic.*

And we didn't. I enjoyed every playtest, and often played *Law-Breakers* twice a day. I frequently emerged from these melees with my employees as the victor, not because they let me win, but because, at forty-one years old, I was still damn good. You couldn't easily frag CliffyB! My concerns about having heroes and MOBA elements also faded. Nexon's CEO, Owen Mahoney, called me one day to say the game had finally clicked for him.

"I didn't get it until I played the map 'Vertigo,'" he said. "I saw the chaos of verticality that the game enabled—"

"The gravity orbs are cool, aren't they?" I said.

"It works," he said.

Overwatch continued to explode in popularity. A similar game called *Paladins* was getting decent traction, yet Randy Pitchford and Gearbox's game *Battleborn* appeared to be limping along, which worried the shit out of me. Randy and his team had a miss with a game based on the *Alien* franchise, but they seldom created products that flopped. Lauren and I played a lot of *Overwatch*. I enjoyed playing as the high-flying, rocket-slinging Pharah, and Lauren liked the winged healer Mercy.

The game grew on me, but I noticed things that bothered me, that only someone who was steeped in years of shooters would see. The game felt floaty; the characters didn't seem to have much weight to them. The collision boxes on some of the projectiles felt overly generous; for example, the archer Hanzo could easily pick people off at a distance with his bow and arrow. When I took a closer look, I saw the tip of his arrow at impact appeared to be the size of a basketball. Little things like that bothered me, but they clearly didn't bother anyone else.

t's okay to do that," I lamented to the folks at Boss Key who were willing to listen. "Just make the tip of his arrow a fireball that matches the size of the fucking collision!"

The message got through. One day an artist burst into my office and blurted out: "LASER SHOES, DUDE!"

I didn't look up from my monitor. "What?"

"No, hear me out," he said. "We need a hero who has boots that fire lasers out of them. Players can use them to traverse the map, like a jet pack, and they can also give enemies one helluva kick!"

"That's completely stupid," I said. "And I love it."

One of our coders, overhearing this, waved his hands as if pleading with us to stop. I smiled at him and said, "Dude, sometimes you have to say, 'Fuck it, this sounds cool.'"

Still, I had never experienced the level of second-guessing and self-doubt that plagued me as we tried to polish *LawBreakers* and get it ready for market. It wasn't just nerves. It was mental malware. I was frustrated by the way the art was coming together, despite loving it previously. Technically, it looked great. But now it lacked a distinctive style, that special something that would make it stand out. I also started thinking that all our maps were too similar. Two bases on either side, an objective centrally located, and low gravity in the middle. Over and over again. Why hadn't I seen these things before?

Late in the year, Arjan, Lauren, one of our senior designers, and I made a pilgrimage to South Korea to meet with Nexon executives in person. They sprang for business class for all of us, and we darted off to Asia in an Airbus 380. The plane had a bar and a duty-free shop on it. All of us hung out in the bar for the first hour and a half, chatting up a large, older Texas oil baron with a young, pretty woman by his side who he introduced as his daughter, although we thought otherwise from the way they interacted after a couple of rounds.

Eventually we were urged back to our seats by a concerned flight attendant who said we were making too much noise and people were trying to sleep. "You put a bar on your plane, what do you think will happen?" Lauren chuckled as we buckled up again.

Nexon's headquarters were technically nice but had very, very little character to them, kind of like the movie trope in which a teenager is adopted by a rich couple with an ultramodern but cold home. At a press junket, I gave a presentation on *LawBreakers* that included one of our trailers. I knocked it out, and we had a dinner that night with our hosts, who expressed their support and eagerness to get our game out. The only complaint came toward the end of the night when one of the higher-ups complained to me about Arjan.

"He's so mean," he said.

"He's a no-BS guy," I said. "He expects results."

Before we left Seoul, I sat in the bar over a plate of spaghetti and a glass of pinot grigio and watched CNN International report that Donald Trump had defeated Hillary Clinton on his way to becoming the forty-fifth president of the United States. As a teenager I'd looked up to Trump, seeing him as a symbol of American strength and capitalism. However, as an adult, I realized he was a bullying buffoon. The qualities that many liked about him—"He tells it like it is" or "He's a businessman"—made little sense to me now. He had turned U.S. politics into the WWE.

How had this happened? How did we get this giant orange brat as our president after eight years of an eloquent, gentle, and principled leader?

On the flight back, the answer hit me. Gamergate! It was fucking Gamergate. It had been a dress rehearsal for the 2016 election. Memes. Pepe the frog. 4chan. Bots. Russian troll factories. The alt-right had waged an online guerilla-warfare campaign against the left and won. Trump had stoked distrust of traditional media, dubbing anything he didn't like or agree with as fake news. He created his own facts. Why read an actual well-researched article with sources cited when you could just share a crude meme or a catchy slogan that confirmed what you wanted to hear? Like maybe Hillary was running a secret child sex ring in a pizza parlor basement in DC.

It was all too late. The damage was done. The internet had given America a barely literate, power-hungry, wannabe tyrant for president.

The finish line was in sight. In early June, we hosted a pair of events at Boss Key for mid-tier and up-and-coming Twitch streamers. We flew them to Raleigh, wined and dined them, and gave them exclusive access to the full game. In return, we captured video of them as they played, and streamed their experience to their fan base. All of them seemed to have fun. The main question they had was whether *LawBreakers* would be an esport. "We'll see; fingers crossed," I said. "We want to make a fun, compelling, competitive game first."

A couple of weeks later, we hit E3. I had pushed Nexon hard

on the marketing, and it showed. We had an enormous banner on the outside of the LA Convention Center. You couldn't go inside without seeing it: *LawBreakers: Gravity—Defying—Combat.* I promoted the game all week. I think it would have been impossible to attend E3 that year and not know *LawBreakers* would be available on August 8—and for the lower price we had decided on of $29.99. "None of that sixty-dollar multiplayer-only bullshit!" I said during my presentation, to big applause.

Before I got back to Raleigh, though, *Overwatch* fans were pushing back online. "I'm perfectly happy with my sixty-dollar multiplayer bullshit, thank you very much."

At the end of the month the game went gold, and we had a party at the Watts and Ward speakeasy owned by my restaurateur friend Niall Hanley. Lauren showed up in a costume she'd made after our female hero Maverick. Then it was time for our two crucial betas—the first was closed and only for those with access keys; and two days later, on June 30, we opened the game for free to everyone who wanted to play. It was a dress rehearsal, our version of previewing the show before opening on Broadway.

Everyone got to the studio early on the thirtieth and spent the next five days of the open beta glued to their monitors, analyzing the data. I would've been happy starting with twenty thousand concurrent players and building to forty or fifty thousand. The reality was not just half that number, it was dismal. At our peak, we had over seven thousand concurrent players—not good for a free beta. By the time the full game came out on August 8, that number had plummeted to three thousand. In September, it was down to one thousand.

The mood at the studio was grim. The team desperately tried to make new content to keep the game in the news, a new hero was prototyped, new maps were released. None of it made a dent. After nearly three years of hard work, passion, and hope—not to mention about $40 million—*LawBreakers* was dead on arrival.

I made the mistake of watching the YouTube hot takes that poured in. The schadenfreude was powerful. The online community fileted and roasted me, my studio, and my game. Everyone had an opinion on why we failed. *Overwatch* crushed us. My ego. Nexon's poor marketing. Our art style and characters didn't have broad-enough appeal. We leaned too heavily on the skill-based aspects of our game, leading to new players getting decimated by those who were in the betas. Just like when a plane crashes, there are multiple cascading failures that cause it. We had shipped the game version of that disaster.

Many months earlier, Lauren had booked a trip for us and her family to Japan in September. We'd said it would either be a celebration or an escape. Escape it was. I couldn't wait to get on the plane. I feared that traveling to the other side of the world would look like I was abandoning my team, but everyone needed time to regroup, not just me, and I landed in Tokyo with a relatively clear conscience and a strong desire to disappear into anonymity.

For ten days, we were tourists. We visited the Tokyo Skytree, Tokyo Disneyland, karaoke bars, the Robot restaurant, and Akihabara. We ate Wagyu beef, ramen, and sushi. We even found our way into a temple, where we befriended a monk and meditated with him. I didn't expect a profound experience from sitting in a quiet room with my eyes closed, and neither my life nor my outlook changed, but slowing down and just existing inside my breath for thirty minutes did allow me a rare interlude of absolute quiet, as well as the chance to hear the enormity of the universe and pray that everything would be okay.

One night Lauren and I met Hideo Kojima and his producer-translator Ken-Ichiro Imaizumi for dinner. I had texted Ken to let him know I was in town and would be honored to take him and Kojima-san out to dinner. They accepted. We met at a yakiniku restaurant that Ken picked, and the food seemed to come for hours.

We ordered bottles of sake and I told Kojima-san about my journey with Boss Key, including my disappointment and sense of failure.

To cheer me up, Kojima-san invited me to visit his studio and have my likeness scanned for his upcoming *Death Stranding* game. I turned him down. I wasn't in the mood to be visible, I said. I felt like an ugly failure inside and out. He put his drink down and looked straight at me without speaking until it was almost uncomfortable.

"What matters is that you did it," he said. "You left the comfort of Epic, got funding, started your very own studio, and shipped a game. Very few people can say that. I haven't even shipped my game with my new studio."

He refilled my sake glass.

"You did it. You took the risk of a true artist."

I spent the long flight back home reflecting about why the game face-planted. It was the perfect storm waiting to happen, I supposed. The market was flooded with hero shooters, and gamers didn't grasp what I felt were the things that made us unique. The game came up for air with press and alphas and betas too many times, often without enough new content. Changing from a free-to-play arena shooter into a $29.99 hero shooter caused confusion. The eclectic look of the finished product may have been off-putting to a generation that adored big-eyed anime characters and bright, pastel palettes.

Finally, I was sure my politics didn't help. Numerous gaming websites wrote that this futuristic shooter had gender-neutral bathrooms.

Despite all of the above, I continued to be mystified by our lack of players. I understood the finale of *Lost* better than I did our minuscule streams. Why didn't it work? Why do some ideas stick and others don't? Why do some motor along and others turn into a phenomenon?

In 1999, Japanese manga author Koushun Takami wrote *Battle*

Royale, a gripping novel about a group of high school students kidnapped by a fascist regime and given twenty-four hours to start killing each other—or else be killed all at once. In 2008, author Suzanne Collins published *The Hunger Games*, a literary phenomenon that injected the same *Battle Royale* concept into the Western world's bloodthirsty consciousness. Gaming tapped into a similar vein. *Unreal Tournament* had the elimination mode Last Man Standing, and *Counter-Strike* was based around a version of the same idea.

But the *Battle Royale* concept didn't catch fire in gaming until persistent Irish programmer Brendan "PlayerUnknown" Greene, a veteran modder, published an early-access beta of his last-man-standing shooter *PUBG*—short for *PlayerUnknown's Battlegrounds*. It attracted tens of thousands of players, including some savvy developers at Epic Games, who applied the idea to *Fortnite*, creating the greatest pivot in video game history.

At the time, *Fortnite* was languishing and limping along as a tower defense game—collect resources, build a fort, and defend it against waves of zombies. It was simple and distracting enough. But that genre had faded in popularity as *Battle Royale* exploded. In August 2017, as *LawBreakers* was face-planting, Brendan's latest version of *PUBG* took off, beginning a run that would ultimately result in sales topping seventy million copies. The following month, Epic released *Fortnite: Battle Royale*, and it turned into a worldwide phenomenon that would generate billions of dollars and attract hundreds of millions of players.

I was shocked. Dumbfounded. And depressed.

Epic could barely keep up with demand for *Fortnite*. I wished Tim, Mark, and everyone else nothing but success. I took a modicum of pride in the game. I had advocated for it when I was at the company and it was going through a gestation period. I had even helped name it. I had also felt sorry for the developers as it limped along. Now I rued its existence as online trolls used it as a means of torturing me after my recent failure. "Hey, aren't you the guy who announced *Fortnite*?" they said.

One day I was lamenting our lack of players, and our senior producer pointed to his monitor and said, "You want to know where everyone is? This is what the kids are playing." I looked at his screen and saw a streamer playing *PUBG* while a series of physics bugs stacked up, creating a surreal dance of nightmare fuel that the broadcaster thought was the funniest thing he'd ever seen. Arjan leaned over my shoulder. "Dude, this is what *my* kids are loving. They eat this stuff up. I don't get it."

"Why even try?" I sighed, defeated and annoyed. "We spent three years lovingly crafting something polished, and they go for this schlock?"

To me, *PUBG* looked like shit. Poor animations and lighting made the game look like it had come out ten years earlier. But the aesthetics didn't matter as much as the outcome—who was left standing at the end. The gameplay of one hundred players parachuting onto a remote island, picking where they landed to scavenge for weapons they could use to hunt one another as a toxic wall of death closed in around them, proved far too compelling. That and the fact that only one player could survive every match. If you died, you went back into the queue and waited for another match.

By this time, Rohan—arms folded, beret on, steely-eyed glare through his LA hipster glasses—had joined the huddle and said, "It's virality, dude. They love the jankiness of the game. It makes 'em feel like they're seeing something they shouldn't."

"Yeah, they know there will be bugs," Arjan said. "Might as well make it a feature for them to laugh at. We could totally do something like this in a matter of months."

We could do that, I thought, and we'd have another game in the market. It wouldn't be perfect or pretty but . . . that was the point, right?

"Fuck it," I said. "Let's do it. Let's embrace the jank. Let's just make sure we put our own fucking spin on it."

I walked away knowing we needed another major publishing deal to stay in business. I had an idea for a game with dragons that would cost tens of millions to make. *Game of Thrones* had made them hot, but I'd always been into dragons, since my first game, and as proof, I had a dragon tattoo on my back that I got at age nineteen. Arjan and a producer also had an idea for a triple-A game set in a prison. It didn't sway me from dragons. But I also saw merit in making a small, janky game. It might keep the lights on a little longer and rally the troops, which I could tell was badly needed.

I shared a *Battle Royale* concept about warring gangs that could be done on the cheap and quickly, but our young animator Zach Lowery pitched his own idea for a down-and-dirty game that had a cool eighties-pop-culture vibe and won us over. Titled *Radical Heights*, it was a third-person *Battle Royale* by way of the movie *Running Man*. The game was set in a giant dome where players competed for cash and prizes, just like the old arcade shooter game *Smash TV*, while they battled one another—not on motorcycles, jeeps, or tanks, but on old-school BMX bikes. Arjan giggled: "I love it." Rohan crowed: "Brilliant."

"I'm ready to go full-on Schwarzenegger," I said. "But apart from the theme and the bikes and buying stuff, what else will help us stand out? What about the map becoming hazardous to force conflict?"

"We'll figure it out," Zach said.

"Just try to make the craziest shit you can," I said. "Like instead of everyone parachuting into the game, maybe have them launched out of cannons—you know, stuff to get the streamers yammering."

Zach listened politely. He got it and accurately said, "If we can pull anything off, it'll be a miracle."

That made sense. It was exactly what we needed. A miracle.

PULLING THE PLUG

The most difficult and demanding part of the hero's journey isn't about waging war against enemies and slaying opponents. No, the truly hard and scariest part comes at the end when the hero returns home, looks in the mirror, and sees the biggest challenges are still there. They are inside them. Everything that came before, all the uncertainty, risk, and battling was about this moment, about confronting their personal demons.

I tried to hide it for as long as possible, but this was my moment of truth. I brought on an experienced executive producer named Joe Halper to help with everything—all the work of running a business that had piled up, as well as our last-ditch efforts to make games that would save Boss Key, our jobs, and my reputation, but there was no denying the ship had hit an iceberg when I sat across from Arjan and Joe one night in the office after everyone left and saw the level of concern on their faces. Epic had just poached JayHawk. I didn't blame the guy for going. He had responsibilities.

I looked across the studio at the Christmas tree we'd put up as the holiday neared. Then Arjan sighed.

"The tank is on empty," he said, though his voice sounded more like a groan. "At our current burn rate, we're about six months from shutting down."

This was the point where I could've jumped in my Lamborghini and sped off into the sunset, a cheap, callous, uncaring, selfish coward with a personal fortune that would cushion me and my wife for the rest of our lives. It would've been easy. The keys were in my pocket, and I could have uttered as a final directive the last words Captain Edward J. Smith said to his crew on the *Titanic*: "Well, boys, do your best for the women and children, and look out for yourself." But I didn't, couldn't, and wouldn't ever have been able to live with myself. The true hero's journey begins when facing certain defeat.

"No one waves the white flag," I said. "We're still here, we're still fighting."

A plan emerged. *Radical Heights* moved along as fast as a skunkworks game could. The hardest part was getting artists to make things as fast as possible and "just good enough" to get into the wild. As perfectionists, they had a hard time downshifting to being "just good enough." Then I got a call from a former colleague who had worked on *Unreal 2* and was now spearheading Twentieth Century Fox's interactive division. He had the rights to the *Alien* franchise and said Fox was looking to do a triple-A game in that space. Were we interested in making that game? Without sounding desperate, I said yes, we should meet. Arjan said, "Oh shit, that could be . . ." I agreed.

Finally, there was my dragon idea. This was the big, expensive game that would cost tens of millions of dollars. But I saw it in my head. *How to Train Your Dragon* . . . but badass. I saw it as a boy-and-his-dog story—only the dog weighed tons, could fly, and breathed fire. "Let's step it up a notch or two," one of our animators said. "Dragons versus zombies. The players are ninjas. Ninjas with dragons fighting zombies." I liked it. The ultimate mash-up of all things cool, we called the game *DragonFlies* and worked up a presentation to take to publishers. My agent, Ophir, set up meetings.

I always believed the path to success was simple: if I made cool shit, the money would come, and I could make more cool shit. It had been that way my whole career, my whole life since I made my first game as a teenager. There might be more, but I'd yet to experience it, and so I chose to believe we were on our way to finding the key that would unlock the door to the special power that would save Boss Key.

I had always been able to find the key.

Our first meetings were with Electronic Arts and 2K Games in San Francisco. The night before, I lay in my hotel room bed, curled up in the fetal position, moaning that I couldn't do the pitch. Lauren talked me through the crisis, and the next day I powered through our pitch at both places, mustering as much excitement and charisma as I could, with Arjan and Ophir chiming in as needed. The next day we met with Microsoft in Seattle. Then we parachuted into LA for meetings with Warner Interactive and Activision.

Each stop was the same. People whom I had known for years greeted me with hugs and handshakes, listened attentively, even enthusiastically, asked good questions about the game and tough questions about the budget, which we were able to answer, and then the air in the room disappeared when they inevitably asked, "Why do you think *LawBreakers* failed?" Even though we left each meeting with folks promising they were going to talk among themselves and run the numbers and get back to us, and hopefully we'd work together, I walked back to our waiting car feeling sick to my stomach.

After the New Year, we waited to hear back from publishers. Arjan bristled with impatience every time he heard me on the phone with Ophir telling me to sit tight. Then we heard the *Alien* game was a no-go after Disney's acquisition of Fox. I got an email that began: "Sorry, Cliff, but . . ." For Arjan, that was the final blow. One day he and Joe asked if I could join them for coffee and chat. We walked to our local coffee shop, and I ordered a latte from the hipster barista with the ponytail, glasses, and chipped fingernail polish.

"Okay, what's up, boys?" I asked.

Arjan took a deep breath and looked me in the eyes. "I had lunch with the Epic guys, and they made me an offer."

I felt like I'd been shot. "What the fuck, dude?"

"Sorry, man," he said. "It's a really great deal. I need to consider it."

I looked off in the opposite direction and shook my head. I couldn't believe it.

"Arjan and I have been talking most of the day about this," Joe said. "He told me he's going to sleep on it tonight and get back to us tomorrow."

Later, I learned that Joe had pushed Arjan to set up a meeting with Tim Sweeney and Mark Rein to ask them to work *Radical Heights* into the Epic store as a complement to *Fortnite*. It would be good karma for Epic and a lifeline for us. Instead, they offered Arjan a job, including what I heard was a fat signing bonus.

"If he leaves, I'm confident I can pick up the slack," Joe said.

I turned to Arjan. "I get it. Family first. We always said that. But you're breaking my heart over here, dude. We still have a shot with *DragonFlies*!"

"I'm sure things will work out," he said. "Just not with me."

was mad and had to get it out of my system. I messaged Tim on Twitter: "Stop stealing my guys." No response—and of course, none needed. I told the staff and gave them time to digest the news. "Folks, we are not done here," I said. "We are full speed ahead with *Radical Heights*. We are waiting to hear about *DragonFlies*. Boss Key is still in the business of making games—and will be for a long time."

The news of Arjan's departure did not play well with those who were mulling our pitch for *DragonFlies*. One by one, they sent rejections. EA felt it was too similar to their multiplayer RPG *Anthem*. Activision was fully engaged with *Call of Duty* and didn't want to make new IP. Microsoft said simply, "We're going to let this one go. Good luck placing it with someone else." And so on.

We had one play left, our Hail Mary. On April 10, 2018, we released *Radical Heights*. We teased the game the day before its release and then dropped it out there. Not the most elegant strategy, but I imagined Captain "Sully" Sullenberger wasn't concerned about appearances when he landed US Airways Flight 1549 in the Hudson River. He just wanted to get all the passengers out of the plane alive.

I had never been prouder of my team and all that they managed to pull off. We had one large map with locations such as Short Round, Venus Beach, and Garden Grove. We pedaled our bikes madly across this sprawling landscape, occasionally misjudging a jump and tumbling down a hill, end over end, just like we did as kids. The game felt like *Lord of the Flies* by way of Chuck E. Cheese. The whole studio played it endlessly to produce AI foes to fill in the gaps if the player count dipped after it went live. The spirit inside Boss Key was unbelievable. It was intoxicating—and dammit, the game was fun.

Spring was in bloom all over Raleigh after what felt like the longest, coldest winter I'd experienced since moving there in 1998, and I convinced myself it was an omen. We were due to bust out of our own cold spell. *Radical Heights* gave social media a new topic to chew on and the gaming press lit up. Everyone knew our building was on fire. The collective *Fortnite*/*PUBG* players caught wind of it and many of them put down their toys long enough to check out this new challenger in the *Battle Royale* arena.

One of the early adopters was Dr. Disrespect, an extremely popular online gaming personality who started firing up *Radical Heights* on a regular basis and genuinely seemed to like the game. Each time the good doctor played *Radical Heights* we saw a spike in users . . .

and hope rose. We had a few thousand players a day, not a ton, not enough to sustain a business like ours, but it was a jumping-off point for a living product. We could make new assets for a janky game like this far faster than we could for *LawBreakers*. One day Joe came into my office and asked if I had seen the data—we were number one on Twitch!

It happened enough times that we were able to see a pattern. When *Fortnite*'s servers were down, people switched to *Radical Heights*. They liked the game.

That's when the cheating started. In the early days of a freshly released game, streamers, journalists, and influencers wanting to be ahead of the curve craned their necks to find new IP and check it out. Others were on the lookout too—but for a different reason. They were the cheaters, people who got off on destroying new games. They combed the beach for new sandcastles they could kick, like a bully straight out of those Charles Atlas comic book ads.

They found *Radical Heights*, and suddenly we had players running through our world at four times the normal speed, crashing through walls and shooting with superhuman aim. Gameplay devolved into chaos. We had shipped without cheat protection, and now we were paying the price. A fan sent me a screenshot of a message posted on 4chan: "No cheat protection? Check. You know what to do boys!" Another message said, "This Blowzinsky guy still at it? Let's ruin this f*ggot." Those were just two of many, but the damage was done. Our player count plummeted.

We had one last chance. Joe went to GDC and met with Twitch, and they agreed to get behind *Radical Heights* in a worldwide event where their influencers would play the game for prize money that Twitch put up. It was set for early May. Then Epic announced they were celebrating the new season of *Fortnite* in a crossover event with the new Marvel movie *Avengers: Infinity War.* They scheduled it for the same day as our Twitch event. There was no use even pretending we could compete.

"Nobody's going to watch the panels on Twitch," Joe said.

My stomach burned. "I agree," I said.

"You know, Cliff, the lease is up on the building. This place is ridiculously expensive. We're losing employees left and right. It's time."

It was, and on May 14, 2018, we pulled the plug.

Joe worked with our lawyers to draw up a severance package for the remaining employees. Two weeks of salary with two months of healthcare coverage was the best we could do. Lauren helped me through the worst moments. We hunkered down at home. We cooked stews and tacos and snuggled in front of the TV. We binged *Silicon Valley*. I was barely able to watch the scene where Thomas Middleditch's character vomits in his office trash can before addressing employees on his company's failure.

Before we closed the doors for good, Joe pulled me aside for a private conversation. "Look, man, I know how devastating this is," he said. "I know how hard it is. But you've got a lot to be proud of. You created a studio. You got some of the best people in the business to work here. You made games. You're still friends with people. Nobody made any enemies here. The studio failed, but you didn't. And neither did anybody else."

Boss Key had a life span of four years, 2014–2018. I didn't want it to rest in peace as much as I wanted it to live on as a splendid effort. In the last days of our lease, Lauren and I went to the office to say goodbye to the space and all the memories that remained there. I walked through in silence, full of mixed feelings, mostly melancholy, as if the space were talking to me, whispering, like Clementine in the movie *Eternal Sunshine of the Spotless Mind*: "Remember me. Try your best."

It was all good until it wasn't. Suddenly, I tore up the backdrop for our livestreams as I screamed, "Fuck you."

Afterward, I calmed down and apologized to Lauren. "I couldn't help it. I had to get it out of my system."

I couldn't wait to get home. I had lost that after my dad died, and now home was what I had left, and it was everything I really wanted and needed. A few days later, I got a new tattoo: an antique key with text below it in an old typewriter font that said "Finally home."

I arrived at a conclusion about my hero's journey. It wasn't necessary to win every battle, to always get the high score. Sometimes getting past the baddies and through the tough times was enough. Surviving and learning that you could survive was enough. Sometimes it was more than enough. If you're going through hell, keep going! In the weeks and months after, I wondered when I was going to finally cry, and then I wondered why I hadn't cried, but all that changed when I had to put down my beloved dog and longtime best friend, Teddy. He'd been sick for a while and no longer had anything left. I lay on the kitchen floor next to him the whole night and couldn't stop the tears. Lauren crouched down, wiped my eyes, and hugged the two of us.

The next day I kissed Teddy's muzzle and cradled him in my arms as he drew his last breaths and crossed the rainbow bridge. It was one of the hardest days of my life.

After Boss Key, I went through a long period of grieving what I perceived as failure. It wasn't, just as Joe and Kojima-san had told me. But I needed a while before I could see that. I'd tried to do my own thing. I made good friends. We made a couple of really fun games. I still had the love of my life next to me. It was the ultimate boss fight, and it was with myself. I emerged from it better, stronger, and wiser. And no longer needing to fight.

I had no immediate plans to do anything else, no urge to figure out what was next, and of course that's when a little sumpin' fell in my lap: Broadway. Through a friend, I was invested in the play *Hadestown*, which became a smash and won a slew of Tony Awards, including the big one for Best Musical. Another small investment in a revival of Terrence McNally's *Frankie and Johnny in the Clair de Lune*, starring Audra McDonald and Michael Shannon, let me live out the thrills and dreams of a high school drama nerd. It has taken me forty-seven years to figure out that I didn't have to spend every day trying to prove myself or fix something. I knew my father would have been proud—maybe even amazed. I could relax and enjoy my life.

In July, Lauren and I made our annual pilgrimage to San Diego Comic-Con. I had mixed feelings about being at the world's greatest nerd prom. I wanted to have the kind of fun we always had there, but I was self-conscious about being seen at the panels and parties after such a public failure. It didn't take long, though, before I realized that no one saw me that way, not even the former Boss Key employees I ran into, many of whom had already landed new jobs. A few of us took a photo together. "We're family," one of them said, and I swear I teared up. Later, I caught up with an exec from Marvel, who congratulated me on taking a shot at my own thing with Boss Key. "You've got nothing to prove," he said. "Just be you."

Later that night, I was dancing with Lauren at one of the parties. My shirt was soaked, I was surrounded by friends, former colleagues, and fellow nerds. The DJ was spinning Big Sean's "Live This Life," the song I put on repeat after Tencent invested in Epic and I felt like the world had handed me a winning lottery ticket. Some random guy with his girl spotted me on the dance floor and made his way over. "Hey, Cliff! CliffyB! Dude, *Gears of War* rules! Man, thank you for my childhood!"

Lauren gave my butt a little squeeze and leaned in close. "Just be you."

ACKNOWLEDGMENTS

In the first draft of this book, I mentioned everyone with whom I worked, knew as a kid, and engaged with on social media. Rest assured, if I met you, your name was in that draft. It was like an alternative to LinkedIn. Then I was told there were too many names, it was too hard to keep track of everyone, and the book had to be a reasonable length. So I began cutting. I knew I'd be hurting some feelings. Please know you only hurt those you love. I have had good times—no, great times—and owe gratitude to so many of you, too many to name. It's also important to acknowledge that games are made by many people, especially the games I've been involved with. Everybody brings talent and makes key contributions. I couldn't possibly go into that kind of detail in this book. If you really want to know how the sausage is made, get a job in the industry and learn to make the sausage. I never intended to write a tell-all as much as a tell-on-myself—and make it entertaining.

All that said, I do want to thank specific people. At Epic I'd like to thank Tim Sweeney and Mark Rein for taking a chance on a bright-eyed and eager-to-work young creative. I'm sorry I couldn't stick around to see your plans for world domination come to fruition. It was time for me to walk away from the job, but never from our friendship and my gratitude.

Thank you to everyone I worked with over the years at Epic Games. Rod Fergusson is still the hardest-working producer I've ever known. Shout-out to Mike Capps for keeping me honest as my nerd stardom took off. Also, I'd like to thank Phil Spencer from Microsoft for betting big on the vision I had. It worked! It's a classic. As Marcus Fenix might say, all those memories, all that work, it still warms my heart.

To everyone who took a chance and came to work at Boss Key, I am forever appreciative. We were in a foxhole together; it was a memorable time where I got to witness your talent and toughness, loyalty and pride. Thank you for believing in me and my vision. I will always feel the same way about you. Thank you.

Shout-out to all the public relations people who dealt with an eager young man who just wanted to be popular and seem cool. I want to thank my agents Ophir Lupu and Albert Lee from UTA, and their assistant, Laurie-Maude Chenard. It still blows me away that I have big-time agents and can say to folks, "Let me talk to my people," and know that my people are excellent.

I knew it took a lot of people to make a video game, but I never would've guessed it's the same with a book. Now I know. Many thanks and much appreciation to my editor at Simon & Schuster, Sean Manning, for reading this book and raking it over the coals and making it the compelling and interesting story I had in me. Oh, and of course, everyone else at S&S: assistant editor Tzipora Baitch; executive director of publicity Julia Prosser; associate director of publicity Anne-Tate Pearce; publicity manager Brianna Scharfenberg; marketing manager Leila Siddiqui; director of subsidiary rights Marie Florio; managing editor Amanda Mulholland; art director Alison Forner, for the cover; CEO Jon Karp; associate publisher Irene Kheradi; and publisher Dana Canedy.

Todd Gold, I'll forever be in your debt for teaching me how to actually write.

Thanks to childhood friend Ralph Barbagallo for teaching me so much about game theory and design.

For being there for me on a nearly daily basis, my older brother Tyler. Thanks for always looking out for me and giving me Yoda-like advice on the regular.

Thank you to Broadway actor Alex Boinello for reaching out to me to co-produce *Hadestown*, as well as Hunter Arnold and Kayla Greenspan from TBD productions for facilitating it all. At my lowest moment, after my studio closed, you all provided a much-needed win for me. It helped heal a lot of bruises. Being in Radio City Music Hall as the play won eight Tony Awards is something I'll always cherish.

To Niall Hanley, my restaurant business partner, you giant Irish a-hole—I love you and thank you for so much sage advice over the years, and for showing up with a hose at my condo at four a.m. when my enormous fish tank broke, so I could drain the water out the window.

To the many people in the industry who inspired me from childhood through today and no doubt into tomorrow: thank you. I hope I have done the same for others. We're in a conversation with one another, not competing but learning from our failures and building on our successes. I don't think I saw that twenty years ago. I do now.

To everyone who has ever enjoyed any game that I've had a hand in, thank you, especially to those who got tattoos or built cosplay showing their love of it, and most of all to those of you who have found escape, peace, empowerment, hope, and maybe even a little bit more of yourself when playing the games. It is truly the ultimate honor that one can have as a creative. If you've played my games, you know me. I always look forward to meeting and getting to know you.

Finally, to Lauren, my forever person. It took a lot of trial and error to finally find you, but here you are, brightening my life every single day and night. Thank you for supporting me in all my pursuits, especially the one where I chased after you! I couldn't have made the moves and taken the risks I have without you by my side. Neither would I have wanted to. I feel the same about today, tomorrow, and beyond. You truly are an angel sent from above. Thank you. And I love you.

POST-CREDITS SCENE

It took two years, but I landed on the floor of my office, with a notebook in my lap, writing out ideas for a new video game. Then came another. Then came an idea for a graphic novel. Then came an offer to consult on a game someone had in development. I didn't know where any of it would take me and didn't really care. I was being me and doing what I believed I did best and loved most—being creative.

Technology and the video game industry, joined at the hip as they always have been, move insanely fast. In the time it has taken me to write this book, I've seen the rise of cryptocurrencies, NFTs, and virtual real estate as nearly every company seems to be staking out ground in the metaverse. It feels like the world is marching toward the real-life version of *Ready Player One* and the tech titans that rule our daily lives are leading the charge. The *Washington Post* declared the "feeding frenzy for video game makers is now fully underway." Microsoft is spending almost $70 billion to acquire Activision Blizzard. Sony is purchasing Bungie. And Take-Two Interactive Software is buying Zynga.

Why is this happening?

Two reasons. First, gaming is still growing. The worldwide gaming market is projected to increase from $180 billion in 2021 to $219 billion in 2024. The people like me who started playing games in the eighties are still playing games, and every generation since has jumped on board. The second reason for all this consolidation should be obvious to even non-gamers. Technology is taking over our lives. Seniors are yelling at Alexa and kids are yelling for VR headsets. As I was once told, if you want to see the future, look to the East, but I'm going to add also look to Silicon Valley, Los Angeles, Raleigh, and other tech hubs in the U.S. And then look inside yourself. I've learned that's where you'll really get a glimpse at the future.

I reflect on my time in the business on a daily basis. I still have dreams of puttering around a game studio, checking out the exciting things that the developers are crafting and giving enthusiastic feedback. Oddly enough, I talk more with former Boss Key employees than those from Epic. It didn't work as a business, but damn we had fun. I still have fans on social media asking me to return to *Gears* to "fix it," even though the last two installments have been pretty spiffy, if you ask me.

There's a trope that's used quite often in video games—usually toward the end of the game—when you have to fight yourself. In *The Legend of Zelda*, the protagonist, Link, fights the Dark Link. Writing this book has very much felt like that. Revisiting the highs and lows of my childhood and adult life has been a confrontation between all sides of myself, light and dark and various shades in between, and though some days I feel old—at least parts of me do, like my lower intestines—and like I've been through a lot, the truth is, I'm not old, and most days I feel like the best and most exciting days are still to come.

I've learned that you can either obsess over the past or gather up all that you've learned and get ready to rock the future. I remind myself of that endlessly.

The one constant is change in this world and that adage is 100 percent true for the video game industry. Through the many interviews I've given throughout my career, I've been asked so many times where I think the industry will be in three years. The truth is that no one knows. Maybe Tim Sweeney. But maybe not even him. Though I think it's safe to bet we'll see new updated versions of *Call of Duty* for the next God-knows-how-many years. I just hope we don't see *Call of Duty: American Civil War 2026*, you know what I mean?

What's next? I don't know. I'm intent on producing more Broadway shows. One of these days I'll get around to telling a crazy story I have in mind about a crawfish *kaiju* attacking New Orleans. Maybe I'll find a way to finally create a game with dragons. Maybe I'll rejoin Delta Squad. Maybe I'll invest in more restaurants in Raleigh (I co-own two) and learn to bartend. If I do, come by and see me. (I'm partial to a Ketel vodka with soda and a splash of ginger beer, and my favorite toast is "Cheers, motherfuckers!") One thing I'm certain of? I'll never be CEO of anything ever again.

I do think we're in for a wild ride. People are using anime avatars to craft personas that they stream in character while playing video games. The megahit *League of Legends* has a virtual K-pop band that keeps fans glued to the screen. Young men would rather have a virtual *waifu* than interact with real-life humans. Are they plugging into the Matrix sooner than the rest of us? Is the real world that crappy?

For those who think it is, video games provide an alternative. And for those who don't want off? I think video games have given us the blueprint for unraveling the Matrix. It's on humanity to figure out where to go with that power.

But enough with the forecasting and pontificating. For those who want to know what I'm playing right now—and that's always the question us gamers ask each other—it's *Mega Man 11*. Lately I'm all about retro side-scrolling platform games. Like *Jazz*.

As always when I get into a flow at my computer, my dogs are pestering me to take them outside. Before I go, indulge me this. If there's one takeaway from all these tales I've told, it's this: "You go into video games because you want to remake the world as you